AFRICA AND THE NEW GLOBALIZATION

Africa and the New Globalization

GEORGE KLAY KIEH, JR.
Grand Valley State University, USA

Routledge
Taylor & Francis Group
LONDON AND NEW YORK

First published 2008 by Ashgate Publishing

2 Park Square, Milton Park, Abingdon, Oxfordshire OX14 4RN
711 Third Avenue, New York, NY 10017

Routledge is an imprint of the Taylor & Francis Group, an informa business

First issued in paperback 2018

British Library Cataloguing in Publication Data
Africa and the new globalization
1. Globalization - Economic aspects - Africa
2. Globalization - Social aspects - Africa 3. Africa - Economic conditions - 21st century 4. Africa conditions - 21st century
I. Kieh, George Klay, 1956-
338.9'6

Library of Congress Cataloging-in-Publication Data
Africa and the new globalization / edited by George Klay Kieh, Jr.
p. cm.
Includes index.
ISBN 978-0-7546-7138-1
1. Globalization--Economic aspects--Africa. 2. Globalization--Social aspects--Africa. 3. Africa--Economic conditions--21st century. 4.Africa--Social conditions--21st century. I. Kieh, George Klay, 1956-

HC800.A553316 2007
337.6--dc22

2007013632

ISBN 13: 978-0-7546-7138-1 (hbk)
ISBN 13 978-1-138-38280-0 (pbk)

Contents

List of Tables

About the Contributors

Pablo. L.E. Idahosa is Director of the African Studies Program and Professor of African and Development Studies at York University, Toronto, Canada. His research interests are in the areas of development studies, African political thought, African modernities, social capital and welfare. His publications include: *The Populist Dimension of African Political Thought and Somali Diaspora.*

George Klay Kieh, Jr. is Professor of Political Science and African Studies at Grand Valley State University. Michigan, USA. and Senior Research Fellow in the Program in Ethnic and Federal Studies at the University of Ibadan, Nigeria. He has published extensively in the areas of civil conflicts in Africa, security studies, democratization and development in Africa and American foreign policy. His most recent book is an edited volume on *Beyond State Failure and Collapse: Making the State Relevant in Africa*, Lexington Books, 2007.

Jacques Mangala is Assistant Professor of Political Science and Director of the African and African-American Studies Program at Grand Valley State University, Michigan, USA. His research specializations are in the areas of international law and organization, human rights, refugees and international migration, African Diaspora and African Politics. His works have been published in journals such as *Quarterly on Refugee Problems*, *The International Law Review*, *Refugee* and *The African review of International and Comparative Law*. He has a forthcoming book on *The Status of the Protection of Refugees in Africa*, Bruylant-Academic, Belgium.

John Mukum Mbaku is William Eccles Professor of Economics and John Hinckley Fellow at Weber State University, Ogden, Utah, USA. His present research interests are in public choice, constitutional political economy, trade integration, inter-group relations and institutional reforms in Africa. He has published extensively in the aforementioned areas. His most recent book is *Corruption in Africa: Causes, Consequences and Cleanups*, Lexington Books, 2007.

Amy Patterson is Associate Professor of Political Science at Calvin College, Michigan, USA. Her research interests include gender and development, African democratization and development and the politics of AIDS in Africa. Her works have appeared in journals such as *Journal of Modern African Studies*, *Africa Today*, *African Studies Review*, *Canadian Journal of African Studies* and *PS: Political Science and Politics*. Her most recent book is *The Politics of AIDS in Africa*, Lynne Rienner Publishers.

E. Ike Udogu is Professor of Political Science and African Politics at Appalachian State University, Boone, North Carolina, USA. His research interests includes ethnicity and politics in Africa, the national question in Africa, human rights and democratization in Africa. He has published extensively in these areas. His most recent book is *African Renaissance in the Millenium: Political, Economic and Social Discourses on the Way Forward*, Lexington Books, 2007.

Preface

Globalization is not a new phenomenon in the international system. This is evidenced by the fact that various efforts have been made over the last several centuries to establish a so-called "global village" with multiple spheres – cultural, economic, ecological, political, social, etc. However, the various phases of globalization have had divergent scope, actors, dimensions and dynamics. Hence, each of the phases of globalization can be differentiated using the aforementioned markers. Since 1990, the "new globalization" has emerged as the current phase of the phenomenon. Among other things, the "new globalization" is the most expansive and technological advanced of all of the phases of globalization. For example, the "new globalization" has occasioned, inter alia, the integration of virtually all states of the world and non-state actors into the global capitalist system. The resultant consequences have differed from country to country and region to region.

Against this background, the African Studies and Research Forum (ASRF) of the Association of Third World Studies, as part of its "Research Program on Africa," assigned me the task of assembling a group of Africanist scholars to examine some of the effects the "new globalization" has, and continues to have on Africa. I would like to thank Professor John Mukum Mbaku, the former President of the ASFR, and Professor E.Ike Udogu, the former Director of Research and Publications of the ASRF, for the support and encouragement they provided for the project from its conception to completion.

Also, I would like to express my gratitude to the contributors to the research project and this volume for the time and effort they committed to the project. Particularly, their very insightful chapters on some of the frontier issues confronting Africa in the age of the "new globalization" will help this volume to make a significant contribution to the scholarly literature on globalization as well as the on going debate in various circles.

At Ashgate Publishing Company, Kirstin Howgate, the Publisher of International Relations, deserves thanks and gratitude for working with me very patiently first on the prospectus and subsequently on the research and writing of the book. Also, I am grateful to the anonymous reviewers for their very insightful and useful suggestions which definitely helped to improve both the foci and quality of the book. In a similar vein, I would like to thank the Production Department for working with me as the volume proceeded through the various stages of the production process.

Finally, I would like to thank my dear wife, Doris, for her usual understanding, support and encouragement. Particularly, she allowed me to devote a substantial amount of time to researching and writing my own chapters for the volume, and in the labor intensive process of editing and preparing the volume.

Acknowledgement

John Wiley and Sons granted permission for parts of John Mukum Mbaku's article, "Improving African Participation in the Global Economy: The Role of Economic Freedom", *Business and Contemporary World*, Vol. 10, No. 2, 1998, pp. 297–238, to be used in chapter 7 (The New Globalization and the Environment in Africa) of this volume. I am grateful to the publisher for the permission.

Chapter 1

Introduction: From The Old to the New Globalization

George Klay Kieh, Jr.

Introduction

The end of the Cold War witnessed the singing of a requiem for the previous global order and its attendant ideological rivalry that handcuffed cooperation and interdependence. The disintegration and collapse of the Soviet Union robbed Stalinist socialism of its pre-eminent "heavyweight," and removed the major ideological, economic, political and military-security barriers to the consolidation of the global capitalist order as the systemic suzerain. Thus, the stage was set for the consolidation of global capitalism in virtually every corner of the world. The emergent nascent global order referred to as the "new globalization" has taken the world by "storm," since its inception in 1990. As Halliday (2001, p. 60) observes," Globalization has become from the early 1990s onwards the central topic of debate in social sciences and in much public debate, in both developed and developing societies." Similarly, as Kiggundu (2002, p. ix) notes,

> Globalization has come to characterize the end of the twentieth century and the beginning of the new millennium. It makes and unmakes individuals, families, organizations, communities, and nation-states. Some think it will save the world; others are convinced it will destroy it.

The new globalization has unleashed a whirlwind in virtually every area of human endeavor. For example, there is the dawning of new technologies, dramatic medical advances, an information explosion, and a rapidly growing global economy (Watch Tower, 2000, p. 2). Adams et al. (1999, p. 1) capture the essence of the cascading effects of the new globalization thus:

> Globalization is the defining characteristic of our time. The modern system of independent nation-states and distinct national economies is being replaced by a single transnational political economy. Power and authority are steadily shifting to global institutions and corporations. National governments have seen their sovereignty and control over domestic political and economic affairs rapidly diminished.

In effect, the dominant thinking in development today sees globalization as a matter of life or death for less developed countries (Heredia, 1997, p. 383). If embraced, it is argued, globalization will quickly propel developing nations into modernity and affluence; if resisted, it will either crush them or throw them by the way side (Heredia, 1997, p. 383). The bottom line is that the new globalization makes and unmakes individuals, families, organizations, communities, and the nation-states (Kiggundu, 2002, p. ix). Some think it will save the world; others are convinced it will destroy it (Kiggundu, 2002, p. ix).

However, on the other hand, the new globalization is confronted with daunting challenges. There is burgeoning increase in the incidence of civil wars and the associated humanitarian crises. Particularly, in the case of Africa, this reflects a deepening crisis of the neo-colonial state. By the year 2020, non-communicable diseases are expected to account for seven out of every ten deaths in the developing regions, compared with less than half today (Watch Tower, 2000, p. 2). Some experts claim that by 2010, 66 million few people will be alive in the 23 countries with the most severe AIDS epidemic (Watch Tower, 2000, p. 2).

Against this background, the purpose of this chapter is three-fold. First, the chapter will examine the nature, dynamics and effects of the old globalization on Africa. The rationale is to situate the new globalization in Africa within the appropriate historical crucible. Second, the objectives of the book will be discussed. Third, the various chapters in the book will be summarized.

The Old Globalization

Background

The old globalization developed in three major phases concurrent with the evolution of the international capitalist order. The motor force was the union of industrial and bank capital into monopoly capital and its spillover across the boundaries of European states, and the consequent creation of a world order which closely linked the economies of various countries (Nnoli, 2003, p. 1). The first phase, which Roskin and Berry (2002, p. 259) refer to as the "Victorian globalization," started in 1960 and declined in 1914. This initial phase was the formative epoch of the global capitalist order. It commenced with the inception of the industrial revolution. The resultant technological capacities introduced by the industrial revolution boosted economic production unprecedented in the annals of human existence. The productive process requires the availability of raw materials and markets to sell the products. In turn, these imperatives necessitated efforts to expand the ambit of the Euro-centric international system, the undertaking of colonial and imperialist adventures in the developing world and the efforts to promote global trade. The imposition of colonialism on the peoples of the Third World was the highlight of the project of conquest and control. However, the formative phase was aborted by the eruption of the First World War.

The end of the First World War witnessed the intensification of efforts to complete the formation of the international capitalist order and to extend its tentacles to virtually every corner of the globe. Accordingly, the signing of the Versailles Treaty in 1919 commenced the expansionist phase of the old globalization. This era witnessed efforts to create a "global village" principally through the acceleration of trade and investment. However, the "Great Depression" and the Second World War derailed the expansionist phase of the old globalization.

With the end of the Second World War in 1945, the second phase of the old globalization began. This epoch was propelled by improvement in communications, increased international investments, especially by American corporations in Western Europe and increased trade. The second phase (1945–1990) had several distinctive features. At the vortex of the emergent global political economy was capitalist suzerainty, despite the ideological challenge posed by Stalinist socialism. In other words, the capitalist mode of production and its attendant structures, relations and processes constituted the kernels of the overarching framework of the old globalization. Another major feature was the reconfiguration of global power relations: Power shifted from continental Europe to the United States and the Soviet Union, as the two superpowers. The two superpowers became locked in an intense rivalry for global domination. The rivalry occasioned, inter alia, the burgeoning increase in the global arms race, including the two superpowers' respective nuclear arsenals. Similarly, both superpowers engaged in unprecedented arms transfers especially to client regimes and groups. Also, the superpower rivalry had a deleterious impact on the promotion of international cooperation, since states were forced to align with one power bloc or the other. Ultimately, the globalization project was handicapped by the existence of two competing international economic systems: The global capitalist and the global Stalinist socialist systems. The former, which was under American leadership, had several major features. Trade in the "American orbit" was conducted under the framework of the Generalized Agreement on Tariffs and Trade. Also, financial and economic relations were managed through the "Bretton Woods Institutions" comprising the International Monetary Fund (IMF) and the International Bank for Reconstruction and Development (IBRD) or the "World Bank Group." By the 1950s, the ambit of the capitalist sphere was expanded to incorporate the emerging independent states in the periphery. The North Atlantic Treaty Organization (NATO) served as the "security shield" against the Soviet Union and its allies. On the other hand, the Stalinist socialist system was under Soviet leadership. It primarily consisted of the Soviet Union and Eastern and Central Union states. The Council for Mutual Economic Assistance (COMECON) served as the framework through which economic relations between and among the members states were coordinated. At the military-security level, the Warsaw Treaty Organization served as the countervailing force to the North Atlantic Treaty Organization.

The old globalization ended in 1990, with the collapse and subsequent disintegration of the Soviet Union. Also, the various Soviet client states in Central and Eastern Europe abandoned the Stalinist socialist path to development and decamped to the American-led capitalist bloc. Moreover, even China, the self-appointed guardian of so-called "pure scientific socialism" shifted its mode of production from "Maoist socialism" to capitalism. The end of the second and final phase of the old globalization came with the end of the ideological rivalry between capitalism and Stalinist socialism.

Africa and the Old Globalization

Africa's relations with the old globalization proceeded in various stages. Africa's initial contact with the old globalization was made in the sixteenth century through trade relations with various European imperial agents. From their inception, Afro-European relations were conducted under a framework of unequal exchange and exploitation, prompting Palmberg (1983, p. 5) to characterize these relations as "the extension of [European] piracy that was going on along the Mediterranean coast." Basically, the Europeans traded inferior goods that were no longer marketable in Europe for high quality African goods. The resultant "system of unequal exchange" was propelled by the European traders' abilities to cajole and deceive backed by their reliance on their home countries' repository of force.

Enticed by the lucrative nature of the "system of unequal exchange," the Europeans made the determination that Africa was endowed with substantial human capital. Hence, based on the exigencies of their dominant feudal mode of production, especially the need for physical labor, the Europeans decided to use African slave labor. Accordingly, the Europeans established a diabolical slave system replete with the trappings of cruelty, barbarity, exploitation and abuse as the *dues ex machina* for obtaining cheap labor from the continent. Importantly, the slave system was designed to rob Africa of the cream of its human capital; thus, the Europeans focused on Africans between the ages of 16–25. Operationally, the Europeans used various methods. One major instrumentarium was kidnapping. Like brigands and criminal gangs, the Europeans roamed various communities on the continent and abducted young men and women. Another method was so-called "purchasing." Under this arrangement, Europeans "bought "African as slaves from African political elites. Importantly, the impetus for the establishment of the slave selling industry in Africa was provided by the European slave traders. That is, to use the capitalist parlance, the European slave traders' "demand" for slaves stimulated the "supply" in Africa.

So, Africans who were kidnapped and "purchased" by European slave traders were chained and packed into ships bounded for Europe, the Americas and the Caribbean to work as slaves on various European-owned plantations. Given the horrendous conditions, scores of Africans died during the journey across the Atlantic Ocean. Similarly, against the backdrop of the inhumane conditions on the various plantations, thousands of Africans also died. Significantly, those Africans who survived the recurrent cruel and inhumane treatment provided the free labor that was epicentral to the production of the wealth that constructed European states and the United States.

Excited by the immense profitability of the "system of unequal exchange" and slavery, the Europeans decided to formally colonize Africa. But, there was a major conundrum: Since the European states had data about the economic topography of Africa, all of them were desirous of colonizing these lucrative areas. Accordingly, fierce competition emerged based on a "zero sum game". As Fetter (1979, p. 7) argues, "By 1884, competition for the … territories of Africa had become so intense that the rulers of the colonizing nations concluded that it was necessary to regulate the process of annexation by international agreement." Accordingly, under the German-French initiative, the various colonial and imperialist powers met at the

Berlin Conference (1884–1885) to develop a framework for regulating the process of territorial conquest and annexation in Africa. Under the framework appropriately dubbed the "scramble for Africa," the various colonial and imperialist powers carved up the territories of Africa in a manner akin to hunters dividing meat after a hunting expedition.

Having carved up African territories, the imperialists sent armies to Africa in order to turn the boundaries on their maps into frontiers on the ground (Birmingham, 1995, p.3). Owners of the land who resisted the arrival of the self-styled force of "civilization" were to be "pacified "by conquest (Birmingham, 1995, p. 3). With the process of territorial conquest and annexation completed, the imperialist powers than established what Kieh (2007, p. 3) calls the "Berlinist state." Although the "Berlinist state" had variations – Belgian, British, Dutch, French, German, Italian, Portuguese and Spanish –, its single *raison d'etre* was to serve as the "Leviathan" for facilitating imperialist plundering and pillaging of Africa. The Berlinist state had several core features, prominent among which was its absolutist character. Ake (1996, p. 2) provides a comprehensive summation of the pedigree of the totalitarian colonial state:

> The colonial state redistributed land and determined who should produce what and how. It attended to the supply of labor, sometimes resorting to force labor; it churned out administrative instruments and legislated taxes to induce the breakup of traditional social relations of production, the atomization of society; and the process of proletarianization. It went into the business of education to ensure that workers could do the jobs they were required to perform and would remain steadfast in the performance of their often tedious and disagreeable tasks...Indeed, it controlled every aspect of the colonial economy tight to maintain its power and domination to realize the economic objectives of colonization.

Despite the ubiquity and brutality of the colonial state, Africans in the various colonies organized broad-based movements as the vehicles for waging the struggle for independence against the colonialists and the imperialists. The struggles assumed several forms in the various colonies – ranging from protest to the armed struggle. Characteristically, the colonial and imperialist powers responded to the agitation for independence with increased repression. However, a confluence of factors – the toll of the pro-independence struggles; the devastation visited on the economies of the imperialist powers by World War Two; the consequent domestic pressure within the various imperialist powers urging a shift in focus form empire building and maintenance to national reconstruction; and the shift in the global "balance of power" from Europe to the United States and the Soviet Union – forced the imperialist powers to give up their respective colonies. Accordingly, the 1960s was Africa's *annus mirabilis* evidenced by the wave of "flag independence" that began to sweep across the continent. However, the Portuguese remained intransigent in their refusal to dismantle their colonial empire on the continent, until 1975.

Significantly, the end of colonialism did not mean the end of imperialist control over the continent. As Okigbo (1993, p. 29) observes, "Having lost direct authority... the colonial powers sought to retain colonial control through a series of undeclared protocols: economic and political ties and traditions linking the colonial territories to the metropolis..." Within the broader context, the newly independent African states were formally incorporated into the "old globalization" as peripheral players with the continuing responsibility of serving as plantations for the production of raw materials – agricultural, mineral and oil – to cater to the insatiable appetite of the industrial-manufacturing complexes of the metropolitan powers. Domestically, with very few exceptions, the newly emergent ruling classes within the various African states failed to deconstruct, rethink and democratically reconstitute the colonial state. Instead, they adopted the colonial state in its neo-colonial incarnation.

Overall, the "old globalization" robbed Africa through its insidious "system of unequal exchange," slavery, colonialism and neo-colonialism. Specifically, African was stripped of the human and material resources exigent for national development. Instead, these resources were stolen by the imperialist powers and used to promote development in their respective countries. So, during the "old globalization," in dialectical terms, the underdevelopment of Africa facilitated the development of European states and the United States. In essence, with the collusion between the Africa ruling classes and their patrons in the metropolis, the "old globalization" was pivotal to the development of the multifaceted crises of underdevelopment that engulfed the continent from the 1960s to the 1990s.

The Transition to the "New Globalization"

Background

As has been indicated, the "new globalization" emerged beginning in 1990, replacing the "old globalization." The transition was necessitated by the various changes that were taking place in the international system. At the vortex was the phenomenal advancement in technology and its consequent impact on virtually all spheres of human activities. The other major factors included the end of the Cold War and the so-called "triumph" of capitalism; the absence of a global challenge to capitalist hegemony; the availability of the old "Soviet sphere of influence" and the People's Republic of China for incorporation into the global capitalist system; and the resultant emergence of "new enclaves" to serve the profit-maximization agendas of multinational corporations and the other suzerains of the international capitalist system. Against this background, the "old globalization" was deemed incapable of dealing with these new developments.

The Incorporation and Re-incorporation of African States into the Global Capitalist System

On the African continent, all of the states that were charting non-capitalist paths to development virtually crumbled under the "weight" of the "new globalization." Accordingly, all of them adopted the peripheral capitalist mode of production and its associated political economy. As for the "old" peripheral capitalist African states, they were simply re-incorporated into the international capitalist order. Interestingly, outliers such as Mauritius and Libya that experimented with social democracy and Arab socialism respectively have also been fully incorporated into the international capitalist system. In short, all of the states in Africa have become appendages of the "newly globalized capitalist system."

Against this background, the "new globalization" has set into motion the second phase of neo-colonial domination, plunder, pillage and exploitation in Africa. Given its unbridled hegemony, the "new globalization" is rendering African states incapable of designing and implementing their own independent national development agendas, and controlling the various transactions – economics, etc – that are taking place within their respective territories. To make matters worse, African states have failed to develop the requisite structures and policies to effectively tackle the multiple cascading effects of the "new globalization." Even in cases where such architectures are developed, they tend to reinforce Africa's subordinate role in the "international division of labor" and the other structures of the "new globalization." For example, the "New Economic Partnership for Africa's Development (NEPAD) is a recipe for cementing the dependency relationship between the developed capitalist states and African states (Kieh, 2003). This is because NEPAD accepts the unjust international capitalist system and its vagaries as givens (Kieh, 2003). Unchallenged and emboldened by the subservience of the ruling classes in Africa, the forces of the "new globalization" are succeeding in their efforts to re-colonize Africa, particularly, to continue using the continent's vast resources – oil and minerals – for promoting development, including the advancement of the standard of living of the citizens of the advanced industrialized capitalist states. On the other hand, the multifaceted crises of underdevelopment on the African continent are getting worse. For example, as the various annual human development reports published by the United Nations Development Program show, the vast majority of Africans are being increasingly swallowed by the "quicksand" of abject poverty, mass unemployment, burgeoning rates of illiteracy, the lack of access to health care, safe drinking water and sanitation and the resultant high rates of malnutrition, vulnerability to diseases, infant mortality, maternal mortality and deaths. In short, overall, the "new globalization" is sharpening the dialectical tension between development in the advanced industrialized capitalist states and underdevelopment in African states.

The Focus of the Book

The central problematique that the book seeks to address is the impact of the "new globalization" on Africa. In order to address the core research problem, the chapters in the book examine various frontier issues in Africa – the debt crisis, human rights, development, state sovereignty, the environment and the HIV/AIDS pandemic – in terms of the ways they are conditioned and framed by the "new globalization" and the resultant effects on the region.

Based on the analysis of the nature and impact of the "nee globalization" on Africa in the aforementioned frontier areas, the various chapters then suggest some ways in which Africa could be repositioned to address the effects in ways that benefit the continent. The underlying premise is that given the ubiquity and the attendant commanding power of the "new globalization" African states need to develop the requisite structures and policies to help manage the consequences of the phenomenon.

The Organization of the Book

The book consists of three parts embodying nine (9) chapters. In chapter 1, George Klay Kieh, Jr. attempts to put the "new globalization" in historical context, by, among other things discussing the "old globalization" and its various phases. Kieh then examines the impact of the "old globalization" on Africa by addressing issues such as slavery, colonialism and neo-colonialism. He then links the "old globalization" to the "new one," by deciphering some of the major factors that led to the transition from the former to the latter. This is followed by a discussion of the central research problem of the book. Finally, he summarizes the various chapters that constitute the volume.

Chapter 2 provides the analytical framework of the book. Specifically, Kieh examines the scope, ideological underpinnings and the dimensions and dynamics of the "new globalization." According to him, the "new globalization" differs from the "old one" in two major ways. First, the "new globalization" encompasses the totality of the actors in the international system – state and non-state. Second, the "new globalization" is anchored on unprecedented technological developments. In terms of ideology, like the "old globalization," the "new globalization" is a handmaid of international capitalism. The chapter ends with a discussion of the multidimensionality of the "new globalization."

John Mukum Mbaku tackles the issue of the debilitating debt crisis in Africa in chapter 3. He begins by placing the debt crisis within the broader context of the crises of underdevelopment that have plagued the continent since the dawn of the post-colonial era. He then examines the nature and dynamics of the various debt forgiveness programs proffered by the developed capitalist states and the Bretton Woods international financial institutions – International Monetary Fund (IMF) and the World Bank – in the context of the "new globalization." He argues that the current debt forgiveness programs will not help lift up Africa from the abyss of underdevelopment because they are decoupled from the critical exigency for state reconstitution in Africa. Alternatively, Mbaku proposes debt cancellation as the best solution to the crisis. But, importantly, he argues that in order to have the desired impact, debt cancellation must take place in the context of state reconstitution. Such a process must be anchored on institutional reforms. These reforms must occasion the creation of transparent, accountable and participatory governance structures that would curtail the propensity of some African policy makers to engage in reckless borrowing and/or corruption. Additionally, he suggests that African states should create wealth and promote indigenous entrepreneurialship as strategies for helping to alleviate poverty.

Chapter 4 focuses on the vexatious issue of human rights. E.Ike Udogu probes the travails of human rights in the continent using the African Charter on Human and Peoples' Rights and various international human rights regimes as the evaluative frameworks. He concludes that despite the emphasis of the "new globalization" on, among other things, the promotion of political rights and civil liberties, the state of human rights in Africa remains generally poor. Against this backdrop, he proposes various modalities for improving the state of human rights, including human rights education and an increased role for human rights based non-governmental organizations.

Pablo Idahosa examines the roles and relationships between the state in Africa and non-governmental organizations in the critical area of development in chapter 5. He argues that since the advent of the "new globalization" NGOs have become major actors in the development arena of African states. By and large, these NGOs have tried to undermine and minimize the roles of African states in their own development processes as part of the "new globalization's" agenda of strengthening the dependency relationship between Africa and global capitalist system. Alternatively, Idahosa suggests that there is a need to establish democratic developmental states in Africa that will recapture and control the process of development in the interests of the African peoples.

In chapter 6, Jacque Mangala probes the challenges being posed by globalization to state sovereignty in Africa. He begins by surveying the scholarly literature on sovereignty. This is followed by an examination of the impact of the "old globalization" on state sovereignty in Africa. Initially, during colonialism, he argues that the "old globalization" wiped out state sovereignty in Africa, and instead made the continent an object of international relations whose interests and destiny were decided by external powers. Similarly, during the post-colonial era, according to Mangala, Africa has not enjoyed the full panoply of sovereignty as embodied in the Westphalian framework. Regarding the "new globalization," he posits that due to, among other things, the aforementioned and other constraints, Africa was not ready to face the challenges of the phenomenon. Mangala then identifies four major effects of the "new globalization" on state sovereignty in the continent. First, the new globalization has limited the abilities of African states to formulate and implement autonomous economic and social policies. Second, the phenomenon obstructs the promotion of democratization. Third, the new globalization inhibits the ability of African states to deal with computer-based crime. Fourth, the phenomenon hamstrings the region's ability to protect and regulate the environment. Mangala suggests that the best way in which African states can successfully face and mediate the challenges of the new globalization is through what he calls "pooled sovereignty based on autonomous regionalism."

Chapter 7 focuses on the state of the environment in Africa. John Mukum Mbaku begins with the argument that the genesis of environmental degradation in Africa can be traced to colonial exploitation and plunder. During the post-colonial era, the situation continued because of African states' poorly specified and unenforced property rights in environmental resources. According to him, this major shortcoming has led to the excessive exploitation of the region's environmental resources by the developed states and their multinational corporations. In terms of the new globalization, Mbaku argues that the phenomenon is affecting the environment on the continent in several major ways. At the core is the increased demand for natural resources, especially oil. This has accelerated the pace of environmental degradation, for example in places like the Niger Delta region of Nigeria. Another adverse effect is that multinational corporations are engaged in various activities that are exacerbating environmental degradation. Also, Africa's continual role as an enclave for the production of raw materials has increased, given the need for raw materials to feed the manufacturing complexes in the developed states. This is contributing to the problem of massive pollution. Mbaku provides various prescriptions for helping to address the continent's environmental conundrum. First, there is a need to reconstitute the state in Africa, and to, among other things, formulate and implement institutional mechanisms that will hold state managers and multinational corporations accountable. Second, African states need to integrate base on changes in the composition of their trade. Third, human capital needs to be developed, so that they can engage in the research and development of environmentally-friendly products.

Amy Patterson addresses the frontier social issue of HIV/AIDS in chapter 8. Her central argument is that due to the uneven benefits of globalization, some aspects of globalization have facilitated the spread of HIV/AIDS in Africa and complicated the continent's ability to address the pandemic. However, on the other hand, other aspects of globalization have helped developed modalities for addressing the disease. Specifically, in the case of the adverse effects of the new globalization on the spread of HIV/AIDS, Patterson identifies four major cases: labor migration, the adoption of neo-liberal economic policies and the correspondingly decimation of the "social safety net" in African states; the increased power of the World Trade Organization and the resultant impact of its intellectual property regime on accessibility to HIV/AIDS drugs; and lack of sustained interest in Africa by the major powers in the current post-Cold war era. On the other hand, she asserts that the phenomenon is having some positive effects: the role of the global media and entertainment industry in promoting awareness; the establishment of transnational advocacy groups; and promotion of global cooperation; and medical advances.

In chapter 9, George Klay Kieh, Jr. attempts to draw the lessons from the impact of the "new globalization" on Africa, and to map out a general trajectory designed to help Africa develop the requisite institutions, rules, processes and policies to address the effects of the phenomenon. Specifically, he identifies four major lessons. First, African states do not have the requisite architecture that would enable them to mediate, contain and address the effects of the "new globalization." Undoubtedly, the neo-colonial state, which has been an agent of the "old globalization", is incapable of shielding the continent from the adverse effects of the "new globalization." This is because by its nature, mission and character the neo-colonial African state is designed to make Africa vulnerable to the pathologies of the "new globalization." Second, African states continue to remain on the periphery of the "new world order." Third, overall, treading along the same line as its progenitor, the "new globalization" is worsening the crises of underdevelopment on the continent. Fourth, the African ruling classes are content to continue"eating the crumbs from the table" of the "new globalization." Alternatively, Kieh suggests three measures that would help strengthen Africa to face the challenges of the "new globalization." At the fulcrum is the urgent need to deconstruct, rethink and democratically reconstitute the neo-colonial state. Another measure is the necessity of fostering serious regionalism. Also, there is the critical need to transform the Non-aligned Movement and the "Group of 77" into a single new multipurpose organization that would serve as a platform for promoting political and socio-economic development in the third world.

References

Adams, Francis et al. (1999), *Globalization and the Developing World: An Introduction.* (London: Macmillan).

Ake, Claude (1996), *Democracy and Development in Africa* (Washington D.C. The Brookings Institution).

Birmingham, David (1995), *The Decolonization of Africa* (London: University College of London Press).

Fetter, Bruce (1979), *Colonial Rule in Africa* (Madison, WI: University of Wisconsin Press).

Heredia, Blanca (1997), "Prosper or Perish? Development in the Age of Global Capital", in *Current History* November, pp. 383–388.

Kieh, George Klay (2007), "Introduction: The Terminally Ill Berlinist State", in G. Klay Kieh, Jr. (ed.), *Beyond State Failure and Collapse: Making the State Relevant in Africa* (Lanham, MD: Lexington Books).

Kieh, George Klay (2003), "Africa, the New Partnership for Africa's Development and the International Capitalist Order.", in *Journal of Comparative Education and International Relations in Africa*, Vol. 5. Nos. 1–2, pp. 111–127.

Kiggundu, Moses (2002), *Managing Globalization in Developing Countries and Transnational Economics* (Westport, CT: Praeger).

Nnoli, Okwudibe (2003), *The Linkage Between Globalization, Development and Democracy in Africa* (DPMF Publications), pp. 1–11.

Okigbo, Pius (1993), "The Future Hunted By the Past" in A. Adedeji (ed.), *Africa Within the World: Beyond Dispossession and Dependence* (London: Zed Books).

Palmberg, Mai (1983), "Introduction", in M. Palmberg.(ed.), *The Struggle for Africa* (London: Zed Books).

Roskin, Michael and Berry, Nicholas (2002), *IR: The New World of International Relations*, 5th edn (Upper Saddle River, NJ: Prentice-Hall).

Watch Tower (2002), *The New Millennium: Dawn of a New Age?* (Brooklyn, NY: Watch Tower Publications).

Chapter 2

The New Globalization: Scope, Nature and Dimensions

George Klay Kieh, Jr.

Introduction

The "new globalization" made it "triumphant entry" onto the global stage, beginning in 1990. Emboldened by the collapse of Stalinist socialism and the "victory" of capitalism, the "new globalization" moved like a whirlwind across the successor Soviet states, the former Stalinist states of Central and Eastern Europe, the People's Republic of China, Vietnam and the rest of the world incorporating these and other areas that were hitherfore outside of the ambit of the global capitalist order.

Since its emergence as the new phase in the development of the international capitalist order, the phenomenon has unleashed aan unprecedented expansion in the various modes of the international capitalist order. For example, there has been the dawning of new technology, dramatic medical advances, an information explosion, and a rapidly growing global economy (Watch Tower, 2000, p. 2). On the other hand, the "new globalization" is confronted with and is contributing to various global challenges. For example, there is a burgeoning increase in the incidence of civil wars and their associated humanitarian crises. Particularly, in the cases of the affected African states, these wars are manifestations of the acute crisis of the neo-colonial state. Also, the assault on the environment continues Given its expansive ambit, the "new globalization" arguably is the most important process affecting relations between states, as well as non-state actors today (Ray and Kaarbo, 2002, p. 486).

Against this background, the overarching purpose of this chapter is to develop an analytical framework for this volume. Based on this, several specific derivatives can be explicated. First, the chapter will examine the expanse of the "new globalization." Second, it will decipher the phenomenon's ideological Weltanschauung. Third, it will discuss the various dimensions of the phenomenon

Scope

The "new globalization" is the most expansive phase of the international capitalist system. It covers all of the regions, sub-regions and countries in the world. Also, the tapestry embodies virtually all non-state actors – international organizations (both intergovernmental and non-governmental), multinational corporations and other businesses, transnational movements and criminal networks.

In geographical terms, the tentacles of the phenomenon are spread over 148.94 million square km of land mass (Union of International Association, 2000<www.uia.org>). Demographically, the phenomenon incorporates and impacts a total of 6.5 billion people (U.S. Census Bureau, 2006 <www.census.govlipc/www/worldpop.html>) in 193 independent states (Rosenberg, 2006, p. 1). In the case of the non-state actors, the "new globalization" envelops about 1,839 inter-governmental organizations (IGOs) and 17,077 non-governmental organizations (NGOs) (Union of International Association<www.uia.org>). As Berrizbeitia (1999, p. 195) notes, "The new globalization has a worldwide reach: its breadth, speed and intensity seem to be substantially larger than they were in the past, and the corresponding impacts on societies and individuals may be correspondingly more intense as well."

The Ideological Panoply

The "new globalization" is conditioned and propelled by a capitalist ideological orientation. The ideological panoply is anchored on several contours. The market is supreme. It, inter alia, determines global "supply and demand." This means that the so-called "market forces" determine the volume and prices of goods – manufactured, semi-manufactured and primary – and services.

Another tenet is the "rolling back" of the state. This means the establishment of a "super minimalist" state that has virtually no role in the ownership of the major means of production and the making of production and distribution decisions. A major part of this process is, as Haque (1999, p. 77) observes, "The replacement of state planning by market forces." Instead, the major emerging role of the state is to provide a conducive environment for the private accumulation of capital by the bourgeoisies – both international and local. Linked to the accumulation function of the state is a "law and order" one. In the bowels of the "new globalization," the redesigned pro-capitalist state is expected to protect the capitalists and their physical assets from destruction by the possible actions of the exploited and marginalized subaltern classes.

The related element is the privatization of state assets. In those countries where the state previously owned and controlled some levers of the mode of production, these assets are being privatized – sold off to various global and local capitalists. The major rationale that has been provided by the forces of the "new globalization" is the rehashing of the old argument by capitalist political economy that the state is not efficient in the management of a business enterprise, irrespective of the sector of the economy in which such entity is based. Alternatively, the myth is peddled that the private sector is more efficient than the state. To the contrary, as the empirical evidence shows, both state-owned and privately-owned enterprises in various countries around the world have been both efficient and inefficient. Hence, there is no basis for the claim that the private sector is more efficient in managing business entities. Clearly, the efficiency of a business entity is determined by a confluence of factors – "public good" versus "private good," the management skills, accountability, etc. So, the private sector does not have a monopoly over economic efficiency. If this was the case, then what accounts for the myriad cases of bankruptcy, "going out of business," and "mergers?"

Also, there is the "folding of the social safety net" tenet. Under this requirement, peripheral states are required to end their various programs in areas such as public education, public housing and public transportation. Alternatively, these social programs should be privatized. For example, the World Bank, one of the major agents of the "new globalization", is pressuring African states to end their investments in public higher education. The alternative is to turn over to private ownership this area that is critical to the development of these countries.

Ultimately, the overarching contour is the facilitation of the rapacious process of capital accumulation by metropolitan-based multinational corporations and other businesses. That is, the capitalist doctrine dictates that all "barriers" to profit-making are to be removed, and the possibilities for the unbridled and unfettered accumulation of wealth be expanded and protected. Significantly, the profit-making imperative takes priority over the provision of basic human needs, especially vulnerable groups, human safety and ecological sustainability. In other words, in the cases in which these objectives conflict with the profit-making project, the latter takes precedence, irrespective of the outcome.

The Dimensions

As has been argued, the "new globalization" is a multifaceted phenomenon with various dimensions – cultural, economic, environmental, military, political, and social, among others. Against this backdrop, this section will map out the nature and dynamics of some of the various dimensions.

Cultural Globalization

The *raison d'être* of cultural globalization is to foster "homogenization." This entails, among other things, the creation of a common global culture. Like the other dimensions of the "new globalization," cultural globalization is propelled by imperialism. Operationally, the essence of the cultural dimension (cultural globalization) of imperialism is the creation of fantasies to escape from misery. It involves the fusion of commercialism, sexuality and conservatism – each presented as idealized expression of private needs, of individual self-realization (Blog City, 2007, p. 7).

Interestingly, the emergent trend of cultural globalization is to design a global culture based on American suzerainty. Accordingly, as Wagnleitner and May (2000, p. 1) correctly note, "To almost any casual observer, it looks as though the popular culture of the United States has spread all over the world: here, there and everywhere. From Argentina to the Congo, the Democratic Republic of the Congo, India to Nigeria..." Significantly, U.S. imperialism as embodied in cultural globalization has two major interlocking goals: to capture markets for its commodities and to establish hegemony in shaping popular consciousness (Petras, 2004, p. 1).

Cultural globalization has several major elements. The food aspect involves the spread of Western products throughout the world. For example, Gerber, Coca-cola, Starbucks, Kentucky Fried Chicken, Häagen-Dazs, and Dunkin' Donuts are readily available in the People's Republic of China (Ray and Kaarbo, 2002, p. 488). Similarly, McDonald's has over 200 restaurants in China with over 150 in Hong Kong alone(Watson, 2000, p. 120). Also, McDonald's largest restaurant is not found in New York City or Los Angeles but in Beijing and second largest is in Moscow (Schiller, 1996, p. 119). In total, McDonald's has 17,000 franchise restaurants in 90 different countries (Official Olympic Website, 1996). Coca-Cola is even more globalized (McAllister, 1997, p. 38). As Barnett and Cavanagh (1994, p. 109) aptly note, "What was once advertised across America as 'The Pause that refreshes' now takes place 560 million times a day every day in 160 countries." The export of American and Western consumption habits to other countries has implications for the latter. One major consequence is the alteration of the diet of the peoples in the various affected countries. That is, over time, the peoples abandoned their indigenous food products. The related problem is that the changes in diet adversely impact local businesses that produce and sell indigenous foods. Some of the negative effects include the loss of revenues due to poor sales, the reduction of the labor force and its implications for unemployment and poverty and closure. For American and Western businesses, this development helps to expand their market reach and their revenue base.

Similarly, jeans, baseball caps, t-shirts and brand name sneakers – Reeboks, Nikes, etc – are becoming common dress for millions of people, especially the youth, all over the world – from Africa to Eastern Europe. The capitalist marketing machine promotes these forms of dress with missionary zeal. Consumers in various countries are socialized to accept the myth that American-styled dress sets the standards in terms of modernity and civilization. Clearly, the propaganda is having the desired effects evidenced by the fact that scores of people around the world are abandoning their traditional dresses and adopting the American ones. Jha (2001, p. 1) captures the impact of American-styled dress on India thus:

> Traditional dress for Indian women, the saree and the salwar kameez, have been cast aside in the bigger cities for Wrangler or Lee jeans with skimpy half-shirts baring the mid-riff. And countless Indian girls have taken to dying their hair blonde, as more beauty parlors pop up to fill the demand.

Movies constitute another major element of cultural globalization. Films from various countries around the world adorn cinemas throughout the globe. However, the majority of the films are American. For example, in 2005, the United States accounted for about 50% of the films that were distributed world-wide(Rosen, 2005).The asymmetry in the distribution of films gives American movies the distinct advantage in helping to shape the perceptions and dreams of ordinary people. Also, the American movies industry is reaping a disproportionate share of global box office sales. For example in 2003, American films accounted for approximately 80% of global box office revenue (Galeota, 2004, p. 22). This translated into about $20.3 billion (Rosen, 2005, p. 3). Hollywood is the fulcrum of American domination of the global movies industry, As Lee (2005, p. 1) asserts, "With economic, institutional and political power, Hollywood has been wielding its influence worldwide without any real competition." Lord Putnam (1999, p. 1) provides an excellent summation of American suzerainty in the global film market:

> I think it's unarguable to assert that American movies now dominate the world's cinema screens. Walk through the downtown streets of just any city in the world and the paraphernalia of advertising is dominated by giant ads for "Event" movies, *Star Wars*, *Matrix* and the Austin Powers sequel. The ubiquity of these movies – and marketing campaigns which support them – is surely the ultimate testimony to the maxim that Hollywood is "not a place, but a state of mind."

Also, since music is an integral part of human history and culture, its is no surprise that cultural globalization has shaped the evolution of music (Boursy, 2007, p. 1). One of the major ways in which this has been done is through the expansion of the geographic scope and reach of music. The international system is being graced with varieties of music form Africa, Asia, Europe, Latin America and North America, as well as hybrid that blend indigenous music with techniques from hip hop, rock or jazz (Boursy, 2007, p. 1). Radios, aircrafts, the internet, CDs and videos have served as major outlets for globalizing music. However, the diversity in the types of music is not matched by the nature of control of the music industry: The latter is oligopolistc. It is controlled by seven major metropolitan-based conglomerates: Sony (Japan), Time/Warner (USA), PolyGram (Netherlands/Germany), Bertelsmann Media Group (Germany), Thorn/EMI (Britain), MCA (United States, and Virgin (United Kingdom). These conglomerates control the music industry in terms of contents, distribution and price. Clearly, their stranglehold on the industry is also translating into huge revenues. For example, in 1990, barely a year after the advent of the "new globalization," the seven corporations collectively earned $13.88 billion in sales (Burnett, 1996, p. 143).

Economic Globalization

Economic globalization is an amalgam of interactions that take place within the structure, decision-making system, the "division of labor" and pricing system of the global capitalist system. Structurally, there is a broad array of actors – states and non-state. The state actors are divided into core – the United States, Japan, etc. –, the semi-peripheral states – Singapore, Taiwan and South Korea, among others –, the transitional former Stalinist socialist states of the Soviet Union and Central and Eastern Europe and China, and the peripheral states – primarily third world countries – that constitute the majority. Among the non-state actors, there are two sets of pivotal players: the Bretton Woods institutions – the International Monetary Fund (IMF) and the World Bank – and multinational corporations. Basically, the Bretton Woods institutions provide the inter-governmental framework through which the core states control the global political economy. For example, the IMF and the World Bank have, and continue to play pivotal roles in the reproduction of capitalist control over the international political economy. Additionally, through the notorious "Structural

Adjustment Programs" (SAPs), the IMF ensures that the peripheral states remain in the state of underdevelopment and subservience to the core ones. The multinational corporations complement the Bretton Woods Institutions by controlling private investment and technological flows. These two critical areas help enable the core states to continue the penetration and control of the economies of the peripheral states. The decision-making system is controlled and dominated by the core states. For example, they design and enforce the "rules" of the system. Essentially, the "rules" are designed to maintain the dominant positions of the core states. Also, under the "international division of labor," the core states produce manufactured goods; the semi-peripheral states and the transitional states produce some manufactured goods and the peripheral states produce raw materials – agricultural products, minerals and oil. The pricing of manufactured goods and raw materials is based on a "system of unequal exchange" under which manufactured goods cost more than raw materials. As a consequence, the peripheral states usually experience terms of trade deficits.

In terms of the modes of interactions, there are several of them. But, for our purposes, we will examine the following: foreign aid, debt, private investment and trade. In the area of foreign aid, there are two major categories: bilateral and multilateral. The various core states – the United States, Japan, Germany, France and Britain, among others – China and the Scandinavian states have bilateral aid programs. For most part, these bilateral aid programs are driven by the national interests of the donor states. For example, for reasons central to its national interests, the United States gives Israel and Egypt the "lion share" of its annual international assistance allocations. In 2005, Israel received $ 2.7 billion, while Egypt received $1.5 billion (United States Agency for International Development, 2005, p. 1). Multilateral aid is provided by various international organizations like the European Union to various regions, sub-regions and states. Overall, the total aid flows from OECD (the wealthy countries) states for 2005 stood at $79.5 billion (Global Issues, 2005, p. 1). The United States was the largest donor of bilateral aid at $27.5 billion (Global Issues, 2005, p. 1). Interestingly, since the dawn of the "new globalization" and the institutionalization of neo-liberal orthodoxy, the core states have been de-emphasizing foreign aid. Instead, they have bamboozled the peripheral states into believing that so-called "free trade" would provide the latter with the capital urgently needed to help spur national development than traditional foreign aid. However, the reality is that the core states are driven by the so-called "aid fatigue," and more importantly by the realization that they would reap greater benefits from increased trade liberalization than through foreign aid.

Similar to the era of the "old globalization," the peripheral states remain in what Payer (1975, p. 1) calls the "debt trap" in the "new globalization." In 2006, for example, the total debt of the peripheral states stood at an estimated $3.6 trillion. Africa's share was over $200 billion (Africa Action, 2007, p. 1). African states spend about $14 billion annually on debt servicing (Africa Action, 2007, p. 1). This means that money that could be used to improve the lives of the peoples of Africa – education, health care, sanitation, clean drinking water, decent public housing, public transportation, etc – is spent on paying the interest on in most cases odious debts. The debts are owed to private Western commercial banks, the core states, the International Monetary Fund and the World Bank. Interestingly, with the failure of the notorious "Structural Adjustment Programs" (SAPs), coupled with the persistent agitation of some peripheral states and private progressive organizations based in the metropolis, the core states designed so-called bilateral and multilateral "debt forgiveness programs." However, the various programs are not unconditionally opened to all indebted peripheral states. Instead, indebted peripheral states must fulfill certain criteria formulated by the core states, in order for them to qualify for "debt relief." The bilateral and multilateral debt relief programs are designed to "forgive the debt" qualified peripheral states owed to the cores states and the Bretton Woods institutions. Thus far, some peripheral states have received debt relief. There are three major problems with the so-called "debt relief." First, debt relief does not include the private commercial banks. Second, there is no guarantee that the money saved from debt servicing and repayment will be spent on the domestic social needs of the affected peripheral states. This is because no mechanism has been put in place to help ensure this. Third and related, debt relief cannot have the desired impact because it is being undertaken within the province of the non-reconstituted neo-colonial state that is intrinsically anti-people, anti-democratic and anti-development.

Another major mode is foreign direct investment. Metropolitan-based multinational corporations remain the linchpins of international private investments. Japan, the United Kingdom and the United States accounted for 73 of the top 100 firms, while 53 were from the European Union (EU) (United Nations Conference on Trade and Development, 2006, p. 6). Since the dawn of the "new globalization," the flows of private investments have experienced marked increases. For example, in 2005, the total global foreign direct investment was $12.6 trillion (United Nations Conference on Trade and Development, 2006, p. 9). Asia is the magnet for attracting foreign investment. Between 2001–2004, the region received nearly one in every four FDI dollars (A.T. Kearney, 2005, p. 33). The average FDI flows to Africa rose to $18.7 billion during the same period (Kearney, 2005, p. 33). However, Africa barely captured 3 percent of total global FDI (Kearney, 2005, p. 33). Two major currents have propelled the growth of foreign investments. The phenomenal development of technology has enabled corporations to spread the ambit of their activities across the global economy. The other is the liberalization of the economies of various states and the attendant opening up of their markets. Given the growing importance of energy, substantial new private investments are being made in the oil sector, especially in various peripheral economies. Ultimately, this will accrue two sets of benefits for the core states and their multinational corporations: a semblance of energy security, given the volatility of the Middle East, and huge profits for the transnational corporations.

The original and continuing fundamental of economic globalization is trade (Waters, 1995, p. 66). Trade is continuously linking together geographically distant producers and consumers, often establishing a relationship of identification as well as interdependence between them (Waters, 1995, p. 66). Also, the volume of trade continues to burgeon. For example, in 2005, the value of world merchandize trade rose by 13% to $10.1 trillion, and the value of world commercial services exports by 11% to $2.4 trillion (World Trade Organization, 2006, p. 1). However, despite the phenomenal increases in the volume of trade, the interaction still remains unfair, unjust and exploitative. That is, global trade is still being conducted under the "global division of labor" and the "system of unequal exchange" and their resulting inequities in terms of the dividends. Because the core states control the global political economy, they also dominate the framework under which global trade is conducted. For example, the trade negotiations that are undertaken under the ambit of the World Trade Organization (WTO) continue to focus on goods and services that are more relevant to the core states than to the peripheral ones. In addition, the overall rules of the WTO tend to serve the interests of the core states than those of the peripheral ones. Moreover, because the peripheral states continue to remain enclaves for the export of raw materials, they continue to account for no more than 2% of the total global trade flows. Furthermore, the volume of trade between and among peripheral states continues to be negligible. This is because as producers of raw materials peripheral states do not have many goods to trade with one another. Hence, the direction of trade from the periphery continues to point to the markets in the core states.

Environmental Globalization

The vortex of the environmental lacunas generated by the "new globalization" is burgeoning economic growth. In turn, this development has precipitated increased economic activities and greater consumption (Esty and Ivanova, 2004, p. 2). These twin phenomena have generated various environmental problems. One of the major challenges is global warming. The changes in the earth's temperature are caused by, inter alia, the release of carbon dioxide and greenhouse gases. And this development has various ramifications. As a consequence of unusual increases in the temperature of various bodies of water – oceans, seas, rivers and lakes –, several countries are experiencing various disasters such as tsunami, typhoons and flooding. Moreover, it is projected that by 2020, the snows of Mount Kilimanjaro in Tanzania may exist only in old photographs (Larson, 2004, p. 1). Also, the glaciers in Montana's Glacier National Park could disappear by 2030 (Larson, 2004, p. 1). And by mid century, the Artic Sea may be completely ice-free during summer time (Larson, 2004, p. 1).

Another major challenge concerns increases in air, land and water pollution. In some cases, the air is being polluted by the efforts to increase agricultural yields through the use pesticides designed to combat the effects of insects. When the pesticides are used, they dispersed in the air and are transported across the borders of several countries. Land pollution is caused by a host of factors, including the disposal of toxic wastes generated from economic production. In the case of water pollution, the sources vary from the drilling of oil to the processing of minerals such as iron ore.

Also, there is increased pressure on oil and mineral deposits. Multinational corporations are criss-crossing the world in search of new oil and mineral deposits in their unending quest to locate new sources of profits. For example, the Democratic Republic of the Congo has become a major source of various minerals, including the one that is used in the manufacturing of cell phones. Similarly, the Gulf of Guinea area along the coast of West and Central Africa has become a prime source of oil. The United States has targeted this area as being critical to its national interest. With the very relaxed and ineffective environmental regulations in African states, multinational corporations in these sectors – oil and minerals – will have a free hand to engage in production activities that would adversely affect the environment – air, land and water pollution.

Moreover, there is the problem of pervasive deforestation evidenced by the felling of trees by corporations and private individuals in response to the demands for logs. In some countries with rain forests, various species of trees are being depleted by the insatiable appetite for making money. One of the other uses of the trees is the making of coal; and this contributes to both air and land pollution.

The onslaught against fisheries and other animals constitutes one of the major problems. It is commonplace for profit-seeking individuals and corporations to engage incessant fishing activities designed to catch huge quantities of various fishes so as to generate increased revenues. Also, selected types of land-based animals are killed and used for various profit-making ventures. Dahl (1998, p.1) perceptively refers to these two interrelated problems as the "global impoverishment of biodiversity."

Given the gravity of the problems being generated, the international community has attempted to establish an environmental regime designed to help address these challenges. The regime is anchored on the United Nations Framework Convention on Climate Change, which was the major outcome of the 1992 "Earth Summit," which was held in Rio de Janeiro, Brazil. In the same vein, the Kyoto Protocol was formulated to complement the convention on climate change. The Protocol went into effect in 2005. The central feature of the Protocol is the establishment of mandatory targets for the reduction of greenhouse gases. The refusal by the United States to sign the Protocol is adversely affecting the international community's capacity to undertake collective action in dealing with a major environmental challenge.

Political Globalization

The centerpiece of political globalization is the increasing challenges being posed to state sovereignty. The Westphalian state that has had a virtual stranglehold on sovereignty is now being challenged by multiple actors – inter-governmental organizations, non-governmental organizations and other private groups – for control over its domestic environment. During the "old globalization," the non-interference norm was sacrosanct: States enjoyed virtual immunity from the uninvited involvement of other actors in their internal affairs. The non-interference norm was given prominence as a major tenet of the Charter of the United Nations and the covenants of all regional and sub-regional organizations. Now, with the creation of a so-called "borderless world," states are losing control over various transactions that are occurring within their borders. Also, the international community has intervened in various civil conflicts without the approval of the authorities of the affected states. For example, in 1991, the Economic Community of West African States (ECOWAS) intervened in the first Liberian civil war without the consent of the beleaguered Doe regime, and imposed a ceasefire on the multiple warlordist factions that were fighting to capture state power. The bottom line as Haj-Yousefi (2001, p. 580) notes, "... the state has become permeable; the impermeability that characterized the classical model of the sovereign state is being challenged." The profundity of these developments, especially their implications for state sovereignty has prompted

Jameson (2000, p. 50) to raise the critical question: "Is [the state] over and done with, or does it still have a vital role to play? The response is no." The "new globalization" has introduced the notion and practice of "multiple sovereignties." That is, while the concept of sovereignty has by no means been rendered redundant, state sovereignty today jostles for recognition alongside novel forms of political power and sites of authority (Held et al., 1999, p. 86).

Specifically, political globalization is manifested in various forms. One of the major ones is the increased importance of the United Nations. For example, the United Nations has become a premier actor in the area of international security. In this arena, the organization has, and continues to play various roles – ranging from peace-making to post-conflict peace-building. Interestingly, the U.N.'s security ambit has now been stretched to include civil conflicts. But both by its constitutional and operational design and the associated *raison d'être*, the United Nations' focus is on international security issues with limited direct involvement in the internal conflicts of states. As Claude(2004, p. xiii) observes, "Since the end of the Cold War, the United Nations has enjoyed – and suffered – a burst of unaccustomed prominence… the United Nations is no longer ignored and neglected; whether its is regarded with utopian idealism or with cynical disdain, it has achieved notable visibility."

Similarly, regional and sub-regional organizations have gained prominence, especially in security matters. For example, the European Union had undertaken peacemaking and peacekeeping roles in various conflicts in Europe. The Organization of American States has been involved in peacemaking and peacekeeping; the most recent case of the latter is in Haiti. Similarly, the African Union had a peacekeeping force in Sudan's Darfur Region. At the sub-regional level, the Economic Community of West African States (ECOWAS) undertook peacemaking and peacekeeping operations during Liberia's two civil wars, the civil war in Sierra Leone, the civil war in Guinea Bissau and the Ivorian civil war.

Another major development is the emergence of a global civil society as reflected in the proliferation of various local and international non-governmental organizations. These NGOs are involved in various spheres – from political to development. Importantly, their activities impact the citizens and governments of various countries and have ramifications for state sovereignty. For example, in countries such as Liberia that are recovering from protracted civil wars, NGOs have virtually taken over the health sector. With the state's incapacity to provide health care for its citizens, NGOs have filled the void by providing needed services to the citizenry.

Also, other non-state actors are becoming important players in the global arena. For example, Hezbollah was locked up with Israel in an unprecedented war in 2006. This was the first time in contemporary international relations that a war was fought between a state and a non-state actor. Furthermore, the war was fought on Lebanese soil, without the participation of Lebanon as a party to the conflict. In addition, various terrorist organizations like Al Qaeda are impacting global affairs.

Another manifestation is the tempting impact of unipolarity on the United States' search for global hegemony. With the collapse of the Soviet Union and the consequent emergence of the United States as the world's only "superpower," some of the neo-conservative members of the bureaucratic wing of the American ruling class holding positions in the current Bush regime made the determination that the time was propitious for the United States to establish global hegemony. Accordingly, Iraq became a "test case" of what was envisioned to be a series of cases involving unilateral intervention by the United States in the internal affairs of strategic states with regimes hostile to the United States. Ultimately, the goal of American neo-imperialism is to create a "new world order" in which the United States would dictate, and every other actor, especially states, would simply obey without question.

The legal transformation that has occurred in the international system is a clear example of the manifestation of political globalization. The major case is the establishment of the International Criminal Court (ICC). The Court will try individuals accused of genocide as defined in the 1949 Geneva Convention (Slomanson, 2003, p. 47); international and internal war crimes, "committed as part of a plan or policy or as part of a large-scale commission of such crimes (Slomanson, 2003, p. 47); and crimes against humanity, which are a "widespread or systematic part of a plan or policy directed against civilians (Slomanson, 2003, p. 47).

Military Globalization

The manifestations of military globalization are many and varied. In this section, some of these manifestations will be examined – the role of the North Atlantic Treaty Organization (NATO), peacekeeping operations and warlordism. NATO has been transformed from a collective defense organization to a "global gendarme." The Washington Treaty that established NATO in 1949 stipulated that the organization was to function as a collective defense organization anchored on the base premise of mutual defense in cases of aggression. Interestingly, NATO has been unilaterally transformed into a global police and military force by the members states without the participation of the non-member states. Since NATO was given a global complexion, it would have therefore made sense for all of the states in the international system to participate in its redesign. Clearly, NATO is now operating outside of the scope of its purpose. For example, in 1999, NATO was used as an interventionist force in the civil conflict between the central government of the former Yugoslavia and the country's Kosovar Albanian population. The fact of the matter was that Yugoslavia had not committed any act of aggression against a member state of NATO. Also, NATO forces are involved in fighting the Taliban in Afghanistan. Again, this is no basis for NATO's involvement in the conflict.

Since the emergence of the "new globalization," there has been a phenomenal increase in the number of peacekeeping operations undertaken by international organizations – global, regional and sub-regional. Weis et al. (2003, p. 49) have referred to this phenomenon as the "rebirth of peacekeeping." For example, since 1990, the United Nations has undertaken 25 peacekeeping operations throughout the international system (Peacekeeping Department, 2006, pp. 1–2).

Another example of military globalization is the increasing prominence of warlordism. In various conflict-plagued countries in the third world, various individuals have organized their personal and private militias. The militias are used to capture and occupy pieces of territory over which the warlords then subsequently establish their rule. The warlordist territory becomes delinked from the rest of the affected country. In resource rich countries like Liberia, Sierra Leone and the Democratic Republic of the Congo, the warlordist militias plunder and pillage the natural resources by selling them and converting the revenues to the personal use of the warlords. Also, the warlords are able to establish external political and economic networks with other states, businesses and criminal syndicates.

Social Globalization

Social globalization embodies a broad array of issues. However, the foci in this part of the chapter will be on health and educational issues. The "new globalization" has affected health issues in several ways. First, it has contributed to the spread of various diseases such HIV/AIDS, SARS and the avian bird flu. This has been done through population movements for a variety of purposes. In essence, the shrinking of the world by technology and economic interdependence allows diseases to spread globally at rapid speed (Fidler, 1996, p. 77). Second, the neo-liberal dogma, which provides the ideological panoply for the "new globalization," has forced peripheral states to reduce public expenditures. The impact of the reduction of state expenditures, including the funding for health programs, leaves states increasingly unprepared to deal with emerging disease problems (Fidler, 1996, p. 77). Third, there have been major advances in the research and development of drugs and other treatments to help combat diseases like HIV/AIDS. In the case of HIV/AIDS, while a cure has not been found, various drugs have proven effective in containing the disease, and allowing those infected to live "normal lives." Fourth and related, various transnational advocacy groups have emerged as vehicles for promoting educational and awareness programs about various diseases and working to focus international attention on these diseases, including the search for cures.

In the area of education, the "new globalization" has occasioned the expansion and increase in the exchange of scholars – faculty and students. For example, in 2004–2005, 2,421 American professors, students and professionals taught, conducted research, studied and provided services at various universities around the world (U.S. Department of State, 2005, p. 2). During the same period, 3.515 foreign scholars taught, conducted research and studied at various American universities (U.S. State Department, 2005, p. 2). In terms of studying abroad, in 2006, a total of 205, 983 American students studied at various universities in Africa, Asia, Europe, Latin America, Canada and Mexico (Institute of International Education, 2006, p. 1). Additionally, schools are establishing degree programs overseas. So, students are receiving American degrees without having to leave home (Prystay, 2005, p. 1). Furthermore, various universities around the world have established online degree and non-degree programs. On the other hand, the "new globalization" is having some adverse effects on education. For example, the neo-liberal framework has been introduced into the educational arena. In turn, this is having two major effects. First, education is being commodified evidenced by the corporate take-over of the sector. There are strong pressures to "roll-back" state regulations, and to transfer a non-market and social sphere issue such as education into the arena of commercial activity. Second, the Bretton Woods Institutions – International Monetary Fund and the World Bank – are interfering with the educational sector in peripheral states.

One of the major thrusts of the intervention is to commercialize tertiary education. Accordingly, the World Bank is pressuring the governments in various peripheral states to shift the funding for public education from the college and university level to the primary level. The resultant sordid state of higher education in several peripheral states has left a void that is being filled by various metropolitan-sponsored universities.

Conclusion

This chapter has attempted to map out an analytical framework for the book by deciphering some of the major features of the "new globalization." Specifically, the chapter discussed the scope, the ideological panoply and the various dimensions of the phenomenon – cultural, economic, environmental, military, political and social. The locus and dynamics of each of the dimensions were discussed.

Finally, the resultant analytical framework has several major tents. First, the "new globalization" has an expansive reach that engulfs all of the various countries and actors – both state and non-state actors. Second, capitalism serves as the Weltanschauung. Accordingly, the primary *raison d'être* of the phenomenon is to promote the private accumulation of capital. Third, peripheral formations are not situated to mediate and address the challenges pose by the phenomenon, including its deleterious effects. Fourth, while the phenomenon is producing some positive results in some areas, the specific distribution of the benefits is skewed toward the core states. Fifth, peripheral states need to design new and innovative approaches in order to be able to impact the phenomenon.

References

Africa Action (2007), Campaign to Cancel Africa's Debt <www.africaaction.org>.

Barnett, R.J. and Cavanagh, J. (1994), *Global Dreams: Imperial Corporations and the New World Order* (New York: Simon and Schuster).

Berrizbeitia, Luis Enrique (1999), "The Process of Globalization", in E. Mayobre, *G-24: The Developing Countries and the International Financial System* (Boulder, Co: Lynne Rienner Publishers).

Blog City (2007), American Cultural Imperialism <www.edstrang.blog-city.com>

Boursy, Richard (2007), "Music Marches to Globalization's Drum", YaleGlobal Online, pp. 1–5.

Burnett, Robert (1996), *The Global Jukebox: The International Music Industry* (London: Routledge).

Claude, Inis (2004). "Foreword", in T. Weis et al., *The United Nations and Changing World Politics*, 4th edn (Boulder: Westview Press).

Esty, David and Ivanson, Maria (2004), Globalization and Environmental Protection: A Global Governance Perspective, Working Paper No. 0402. (New Haven, CT: Yale University Center for Environmental Law and Policy).

Dahl, Arthur L. (1998), *Globalization and the Environment.* Paper presented at the International Seminar on "Globalization: A Challenge for Peace-Solidarity or Exclusion?" October 29–31 (Milan, Italy: International Jacques Maritain Institute).

Fidler, David (1996), "Globalization, International Law, and Emerging Infectious Diseases", *Emerging Infectious Diseases*, Vol. 2, No.2, pp. 77-84.

Galeota, Julia (2004), "Cultural Imperialism: An American Tradition", *The Humanist*, pp. 22-24.

Global Issues (2005), Foreign Aid <www.globalissues.org>.

Haj-Yousefi, Amir (2001), "Economic Globalization, Internationalization of the State and Cooperation: The Case of the Islamic Republic of Iran", *Iranian Journal of International Affairs*, Vol.12. No. 4, pp. 575-586.

Haque, Shamsul (1999), "Globalization of Market Ideology and Its Impact on Third World Development", in A. Kouzmin and A. Hayne (eds), *Essays in Economic Globalization, Transnational Policies and Vulnerability* (Amsterdam: IOS Press), pp. 75–100.

Held, David et al. (1999), *Global Transformations: Politics, Economics and Culture* (Stanford, CA: Stanford University Press).

Institute of International Education (2006), U.S. Students Abroad Top 200,000, Increase By 8 Percent. *Press Release*, November 13 (New York: IIE).

Jameson, Fredric (2000), "Globalization and Political Strategy", *New Left Review*, Vol.4. No. 2, pp. 49–68.

Jha, Srinand (2001), "So Long Saree, Hello Blue Jeans", *Tompaine.Com*, pp. 1–3.

Kearney, A.T. (2005), *FDI Confidence Index*. Vol. 8. Alexander, VA: Global Policy Council.

Larson, Janet (2004), "Toward Global Meltdown?" *The Globalist*, February 16, pp. 1–5.

Lee, Dianna (2005), "Hollywood's Interest in Asian Films Leads to Globalization", UNIORB, pp. 1–3.

McAllister, Matthew (1997), "Sponsorship, Globalization, and Summer Olympics", in Katherine Toland Frith (ed.), *Undressing the Ad: Reading Culture in Advertising* (New York: Peter Lang Publishing).

Payer, Cheryl (1975), *The Debt Trap: The IMF and the Third World* (New York: Monthly Review Press).

Peacekeeping Department, UN Secretariat (2006), *United Nations Peacekeeping Operations* (New York: Peacekeeping Department).

Petras, James (2004), *Cultural Imperialism*, <www.williambowles.infoguests/cultural-imp.html>.

Puttnam, Lord (1999), *A Lecture at the 21st Century Trust Conference: Globalization: Challenges and Discontents*, Akhawayen University, Ifrane, Morocco, September 10-17.

Prystay, Cris (2005), "In Bid to Globalize, U.S. Colleges Offer Degrees in Asia" *Wall Street Journal*, July 12, p. 1.

Rosen, David (2005), *Globalization Blowback: Part I: Globalization and the Culture Industry* <www.digitalindies.com>.

Ray, James Lee and Juliet Kaarbo (2002), *Global Politics* 8th edn (New York: Houghton).

Rosenberg, Matt (2006), "The Number of Countries in the World." *Geography*, December. pp. 1–2.

Schiller, H.I. (1996), *Information Inequality: The Deepening Social Crises in America* (New York: Routledge).

Slomanson, William (2003), *International Law. Fundamental Perspectives on International Law* (Belmont, CA: Wadsworth Publishing).

Union of International Associations (2000), *Yearbook of International Organization, 1999-2000* <www.uia.org>.

United Nations Conference on Trade and Development (2006), *World Investment Report, 2006* (Geneva: UNCTAD).

United States Agency for International Department (2005), *U.S. Overseas Loans and Grants, 2005* (Washington D.C.: USAID).

United States Census Bureau (2006), *Total Midyear Population of the World, 1950-2050* <www.census.govlipc/www/worldpop.html>.

United States Department of State (2005), *Facts and Figures About the Fulbright Program* (Washington. D.C.: U.S. Department of State).

Wagnleitner, Richard and Elaine Tyler May (2000), *Here, There, and Everywhere: The Foreign Politics of American Popular Culture* (Hanover: University Press of New England).

Watch Tower (2000), *The New Millennium: Dawn of a New Age, 2000* (New York: Watch Tower).

Waters, Malcolm (1995), *Globalization* (London and New York: Routledge).

Watson, James (2000), "China's Big Mac Attack", *Foreign Affairs*, Vol.79. No.3, pp.120–134.

Weis, Thomas et al.(2003), *The United Nations and Changing World Politics* 4th edn (Boulder: Westview Press).

World Trade Organization (2006), *World Trade, 2005, Prospects for 2006*, Press Release, 11 April, (Geneva: World Trade Organization).

Chapter 3

The African Debt Crisis and the New Globalization

John Mukum Mbaku

Introduction

In its May 13–19, 2000 issue, *The Economist* (London), called Africa the " hopeless" continent and further characterized the region's prospects for development in the new millennium as practically non-existent. In fact, the magazine argued that the new century has brought primarily disaster to the continent. It went on to state that "[a]t least 45% of Africans [now] live in poverty, and [that] African countries need growth rates of 7% or more to cut that figure in half in 15 years." Despite the fact that this and other Western-based media outlets have traditionally portrayed Africa only in gloomy terms, it is important to note that there is a significant amount of truth in what the magazine has reported.

Available evidence indicates that Africa is in grave trouble. First, few countries in the continent have the productive capacities to achieve the kinds of economic growth rates that would allow them to deal effectively with mass poverty and deprivation. Second, a significant amount of the continent's most productive labor resources, the very people who are supposed to initiate and implement the continent's economic and political renaissance (i.e., people 15–49 years), are being decimated by AIDS. Third, since the mid-1980s, a significant number of the continent's highly educated professionals (engineers, physicians, university professors, accountants, lawyers, and even highly skilled civil servants) have, in response to the continued deterioration in the domestic economic and political environment, as well as the attractive opportunities for migration to the West created by the end of the Cold War and the new globalization, fled to the West. In fact, today, except for universities in South Africa, Botswana, and a few other African countries, most of the institutions of higher learning in the continent have lost a significant number of their senior level instructors to self-exile. In addition, many Africans who have been trained abroad during the last decade and the half have simply chosen not to return to the continent because of deteriorating and suffocative working conditions. Fourth, despite glowing reports from the International Monetary Fund (IMF) and the World Bank about the success of the structural adjustment programs (SAPs) imposed on the continent's economies by the Bretton Woods institutions, more than fifteen years of adjustment have failed to produce any significant and sustainable benefits for the bulk of Africans. In fact, available evidence (see, e.g., Ihonvbere, 1994, Mbaku, 1999a, Cheru, 1989; Ihonvbere, 1996) reveals selectively and capriciously imposed programs which have generated benefits primarily for members of the ruling class, while at the same time imposing significant social, economic, political and human costs on the rest of society. In addition to the fact that implementation, especially since it was carried out capriciously, has resulted in a lot of social disruptions, it has had a significantly negative impact on the welfare of the poor, the majority of whom were never consulted during both the design and implementation phases of these programs. In fact, as the evidence from several African countries that have implemented SAPs has shown, several population groups (especially children, women, rural inhabitants and those forced to live on the urban periphery) have been further impoverished and marginalized by these so-called structural adjustment programs. Fifth, the last forty years in the continent have been characterized by widespread policy failure. Brett (1995, p. 200) finds a lot of evidence for political and economic failure in the continent during most of the post-independence period and argues that its main causes "are clearly structural rather than contingent, since breakdown is almost universal and cannot simply be attributed to particular national circumstances. Instead, they must stem from the nature of institutional arrangements developed under colonialism and hastily modified during the political transition of the 1950s and 1960s." Sixth, post-independence political economy in many African countries has been characterized by destructive ethnic conflict, some of which has produced many of the civil wars that have destroyed a significant part of society's productive capacity and thus, endangered wealth creation and sustainable development. In fact, in some African countries, violent ethnic mobilization, as well as widespread policy failure, including the inability of national governments to maintain law and order and provide the appropriate institutional environment for peaceful resolution of conflict, have been so pervasive as to force the countries to implode – Somalia (1989); Rwanda (1994); Burundi (1996); Zaire/Democratic Republic of Congo (1996); Congo-Brazzaville (1997); and Sierra Leone (1991). Seventh, except in a few countries (notably Botswana and Mauritius), corruption, rent seeking and other forms of political opportunism have become pervasive in virtually all African countries. According to the latest rankings from Transparency International (TI), of the ten most corrupt countries in the world, as perceived by international investors and community leaders, four of them (Cameroon, Nigeria, Tanzania, and Kenya) were in Africa. In fact, Cameroon and Nigeria have, during the last three years been ranked the most corrupt countries in the world. Political opportunism, on the part of civil servants, stunts entrepreneurship and the creation of the wealth that could be used to confront poverty (see, e.g., Mbaku, 1997, 1999b). Finally, according to United Nations Development Program (UNDP, 2000) data on human development, of the 30 poorest countries in the world today, 25 or 83% of them can be found in Africa. Unfortunately, Africa is not only the poorest region of the world, but the one whose prospects for the new century are relatively bleak, as stated by *The Economist* (London), May 13–19, 2000 and supported by the literature on the continent's present economic and political crises (see, e.g., Mbaku, 1999c, 2000; Ihonvbere, 2000).

Why has Africa, which has enormous endowments of both human and natural resources, failed to develop? Why is there so much poverty in the continent? Underdevelopment in Africa has been examined by many researchers (e.g., Ergas,

1986; Mbaku, 1989; OAU, 1981; World Bank, 1981). Identified as important obstacles to poverty alleviation and sustainable development in the continent are (1) bureaucratic and political corruption; (2) political violence and destructive ethnic conflict; (3) *unmanageable external debts*; (4) continued dependence on both primary commodities and the economies of the industrial countries of the (economic) North; (5) pervasive military intervention in national politics and governance; (6) excessive population growth; (7) economic policies of the developed countries, which are said to discriminate against exports from Africa; (8) a chronic shortage of both human and physical capital; (9) racial intolerance; (10) the pervasiveness of several forms of political opportunism, including rent seeking, rent extraction, kleptocracy, prebendalism, etc.; (11) an international financial system that discriminates against traders and entrepreneurs from Africa; and (12) policy mistakes committed by African policymakers. Those who argue that poor macroeconomic performance and thus, the failure to create the wealth that Africans need, can be explained by policy mistakes made by well-intentioned but poorly educated and relatively unskilled civil servants and politicians, have called for the recruitment into the African public services of individuals who are better trained and educated, have higher skills, are more honest and disciplined, and possess higher levels of integrity. This chapter deals with the continent's debt crisis. First, we will review briefly, the historical evolution of the problem. Second, we will examine the role played by the IMF and World Bank imposed SAPs on both African economies and the continent's ability to deal with its external debts. Third, we shall take a brief look at the globalization of the crisis and efforts by Western-based non-governmental organizations (NGOs) to force the developed countries to cancel the continent's debts as a way to enhance the ability of African countries to deliver improvements in the living conditions of citizens. Finally, we shall provide what we believe is a more sustainable way to deal with Africa's debts and ensure sustainable development in the continent.

Background to the Problem and the Involvement of the Bretton Woods Institutions

Since the mid-1970s, many countries in Africa have found themselves saddled with unmanageable debts. By the mid-1980s, the increasing debt burden had become one of the most important constraints to economic growth and human development in Africa. Particularly vulnerable were the already weak and non-viable economies of several sub-Saharan African countries, many of which were now unable to service their debt. Eventually, many of these countries, in an effort to enhance their ability to more effectively deal with rising demands for public goods and services, sought assistance from the international financial community, particularly the International Monetary Fund (IMF) and the World Bank – sometimes referred to as the Bretton Woods institutions. Today, more than fifteen years since they became involved in debt management in Africa, the Bretton Woods institutions are now heavily involved in conditional lending to countries in the continent. In addition, through the so-called structural adjustment programs (SAPs), these multilateral organizations have become seriously involved in institutional reforms and governance in the African countries.

In order for African (as well as other debtor) countries to qualify for additional credits from the international financial community, particularly from the developed market economies, they must agree to implement a basket of institutional reforms that address issues of macroeconomic performance (or in general, resource allocation) and governance. These institutional changes include reduction in the size of the public sector, devaluation of the national currency, deregulation of the international trade sector, and greater reliance on markets for the allocation of resources. Prospective African borrowers must now actively undertake reforms to improve the efficiency of both the public and private sectors in order to continue to qualify for additional credits from the international financial community. In fact, today, a highly indebted African country is not likely to have any access to international credit (either from the public or private sectors of developed countries) without prior "clearance" from the IMF. Thus, African debtor-countries must subject themselves, their governance and economic systems to scrutiny by the IMF in order to acquire the "certification" that is necessary for them to gain access to international financial flows. As a consequence of these developments, Africa's debt management has been globalized and the Bretton Woods institutions have become important players in Africa's post-Cold War transition to more democratic governance structures (see, e.g., Cheru, 1989; Weissman, 1990; Ihonvbere, 1994; UNDP, 1990; Shepherd, 1990).

Baylies (1995, p. 322) argues that the origins of the involvement of the Bretton Woods institutions in institutional reforms in Africa can be traced to "a broader discourse promoted by the World Bank from the mid-eighties which expressed the need for an enabling environment to facilitate prescribed economic reforms." The World Bank argued that a major portion of its development programs in the African countries were not functioning properly because of the existence in these countries, of inappropriate bureaucratic structures and governance systems that were hostile to the private sector and thus, served as a hindrance to economic growth. The Bank intended to force African countries to undertake institutional reforms to improve macroeconomic performance and increase the efficiency of the multilateral institution's projects in these countries. Thus, since the mid-1980s, the IMF and the World Bank have become severely involved in economic and political reforms in Africa and in the region's effort to improve its governance systems.

Although both the World Bank and the IMF are now heavily involved in many aspects of governance in Africa (in fact, during the Clinton administration in the USA , a fund was created to fight AIDS/HIV in Africa and put the World Bank in charge of it, giving the Bretton Woods institution another opportunity to usurp public policy in the continent), they originally were supposed to help African countries resolve an economic crisis that emerged in the mid-1980s and threatened to wipe out most post-independence gains in human development. Throughout the continent, relatively high balance of payments deficits and rising debt levels were threatening to throw many societies in the continent into chaos. In imposing the SAPs on the African countries, the Bretton Woods institutions hoped to provide each African government with a tool to improve macroeconomic performance and significantly increase the ability of the domestic economy to generate the wealth needed to fight poverty and deprivation. Perhaps, more important was the fact that the SAPs were expected to help the African countries manage their debts more effectively and provide them with a way to get off the borrowing "treadmill." As recently as 1994, the World Bank was expressing significant optimism about the impact of the SAPs on the African economies and their ability to improve overall macroeconomic performance. Unfortunately, studies carried out by other researchers have questioned the evidence presented by the World Bank, attesting to improved performance by the African economies that have undergone the SAPs (see, especially World Bank, 1994). While it is generally agreed by many researchers (see, e.g., Lall, 1995; Ihonvbere, 1994; Kayira and Hope, 1997; Magadlela, 1997) that the African economies must be restructured and each provided with institutions that enhance entrepreneurship and wealth creation (e.g., a civil service that is more responsive to the needs of the private sector and a resource allocation system that guarantees economic freedoms), they argue against the approach adopted by the World Bank and other external actors. For public policy to achieve its objectives, its design and implementation must involve the full and effective participation of the relevant stakeholder groups. Unfortunately, as we shall see later, the SAPs are, for all intents and purposes, imported programs that are imposed on Africans, and often implemented capriciously by opportunistic national elites, without the full and effective participation of those whose lives are affected by these programs.

Anyone who has studied Africa's SAPs, since they began fifteen or so years ago, soon realizes that African countries have had virtually no leverage to negotiate effectively with the Bretton Woods institutions. In fact, it could be said that employing the word "negotiate" to describe the process that takes place, usually at IMF headquarters in Washington, D.C., is incorrect since the multilateral organizations have usually dictated terms to debtor countries, most of which are unable to acquire funds from other international sources (Bradshaw and Tshandu, 1990; Dunn, 2000; Plank, 1993; Young, 1995). Despite the fact that the World Bank and the IMF have spent a significant part of the last decade preaching the benefits of democratic governance to African countries, their negotiations with the latter are anything but democratic. Africans most affected by the SAPs are not provided the facilities to participate in the deliberations or permitted to decline the implementation of these programs in their communities, or allowed to adopt locally designed programs that may actually produce more viable, efficient and sustainable solutions to their problems. Instead, the SAPs are held up by the IMF, the World Bank and many of Africa's traditional benefactors as a panacea for all of the continent's economic and political woes (see, e.g., Danaher, 1994). Through out the continent, rural inhabitants and those who have been pushed to the urban periphery, all of whom have been historically marginalized and deprived, usually have no effective input into the design and implementation of these programs. Yet, they are most likely the ones to bear a significant portion of the social and economic costs of the adjustments through higher unemployment rates, cuts in public services, polluted environment, etc.

One, of course, can argue that there are significant impediments to mass participation in the public policy process in the African countries (e.g., economic inequality and its associated causes, including high rates of illiteracy and historical discrimination and marginalization). This, however, is the reason that emphasis must be placed on creating an environment that enhances the ability of these individuals and groups to participate in the design and implementation of policies that affect their lives. While it is true that universal basic education would enhance the ability of these historically marginalized groups and individuals to participate in governance, one should not use the existence of low literacy rates amongst these people, as well as their high levels of poverty and material deprivation as the reason to deny them access to political and economic markets.

SAPs in Africa: 1986–2000

More than 15 years of structural adjustments, as dictated by the IMF and the World Bank, have left most African economies worse off than they were when the process first started. Although they appear to have produced short-term benefits for some economies (e.g., Ghana and Uganda), SAPs have generally had negative impact on the lives of most Africans. The only real benefit to African societies is that the exercise has reminded them of the importance of institutions to economic growth and development (particularly to wealth creation), of the disadvantages and dangers of externally imposed institutional reforms, and of the need to engage the people, especially the relevant stakeholder groups, in comprehensive reforms to provide each society with institutional arrangements that (1) enhance entrepreneurship and wealth creation; (2) adequately constrain the exercise of government agency; and 3) improve the ability of population groups to coexist peacefully.

SAPs, as engineered by the IMF and the World Bank, were supposed to prepare the African economy to properly respond to both negative and positive shocks, including deficits in trade and inflows of foreign resources (e.g., official development aid, private investment, and loans). SAPs have two connected elements: (1) policy changes whose primary objective is to help the African economy achieve both internal and external balances and are considered the responsibility of the IMF and policymakers in the affected or adjusting country; and (2) institutional reforms that force the African economy to rely more on prices and markets for the allocation of resources. Institutional reforms to improve the functioning of market processes are considered the exclusive purview of the World Bank (see, e.g., Lall, 1995, p. 2020). As implemented in Africa since the mid-1980s, SAPs have attempted to (see, for example, Danaher, 1994; World Bank, 1981):

- reduce government ownership and management of productive resources through the sale to the private sector of several state-owned enterprises;
- abolish government-imposed price ceilings on agricultural products in order to improve incentives in the farm sector and increase the production of foodstuffs;
- devalue the domestic currency to make the country's exports more competitive globally;
- reduce government subsidization of domestic consumption;
- reduce government regulation of private exchange and rely more on markets for the allocation of resources;
- implement policies that attract and retain foreign investment; and
- encourage free trade by eliminating protectionist laws and statutes.

Table 3.1 Gross National Product (GNP) Per Capita and Growth Rates for Low-Income African Countries, 1988–1998

Country	GNP per capita, 1998 (U.S. dollars)	Average annual growth rate (%), 1988–1998
Ethiopia	100	0.7
Congo, DR of	110	–9.3
Burundi	140	–3.7
Sierra Leone	140	–5.7
Guinea-Bissau	160	0.2
Niger	190	–2.0
Eritrea	200	2.2
Malawi	200	0.8
Mozambique	210	2.7
Tanzania	210	1.2
Chad	230	1.5
Rwanda	230	–4.6
Burkina Faso	240	0.8
Mali	250	0.5
Madagascar	260	–1.2
Sudan	290	2.3
Nigeria	300	1.3
Uganda	310	3.7
Togo	330	–1.5
Zambia	330	–0.9
Angola	340	–8.5
The Gambia	340	–0.9
Ghana	390	1.5
Mauritania	410	0.8
Senegal	530	–0.1
Lesotho	570	1.3
Cameroon	610	–4.4
Zimbabwe	610	–0.2
Congo, Rep. of	690	–2.2
Côte d'Ivoire	700	–0.2

Source: World Bank (2000), *African Development Indicators, 2000*, The World Bank: Washington, D.C., p. 6.

The view of the IMF's economists is that implementation of the SAPs would allow African countries to manage their debts properly, improve economic performance and lead to much needed growth in national wealth. Despite the fact that economic conditions in the African economies have continued to deteriorate during many years of adjustment, economists at the Bretton Woods institutions have remained optimistic and argue that the SAPs will eventually improve economic conditions

Table 3.2 Gross National Product (GNP) Per Capita and Growth Rates for Middle-Income African Countries, 1988–1998

Country	GNP per capita, 1998 (U.S. dollars)	Average annual growth (%), 1988–1998
Cape Verde	1,060	1.1
Egypt	1,250	2.5
Morocco	1,250	0.7
Swaziland	1,400	1.4
Algeria	1,570	–1.6
Namibia	1,940	1.5
Tunisia	2,150	2.4
South Africa	2,880	–0.5
Botswana	3,600	3.4
Mauritius	3,700	4.1
Gabon	4,170	0.5
Seychelles	6,450	3.1

Source: World Bank (2000), *African Development Indicators, 2000,* The World Bank: Washington, D.C., p. 6.

on the continent and lead to increased national wealth and sustainable development (see, especially the overtly optimistic assessment by the World Bank, 1994; also see Osunsade, 1993).

Since the mid-1980s, most African economies have encountered primarily poor performance. Data provided in Tables 3.1 and 3.2 show that only a small number of African countries experienced reasonable rates of economic growth during the period 1988–1998. Democratic Republic of Congo, which imploded in 1996, had the worse performance of all the African countries during this period, registering a growth rate of –9.3%. The majority of the low-income countries either regressed significantly during this period or registered only modest rates of growth (see Table 3.1). A few of the middle-income countries also performed poorly (see Table 3.2).

In 1998, Ethiopia, with a gross national product (GNP) per capita of US $100, was the poorest country in Africa. In fact, as measured by GNP per capita, Ethiopia is today one of the poorest countries in the world. As mentioned earlier, today, a significant number of the poorest countries in the world can be found in Africa (UNDP, 2000). Presently in the continent, only South Africa and Algeria, and to a certain extent, Mauritius, have viable manufacturing sectors which, can compare favorably to those of the newly industrializing countries such as Brazil, Mexico, Malaysia, and Thailand. Although Libya, Gabon and Seychelles have relatively high per capita incomes, most of the wealth of Libya and Gabon derives primarily from the exploitation of environmental resources, primarily petroleum, and that of Seychelles comes almost entirely from tourism. These countries have not yet developed well-integrated manufacturing and industrial sectors that can allow them to compete effectively in the new global economy.

Table 3.3 Gross National Product (GNP) Per Capita and Growth Rates for Selected Regions of the World, 1988 & 1997–98

Country	GNP per capita, 1998 (U.S. dollars), weighted average	Average annual growth (%), 1997–1998
Sub-Saharan Africa	480	–0.4
East Asia and Pacific	990	–2.2
South Asia	430	3.9
Europe and Central Asia	2,190	..
Middle East and North Africa	2,050	..
Latin America and Caribbean	3,940	0.8

Source: World Bank (2000), *World Development Report, 1999/2000,* Oxford University Press: New York, p. 231.

Table 3.3 provides data on macroeconomic performance in selected regions of the world. During the period 1997–1998, sub-Saharan Africa registered a growth rate in per capita GNP of –0.4%. South Asia, a region that is comparable to sub-Saharan Africa because of its high population growth rates and relatively high poverty levels, encountered reasonably healthy economic growth during the period 1997–1998. It is important to note that despite recent setbacks in East Asia and the Pacific, the region has had relatively healthy economic growth during the last several decades. For example, it registered growth rates in per capita GNP of 7.2%, 7.4% and 5.6% during the periods 1985–1995, 1995–1996, and 1996–1997 respectively (World Bank, 1997, 1998). On the other hand, sub-Saharan Africa regressed economically during the period, 1985–1995 (–1.1%), and grew modestly (1.9%) during the period 1995–1996 (World Bank, 1997, 1998).

In 1998, the weighted average per capita income for sub-Saharan Africa was only US $480 or 12.2% of that of Latin America and the Caribbean and 48.5% of that of East Asia and Pacific (see Table 10.3). Available data show that Africa, especially the part of the continent often referred to as sub-Saharan Africa, remains in crisis. In fact, during most of the post-independence period, the majority of policymakers in Africa have either been unwilling or unable to devote the appropriate level of effort to economic, social and political transformation of their societies. Instead, many public programs, including the SAPs, have been devoted primarily to the extraction of extra-legal compensation for members of the ruling class. In fact, as has been argued by several researchers (see, e.g., Mbaku, 1997; Ihonvbere, 1994, 2000), most of Africa's post-independence leaders have been primarily concerned with crisis management in an effort to (1) enhance the ability of the incumbent to continue to monopolize political space and the allocation of resources; (2) maximize corrupt enrichment by members of the ruling coalition; and (3) maintain a semblance of peaceful coexistence of groups and continue to attract foreign resources. Preoccupation of Africa's ruling elites with crisis management and political survival at all cost, have made it very difficult for these elites to place the appropriate emphasis on national development, the elimination of poverty, protection of the environment, and the improvement of the quality of life for the nation's historically marginalized groups and communities. Perhaps, more important is the fact that such pre-occupation with crisis management has resulted in the stunting of entrepreneurship and wealth creation, forcing the countries to continue to depend on foreign resource flows (primarily debt and official development aid) for survival. Such dependence has forced many of these countries to literally surrender some of their sovereignty to the Bretton Woods institutions in exchange for budget subventions from the international financial community.

If implementation of SAPs was expected to enhance the ability of the African countries to produce the wealth that they need to meet their rising financial obligations, it has not succeeded. As the discussion above has shown, during the last two decades, economic performance in most African countries has been anything but good. As a consequence, the region remains quite poor and deprived, despite more than fifteen years of adjustment.

What effect has adjustment had on debt management and the level of the continent's external indebtedness? In 1980, the total external debt of the African countries stood at US $111,922 million. By 1995, it had risen to US $333,346 million (see Table 3.4). Although it declined to $310,735 million in 1997, the reduction was not very significant. Thus, in 1997, Africa's external debt was nearly three times higher than it was in 1980. Since the nominal gross national product (GDP) for the continent in 1997 was $544,561 million (World Bank, 2000a, p. 21), the continent's foreign debt was 57% of its current output. External debt for sub-Saharan Africa grew faster than that for the continent as a whole during the period 1980–1997, reaching a high of $233,687 million in 1995 before falling to $219,322 million in 1997. Thus, in 1997, sub-Saharan Africa's total external debt was 3.6 times higher than it was in 1980. Except for a few countries, rapid increases in external indebtedness seem to have been universal. In real terms, growth in the continent's total debt was just as phenomenal. For example, in 1980, total external debt in Africa in real terms (1995 constant dollars) was $104,113 million, but by 1997, it had risen to $304,344 million. In 1997, Africa's real GDP (in 1995 constant dollars) was $533,574 million, and as a consequence, its external debt was 57% of the real GDP, an increase from 29% in 1980 (World Bank, 2000a, pp. 17, 45, 176).

Economists use several measures to determine the burden of the debt on national economies. Among these are *total long-term debt*, *debt service*, and *debt service as a percentage of the export of goods and services*. The debt service is usually considered by economists as a more effective measure of the burden of the debt on national economies than, say, total debt because the former (i.e., debt service) represents resources that are actually remitted to foreign creditors by the domestic economy. In the African economies, the resources transmitted abroad are usually *hard currency* derived from the export of goods and services. These are scarce resources that could be used to increase spending on social services, especially in critical areas such as education, sanitation and health care, AIDS/HIV prevention, clean drinking water, nutrition (especially for children), prenatal care, and job training in urban areas. These resources, unfortunately, must be sent abroad to service the debt. Debt service ratios (ex post, depicting the amount actually paid after debt relief and/or arrears;

Table 3.4 Total External Debt in Africa (millions of U.S. dollars, current prices), 1980–1997

Year	Sub-Saharan Africa	North Africa*	Africa
1980	60,641	51,281	111,922
1988	150,535	99,695	250,229
1989	157,351	101,530	258,881
1990	177,400	92,973	270,373
1991	183,595	90,862	274,457
1992	182,555	88,746	271,301
1993	188,707	86,680	275,387
1994	219,670	94,054	313,724
1995	233,687	99,659	333,346
1996	229,462	97,859	327,321
1997	219,322	91,413	310,735

Note: *North Africa as defined here includes, Algeria, Egypt, Libya, Morocco, and Tunisia
Source: World Bank (2000), *African Development Indicators, 2000,* The World Bank: Washington, D.C., p. 176.

see World Bank, 2000a, p. 180) for the African economies in 1997 ranged from a low of 1% in Democratic Republic of Congo to a high of 50% in São Tomé and Principe. The average for sub-Saharan Africa was 13%, that for Africa was 15%, and for North Africa, it was 19%. Africans must devote 15% or more of their export earnings to debt service (World Bank, 2000a, p. 180). The transfer of such significant amounts of resources to the developed countries significantly constrains the ability of each African economy to meet the needs of its people and provide the enabling environment for wealth creation (UNDP, 1990). Throughout most of Africa, it is becoming apparent that many countries cannot continue to send hard-earned foreign exchange abroad for debt service, while millions of people in the continent die from AIDS. Today, many NGOs in the developed countries (e.g., Jubilee 2000/USA), as well as church organizations, are now arguing that spending on AIDS be given priority over debt service.

Since the mid-1980s, a significant number of African countries have subjected their economies to IMF and World Bank imposed SAPs. Unfortunately, macroeconomic performance in these countries has not improved significantly. More important, however, is the fact that external debt levels have continued to rise and, poverty and deprivation levels have actually increased. In fact, many people in these countries are poorer now than they were when their countries began the adjustment programs in the mid-1980s. Although there are several reasons given for the continued deterioration in economic conditions in the region and the fact that the SAPs appear to have had little positive impact on adjusting economies, the most important one is the fact that these institutional reform programs were designed abroad without the effective participation of the relevant stakeholder groups in Africa. Participation and involvement of Africans in the design of the SAPs has usually been limited to the urban based elites who work with IMF and World Bank staff. Critical stakeholder groups, especially about rural peasants and the urban poor who must bear most of the costs of adjustment, are usually not provided the facilities to participate fully and effectively in the design and implementation of the SAPs. Those directly responsible for designing these programs lack time-and-place information, especially social and economic conditions in the rural, as well as peripheral urban areas, that are subjected to SAPs.

Most African countries today have institutional arrangements that (1) do not adequately constrain the state; (2) stunt entrepreneurial effort and thus, the creation of wealth; (3) discourage peaceful coexistence of population groups; and (4) make it very difficult for the private sector to function. In fact, throughout the continent, as already mentioned, corruption, rent seeking and other forms of political opportunism, all inimical to wealth creation, are pervasive. The starting point, then for a reversal of continued deterioration of economic conditions in Africa is institutional reforms. However, the latter cannot be undertaken effectively if the process is dominated by either external actors (as the SAPs are) or controlled by urban elites and their foreign benefactors. In order for reform to function properly and achieve its intended objectives, it must be people-driven – that is, bottom-up, participatory and inclusive. By allowing people at the local level to have more direct control over public policy, the latter is made more "responsive to variations in local demands for regulations, transfers and public services" (Congleton, 1994, p. 16). Granting more people the power to provide input into decisions affecting their lives, puts them in a better position to design regulatory programs that maximize their values and individual needs. Since individuals at the local level have more time-and-place information than the elites at the center, decentralization (e.g., in the design of public policies, including such programs as SAPs) should significantly improve bureaucratic and governmental efficiency. Thus, Africans must be enfranchised and provided the facilities to participate fully and effectively in public policy. In addition, policies such as SAPs must be initiated by Africans themselves, as part of a larger effort to reconstruct the post-colonial state to provide themselves with more democratic governance structures and resource allocation systems that guarantee economic freedoms. Institutional reforms designed primarily to meet the expectations of the IMF, the World Bank and other external lenders and donors in an effort to maintain or increase foreign resource flows, are not likely to provide Africans with long-term solutions to their economic, social and political problems.

While many African governments remain optimistic that World Bank and IMF involvement in their economies would eventually result in improved economic growth and development, most ordinary people in the continent see the Bretton Woods institutions and other such usurpers of African sovereignty as the new colonial masters and SAPs as the tools being used to recolonize them and exploit their resources for the benefit of the metropolitan economies and collaborating national elites.

African countries that have "successfully" implemented the SAPs have been favored by the World Bank, the IMF and the developed market economies with additional resources. The bulk of these resources, however, have not been devoted to the alleviation of poverty, nor have they been invested in providing the necessary economic infrastructures for wealth creation. Instead, most of these resources have been used to feed the enormous appetites of the continent's bloated and parasitic bureaucracies for expensive living and imported European and American goods. Using these resources to provide benefits for politically dominant groups and others with the wherewithal to threaten regime security (e.g., military elites) has enhanced the ability of incumbents to continue to monopolize power and the allocation of resources. As a consequence, while a few individuals and groups continue to maintain a relatively high standard of living, the mass of the people suffer from very high levels of poverty and material deprivation.

Ghana, under military strong-man Flight Lieutenant Jerry Rawlings was held up by the IMF and the World Bank as a shinning example of what SAPs can do for the African economies. From 1983–2000, the government of Rawlings pursued the IMF and World Bank sponsored SAPs with near religious zeal. In return, the international donor community rewarded the country with significant flows of resources. In fact, existing evidence shows that only India and China (PRC), two of the world's most populous nations, received more credit from the World Bank's International Development Agency (IDA) than Ghana in 1988.

In 1980, Ghana's total external debt in real terms (1995 constant dollars) was US $1,331 million (or $123.93 per person) but by 1997, it had mushroomed to $6,117 million (or $340.21 per person). In 1980, Ghana had a real GDP of $4,233 million, implying that its total external debt was equal to 31.44% of its real output. However, by 1997, Ghana's real GDP had grown to $7,042 million and its external debt to $6,117 million in real terms, implying a debt-to-GDP ratio of 86.9% (World Bank, 2000a, pp. 6–7; 17; 45; and 176). Despite World Bank rhetoric about its adjustment success in Ghana, the latter has failed to lower its external indebtedness (World Bank, 2000a) and living conditions for most Ghanaians have either not increased or done so only modestly (Hammond and McGowan, 1994, pp. 78–82). For example, in 1992, Ghana had a human development index (HDI) of 0.482 (UNDP, 1995) but by 1995, it had fallen to 0.466 (UNDP, 1998), and since the 1970s, its GNP per capita has remained below $450. In 1998, it was $390, which is lower than the weighted average of $480 for sub-Saharan Africa, considered one of the poorest regions of the world (World Bank, 2000b, pp. 230–231). It is important to note here that most of the dramatic gains that occurred in Ghana did so immediately after Rawlings seized control of the government through a coup d'état and before the advent of the SAPs. The gains were a reflection of an end to many years of public malfeasance and corruption-driven, opportunistic and perverse economic policies by his predecessors and not necessarily the outcome of the SAPs (see, e.g., Frimpong, 1997, pp. 92–104).

The massive literature on the effects of SAPs on the African economies contradicts the excessive optimism expressed by the Bretton Woods institutions (see, e.g., Danaher, 1994; Hope and Kayira, 1997; Mensah, 1997; Frimpong, 1997; Jacques, 1997, Bandow and Vasquez, 1994; Ihonvbere, 1992). Lall (1995, pp. 2019–2031) argues that SAPs, as promoted by the World Bank and the IMF and implemented by several African governments, have provided little or no benefits to African industry and in addition, have not generated much diversification in manufacturing. Although many African countries still pursue these policies, it has now become evident that most policymakers undertake the exercise primarily because of the benefits provided them and their supporters and not because SAPs are likely to alleviate mass poverty and improve long-term economic growth and development. In virtually all African countries that have pursued SAPs, the latter have been politicized and have become important instruments for elite enrichment and as a consequence, most people in the continent do not view them as a genuine tool to transform the critical domains and enhance the ability of the economy to deliver improvements in the national welfare.

Globalizing the African Debt Crisis

In recent years, especially since the end of the Cold War, Africa's problems with debt have been globalized. The IMF and the World Bank have become more involved in the continent's debt management and poverty alleviation efforts, and individuals and organizations in the developed countries have become actively involved in efforts to help resolve the crisis. The effort by citizens and non-governmental organizations in the developed countries, as well as that by Africans themselves, is directed at two levels: *debt cancellation* and *debt rescheduling*. The former is expected to wipe out all the existing debt of especially the highly indebted African countries and enhance their ability to deal with mass poverty and deprivation. Those who support the debt cancellation initiative believe very strongly that in many African countries, especially those in sub-Saharan Africa, existing debt levels have become the single most important obstacle to human development and must be eliminated in order to allow these people to begin the process of rebuilding their economies and societies. Although debt rescheduling is a relatively complex process, its primary objective is to reduce the amount of resources each debtor country must remit abroad each period for debt service. Under this program, the African country would take longer to repay the debt but will have the opportunity to use "savings" from the reduction in required debt service to increase spending on social programs and provide a more enabling environment (through increased public investment) for wealth creation. Eventually, the domestic economy is expected to achieve the ability, through improved macroeconomic performance, to generate enough resources to properly service its debt and provide for spending on social programs, without further foreign intervention.

Many NGOs in the developed countries consider debt cancellation a moral issue and have called on their legislators to take action accordingly. Since the movement in favor of debt cancellation began, several individuals and organizations have lobbied the IMF, the World Bank and lawmakers in the so-called G7 countries to cancel the debts of the highly indebted countries, many of which are located in Africa. In April 1999, several high-profile individuals, as well as ordinary people, religious organizations, and other non-governmental organizations, met in Washington, D.C. for the *National Mobilization for Debt Cancellation.* The program was sponsored by Jubilee 2000/USA Campaign, an umbrella organization representing national environmental, labor, religious, and social justice groups. In a press release before the rally, the group proclaimed as follows:

> People of faith and all who care about justice for indebted countries in Africa, Asia and Latin America will be gathering on April 9, 2000, at the National Mall in Washington, D.C., to be part of a *massive public witness* supporting debt cancellation for the world's poorest countries (emphasis in original; see <http://www.j2000usa.org>).

The rally was designed to take place exactly one week before the Spring Meeting of the International Monetary Fund and World Bank Executive Board, during which time the two multilateral agencies were expected to discuss the debt crisis in the Third World.

During the last several years, many Africans, including those in leadership positions, have also called for some form of debt relief. In a recent address to the UN General Assembly, for example, the Ethiopian Foreign Minister, Seyoum Mesfin, told participants that unless the African debt burden was dealt with quickly and effectively, the continent was not likely to extricate itself out of its present development crisis. He hoped that during the annual meeting of the World Bank and IMF, the two institutions would seriously consider debt cancellation for the African countries. In a book published in 1999, African intellectuals Professors Thandika Mkandawire and Charles C. Soludo (1999, p. 122) argued very forcefully in favor of debt cancellation for the continent. According to them,

> [Debt cancellation], simple as it sounds, holds the key to Africa's future. All efforts to find out why stabilization or adjustment has not worked, why investment has not resumed, and why the state capacity has been further eroded will fail unless this single but dominant issue – debt overhang – is [addressed].

Salim A. Salim, former Secretary General of the Organization of African Unity, K. Y. Amoako, UN Under-Secretary General and Executive Secretary, Economic Commission for Africa, and Omar Kabbaj, former President, African Development Bank, encouraged the developed countries to find some way to provide highly indebted African countries with debt relief. In a joint statement issued in Ouagadoughou, Burkina Faso on February 5, 1999 at the end of their 9th Consultative meeting, they stated that debt overhang continues to seriously impede socio-economic development in the continent, and called upon the industrial market economies and the multilateral organizations to consider programs that would enable highly indebted African countries to receive debt relief as soon as possible (see <http://www.africapolicy.org>).

In the summer of 1999, African ministers of finance called on the so-called G7 countries, who met in Cologne, Germany in June of that year, to cancel the debts of the poorest African countries. The ministers also pleaded with the G7 countries not to provide debt relief to the African countries at the expense of Official Development Aid (ODA), which they argued, was critical for pulling these countries out of their present economic crises and helping them stay on the road to sustainable development (see, e.g., *ArabicNews.Com*, May 10, 1999).

A year after he became the first sitting U.S. president to travel extensively throughout Africa (that is, in 1999), President Bill Clinton addressed a conference organized by his administration to underscore its efforts to improve ties with African countries, particularly in trade and investment. The conference was named *U.S.-*

Africa Ministerial: Partnership for the 21st Century and was attended by 46 of the 48 countries in sub-Saharan Africa. Sudan, considered by the U.S. as a sponsor of international terrorism, and Somalia, which did not have a properly constituted and functioning central government, were not invited to participate in the proceedings. Most of the African leaders attending the conference wanted the U.S. president to declare that his administration would actively campaign for the cancellation of the debts of 33 sub-Saharan African countries, which are among the 41 countries identified by the World Bank as the world's most highly indebted poor countries. In response, President Bill Clinton called on the developed countries to accelerate efforts to forgive these countries their debts (*Salt Lake (Utah) Tribune*, March 17, 1999).

In an address to the forum of the World Senate at Luxembourg, published in *The Guardian* (March 29, 2000), Dr. Chuba Okadigbo, then President of the Nigerian Senate, argued that Nigerians are not responsible for the huge debts that the country has accumulated during the last several decades and therefore should not be required to repay them. He went on to blame IMF policy blunders and the opportunistic and perverse policies of several illegitimate military governments for placing Nigeria in its present political and economic malaise. He argued in favor of debt cancellation, saying that rescheduling would only prolong the country's agony and deprive millions of Nigerians of the opportunity to improve their living standards. He blamed IMF-imposed structural adjustment programs (SAPs) for Nigeria's debt problems and called upon the developed countries to cancel these debts and enhance the country's ability to produce enough wealth to meet its rising obligations.

Like Dr. Okadigbo, most of the people and organizations that are calling for debt cancellation (e.g., Jubilee 2000/USA) argue that most of sub-Saharan Africa's present debt was accumulated by corrupt, irresponsible, cruel and/or illegal leaders who used the resources to perpetuate themselves in office. At the time the loans were being extended, most of the creditors knew or should have known that the proceeds of these transactions were not to be used for development (e.g., investment in overhead capital) but were destined for the benefit of the leaders and their supporters. Why, according to these supporters of debt cancellation, should the African peoples be forced to pay back loans that were used not to develop their societies but to oppress them and provide privileges for the ruling elites?

In Cologne in 1999, the G7 countries agreed to launch an initiative to provide debt relief for Heavily Indebted Poor Countries (HIPC), most of which are in sub-Saharan Africa. Finance ministers of the G7 argued then that debt relief would provide these poor countries with needed funds for poverty alleviation. When the G7 met in Okinawa, Japan, in July 2000, they reviewed the HIPC Initiative and proclaimed that much progress had been made in helping many countries develop poverty reduction strategies. They noted, however, that several HIPCs were currently affected by military conflicts which, were delaying debt relief and the development of effective poverty reduction programs. They then called on these countries to end their conflicts and embark upon the HIPC process. It was, however, not clear how the G7 were expected to convince the warring factions to stop fighting and allow the HPIC initiative to proceed. In addition, the G7 ministers failed to mention the fact that their arms industries are partly responsible for providing the different sides in these military conflicts the equipment they need to wage war.

Many critics of the G7 debt relief initiative have argued that the developed countries are not really interested in enhancing development in the HIPCs, otherwise, they would support debt cancellation. For one thing, many of the military conflicts that the G7 claimed were delaying the implementation of the HIPC process, these critics claimed, would not have existed if the developed countries had discontinued their arms sales to these countries. Part of the argument being advanced by critics such as Jubilee2000, is that debt cancellation is being held hostage to the international arms trade and that the HIPC is so rigid and complex that few poor countries are actually benefiting from it. In fact, Jubilee 2000/USA argues further that by the time many poor countries in Africa, Latin America, the Caribbean and Asia navigate the complex conditions associated with HIPC well enough to benefit from the initiative, most of their citizens would have been wiped out by poverty and AIDS. Thus, it is incumbent upon the G7 finance ministers to keep the promise they made in 1999 in Cologne and accelerate efforts to help poor countries fight poverty and deprivation. The place to start is to initiate and implement a comprehensive program to cancel the debts of these countries.

Adjustment and Debt Cancellation: Which Way to Sustainable Development in Africa?

SAPs, as promoted by the IMF and the World Bank, were expected to help the African countries manage their debts properly, improve macroeconomic performance and generate the resources needed for poverty alleviation. As argued in this chapter, more than fifteen years of SAPs in Africa have not produced the intended results. So, today, many people and organizations, including some that initially supported the SAPs, are calling for debt cancellation. The question to ask here is: Will debt cancellation really improve economic and social conditions in the continent? Given the fact that most of these unmanageable debts were accumulated through non-transparent public borrowing processes, it is not likely that debt relief will lead to improvements in economic and social conditions unless it is followed by or undertaken together with state reconstruction to provide each HIPC in Africa with transparent, participatory and accountable governance structures. In countries such as Zaire/Democratic Republic of Congo, Nigeria, Cameroon, and Kenya, the public budget process during the last several decades has not allowed for the kind of transparency that would have made it difficult for the government to either borrow recklessly or use the proceeds of these loans to subsidize the consumption activities of bloated and parasitic civil services. Thus, unless each HIPC in Africa is provided with the appropriate governance structures, debt relief would only be a temporary reprieve as governments in these countries would soon be engaged in reckless borrowing and spending, forcing these countries to return to a situation in which they would be forced to ask for further relief.

It is true, as indicated earlier, that many HIPCs in Africa squander a significant part of their scarce export earnings on debt service. As a result, these countries are unable to devote enough resources to such critical development areas as health care, clean drinking water, education, energy development, sewage disposal, especially in the urban areas, nutrition (especially for children and women), and AIDS/HIV education and prevention. Thus, some way must be found to reduce the flow of resources from these countries in the form of debt service. However, to do so without providing each HIPC with institutional arrangements that minimize further uncontrolled borrowing or the corrupt use of loan proceeds, would be counterproductive and would not constitute a sustainable way to deal with poverty and deprivation in the continent of Africa. The appropriate way to deal with poverty in the continent is to combine debt cancellation with state reconstruction through proper constitution making in order to provide each country with governance and economic structures that would minimize the kinds of political opportunism that is responsible for creating the present debt and development quagmire.

Conclusion

SAPs, as promoted by the Bretton Woods institutions, were supposed to improve governance and resource allocation, and significantly enhance the ability of each African country to deal with poverty and deprivation. After more than fifteen years of adjustment, the SAPs do not appear to have succeeded in either helping the African countries manage their debts properly or improve domestic economic conditions. Why have the SAPs failed to transform the African economies and deliver the expected benefits? First, throughout most of the adjusting countries, the SAPs have been implemented capriciously by a civil service whose primary interest has been in generating benefits for itself and not in improving macroeconomic performance. Second, the SAPs were not designed with the effective and full participation of the relevant stakeholder groups in Africa. However, design and implementation have been dominated and controlled by urban-based indigenous elites and their foreign benefactors, most of whom lack time-and-place information that is very essential for the development of effective and viable reform programs. During the last several decades, rural inhabitants, who must bear a significant portion of the costs of adjustment, have rarely if ever, been consulted or provided the facilities to participate in the process of designing and implementing the reform programs. Finally, the SAPs have been forced on African societies by the international lending community. In most of sub-Saharan Africa, these reforms did not originate from domestic efforts to improve macroeconomic performance but from the desire of external actors to control the allocation of aid and to enhance the ability of the African countries to service their external debts. In fact, in the mid-1980s, when it had become obvious that economic conditions in many African countries had deteriorated so much that disaster was just around the corner, many of the leaders still were unwilling to initiate reforms to halt the descend into economic and social "hell."

In Cameroon, for example, it was only after France and Germany, the country's most important benefactors, threatened to discontinue development aid that government officials approached the IMF and began "negotiations" for the implementation of reforms. Given the conditions under which many African governments became involved in institutional reforms, it was inevitable that the process would be reluctant and capricious. Right from the start, civil servants and politicians were reluctant to engage in reforms that were likely to change the *status quo* and only gave in when it became evident that they stood to lose significant amounts of foreign resources from the country's traditional benefactors such as Germany and France.

Reforms imposed on people rarely work. As Africans have completed more than half of the first decade of the new millennium, it is important for them to keep in mind that genuine institutional reforms must be people-driven, bottom-up, participatory and desired by the relevant stakeholder groups. They must be developed by them or with their full and effective participation and implemented with their consent. Perhaps, most important is the fact that reforms must be seen by the stakeholders as relevant and in their best interest. Unless and until Africans are allowed to take ownership of reforms in their communities, macroeconomic performance will continue to be poor and many people on the continent will continue to swelter in poverty and deprivation.

Debt cancellation, as proposed by many individuals, groups and organizations in Africa and the developed countries, sounds like a good idea. However, to provide a sustainable way for Africans to deal with their huge debts, as well as high levels of poverty, debt relief, which could take the form of debt cancellation, must be accompanied by state reconstruction to provide each country with accountable, transparent and participatory governance structures and resource allocation systems that guarantee economic freedoms. Such structures should adequately constrain the exercise of government agency and make it much more difficult for public servants to engage in reckless borrowing or the misuse of borrowed funds. In addition, they should enhance indigenous entrepreneurship and the creation of the wealth that these countries need to deal with mass poverty and deprivation.

References

Bandow, D. and Vasquez, I. (eds) (1994), *Perpetuating Poverty: The World Bank, IMF and the Developing World* (Washington, D.C.: Cato Institute).

Baylies, C. (1995), "'Political Conditionality' and Democratization", *Review of African Political Economy*, Vol. 22, No. 65, pp. 321–337.

Bradshaw, Y. W. and Tshandu, Z. (1990), "Foreign Capital Penetration, State Intervention, and Development in sub-Saharan Africa", *International Studies Quarterly*, Vol. 34, No. 2, pp. 229–251.

Brett, E. A. (1995), "Institutional Theory and Social Change in Uganda", in Harriss, J., Hunter, J. and Lewis, C. M. (eds), *The New Institutional Economics and Third World Development* (London: Routledge).

Cheru, F. (1989), *The Silent Revolution in Africa: Debt, Development and Democracy* (London: Zed Books).

Congleton, R. D. (1994), "Constitutional Federalism and Decentralization: A Second Best Solution", *Economia Delle Scelte Pubbliche* (Italy), Vol. 11, No. 1, pp. 15–29.

Danaher, K. (1994), "Introduction", in K. Danaher (ed.), *50 Years is Enough: The Case Against the World Bank and the International Monetary Fund* (Boston: South End Press).

Dunn, K. (2000), "Tales from the Dark Side: Africa's Challenge to International Relations Theory", *Journal of Third World Studies*, Vol. XVII, No. 1, pp. 61–90.

Ergas, Z. (1986), "In Search of Development: Some Directions for Further Investigation", *The Journal of Modern African Studies*, Vol. 24, No. 2, pp. 303–333.

Frimpong, K. (1997), "Structural Adjustment and the Myth of Its Success in Ghana", in K. R. Hope, Sr. (ed.), *Structural Adjustment, Reconstruction and Development in Africa* (Aldershot, UK and Brookfield, VT: Ashgate).

Hammond, R. and McGowan, L. (1994), "Ghana: The World Bank's Sham Showcase", in K Danaher (ed.), *50 Years is Enough: The Case Against the World Bank and the International Monetary Fund* (Boston, MA: South End Press).

Hope, K. R., Sr. and Kayira, G. (1997), "The Economic Crisis in Africa: An Analytical Perspective on Its Origins and Nature", in *Structural Adjustment, Reconstruction and Development in Africa* (Aldershot, UK and Brookfield, VT: Ashgate).

Ihonvbere, J. O. (1992), "The Military and Political Engineering Under Structural Adjustment: The Nigerian Experience Since 1985", *Journal of Political and Military Sociology*, Vol. 20, pp. 107–131.

Ihonvbere, J. O. (1994), *Nigeria: The Politics of Adjustment & Democracy* (New Brunswick, NJ: Transaction Publishers).

Ihonvbere, J. O. (1996), *Economic Crisis, Civil Society, and Democratization: The Case of Zambia* (Trenton, NJ and Asmara, Eritrea: Africa World Press).

Ihonvbere, J. O. (2000), *Africa and the New World Order* (New York: Peter Lang).

Jacques, G. (1997), "Structural Adjustment and the Poverty Principle in Africa", in K.R., Hope, Sr.(ed.), *Structural Adjustment, Reconstruction and Development in Africa* (Aldershot, UK and Brookfield, VT: Ashgate) .

Kayira, G. and Hope, K. R., Jr. (1997), "Structural Adjustment Policies: An Assessment of the Economic Impact on Southern Africa", in *Structural Adjustment, Reconstruction and Development in Africa* (Aldershot, UK and Brookfield, VT.: Ashgate).

Lall, S. (1995), "Structural Adjustment and African Industry", *World Development*, Vol. 23, No. 12, pp. 2019–2031.

Magadlela, D. (1997), "The Social Impact of Structural Adjustment Programs on the Smallholder Irrigation Farmers in Zimbabwe", in K. R. Hope, Sr. (ed.), *Structural Adjustment, Reconstruction and Development in Africa* (Aldershot, UK and Brookfield, VT.: Ashgate).

Mbaku, J. M. (1989), "Patterns and Levels of Life in Sahel West African Since the 1960s", *Africa Insight*, Vol. 19, No. 1, pp. 38–47.

Mbaku, J. M. (1997), *Institutions and Reform in Africa: The Public Choice Perspective* (Westport, CT.: Praeger).

Mbaku, J. M. (1999a), "A Balance Sheet of Structural Adjustment in Africa: Towards a Sustainable Development Agenda", in J. M. Mbaku (ed.), *Preparing Africa for the Twenty-First Century: Strategies for Peaceful Coexistence and Sustainable Development*, (Aldershot, UK and Brookfield, VT.: Ashgate).

Mbaku, J. M. (1999b), "Making the State Relevant to African Societies", in J. M. Mbaku, (ed.), *Preparing Africa for the Twenty-First Century: Strategies for Peaceful Coexistence and Sustainable Development* (Aldershot, UK and Brookfield, VT.: Ashgate).

Mbaku, J. M. (ed.) (1999c), *Preparing Africa for the Twenty-First Century: Strategies for Peaceful Coexistence and Sustainable Development* (Aldershot, UK and Brookfield, VT.: Ashgate).

Mbaku, J. M. (2000), *Bureaucratic and Political Corruption in Africa: The Public Choice Perspective* (Malabar, FL: Krieger).

Mensah, S. N.-A. (1997), 'Structural Adjustment Policies: Some Lessons for Development Momentum in Africa', in *Structural Adjustment, Reconstruction and Development in Africa* (Aldershot, UK and Brookfield, VT: Ashgate).

Mkandawire, T. and Soludo, C. C. (1999), *Our Continent, Our Future: African Perspectives on Structural Adjustment* (Trenton, NJ: Africa World Press)

OAU (Organization of African Unity) (1981), *The Lagos Plan of Action for the Economic Development of Africa 1980–2000*, (Geneva: International Institute for Labor Studies).

Osunsade, F. L. (1993), *IMF Support for African Adjustment Programs: Questions and Answers*, (Washington, D.C: IMF).

Plank, D. N. (1993), "Aid, Debt, and the End of Sovereignty: Mozambique and Its Donors", *The Journal of Modern African Studies*, Vol. 31, No. 3, pp. 407–430.

Salt Lake (Utah) Tribune, March 17, 1999.

Shepherd, G. W. (1990), "The African Right to Development: World Policy and the Debt Crisis", *Africa Today*, Vol. 37, pp. 191–212.

The Guardian (London), March 29, 2000.

UNDP (United Nations Development Program) (1990), *Human Development Report, 1990* (New York: Oxford University Press).

UNDP (1995), *Human Development Report, 1995*, (New York: Oxford University Press).

UNDP (1998), *Human Development Report, 1998*, (New York: Oxford University Press).

UNDP (2000), *Human Development Report, 2000*, (New York: Oxford University Press).

Weissman, S. R. (1990), "Structural Adjustment in Africa: Insights from the Experience of Ghana and Senegal", *World Development*, Vol. 18, No. 12, pp. 1621–1634.

World Bank (1981), *Accelerated Development in sub-Saharan Africa: An Agenda for Action* (Washington, D.C.: The World Bank).

World Bank (1994), *Adjustment in Africa: Reforms, Results, and the Road Ahead* (New York.: Oxford University Press).

World Bank (1997), *World Development Report, 1997* (New York: Oxford University Press).

World Bank (1998), *World Development Indicators, 1998* (Washington, D.C.: The World Bank).

World Bank (2000a), *African Development Indicators, 2000* (New York: Oxford University Press).

World Bank (2000b), *World Development Report, 1999/2000* (New York: Oxford University Press).

Young, T. (1995), "'A Project to be Realized': Global Liberalism and Contemporary Africa", *Millennium*, Vol. 24, No. 3 (Winter), pp. 527–548.

Chapter 4

Human Rights and the New Globalization in Africa

E. Ike Udogu

Introduction

Arguably, the issue of human rights is fundamentally a twentieth century phenomenon. Indeed, the intellectual discourse on this issue and reaction to it increased after WWII. Before 1945, the primacy of the sovereign nation-state in world politics led to the confinement of the debate on human rights issues to domestic politics. In this respect, the concepts of independence and sovereignty made it difficult for other nations to interfere in what was presumed to be the domestic and internal affairs of a sovereign nation-state. In fact, Chapter 1, Article 2, paragraph 7 of the Charter of the United Nations states: "Nothing contained in the present charter shall authorize the United Nations to intervene in matters which are essentially within the domestic jurisdiction of any state or shall require the Members to submit such matters to settlement under the present Charter" (Charter of the United Nations). Little wonder, then, that the international community has had a problem with tackling human rights problems globally.

Operationally, human rights involve, among other things, the equal protection (within the rule of law) of individuals as well as group rights in a polity. In a broader context, Cyrus Vance, former U.S. Secretary of State, defined human rights to include

- The right to be free of violations of the integrity of the person. Such violations include torture; cruel, inhumane, or degrading treatment or punishment; and arbitrary arrest or imprisonment. They also include denial of fair public trial, and invasion of the home.
- The right to the fulfillment of such vital needs as food, shelter, health care, and education.
- The right to enjoy civil and political liberties; freedom of thought, religion, assembly, and speech; freedom of the press; freedom of movement both within and outside one's country; and freedom to take part in government (Vance: 1979, p. 310).

Although attempts have been made to highlight the problems of human rights globally, at least since 1948, the results have been mixed. In fact, so much have been done by so many groups and individuals to assail this issue. To this end, attempts to improve human rights awareness and practices have been pursued within the general framework of the following:

- The U.N. Charter itself;
- The 1948 Universal Declaration of Human Rights;
- The two 1966 U. N. Covenants on Human Rights;
- The papal encyclical *Pacem in Terris*;
- The Vatican Commission on Justice and Peace;
- The statutes of regional organizations in Europe and in the Americas;
- The provisions of many national constitutions;
- Amnesty International (working to protect prisoners of conscience and the abolition of torture);
- The International Commission of Jurists (promoting the rule of law and the right to fair trial);
- The International Institute of Human Rights;
- President Jimmy Carter's human rights initiatives;
- The Final Act of the Helsinki Conference (Riemer and Simon: 1997, p. 373).

These are just a few declarations, covenants, and endeavors made by individuals as well as groups and institutions to resolve human rights issues globally. In some cases the above manifestos, even though well-intended, have exacerbated the dilemma of individuals and groups in Africa when they seek to assert their rights. For instance, within the context of the 1948 Universal Declaration of Human Rights, Article 1 states that: 'All human beings are born free and equal in dignity and rights. They are endowed with reason and conscience and should act towards one another in a spirit of brotherhood'. This tenet of the declaration while laudable is difficult to attain and, indeed, problematic in many cases – for example, the United Kingdom (Catholics and Protestants in Northern Ireland), in Spain and France (the Basque separatist movement), in Bosnia-Herzogovina (the Muslims, Serbs and Croats), in India (the untouchables) and in Africa (apartheid).

In Africa, the human rights problems are weighty and in many ways analogous to those in Europe and elsewhere. After all, following the Berlin Conference of 1884-1885, Africa was officially ceded to some of the European powers. The ethnic and political clashes in Rwanda, Burundi, Kenya, Zimbabwe, the Sudan and Nigeria have occurred, in part, as a result of the colonial policy of divide and rule. The infractions of the human rights of individuals and especially ethnic minority groups in these areas flow from the politics of exclusion and marginalization. Indeed, separatist movements, internal/irredentist wars and political turmoil in many countries in Africa have their roots in rights violation. To this end, (after over 50 years of the UN Universal Declaration of Human Rights), this study will attempt to do the following within the framework of the contemporary discourse on globalization: discuss concisely a few theories of human rights; highlight the issue of the violation of human rights in Africa; and suggest ways to pacify the problem in the new millennium.

Human Rights: A Theoretical Overview

Human rights issues today, regardless of one's ideological spectrum, are fundamentally global. Indeed, so universal are their scope and attraction within the contemporary global village that such cherished ideas, namely, civil and political rights which gained acceptance in the West are within its purview. Moreover, the concept of egalitarianism of human beings which was one of the central dogmas of the socialist revolution, in the first half of the twentieth century, is subsumed within the context of human rights (Udogu, 2000, pp. 22–23).

But the paradox, in spite of its global saliency, is that not all people enjoy their rights equally in most polities. Nevertheless, conceptually and even theologically, individuals are meant to have identical human rights. Unfortunately, this assumption has not always been the case. In a real sense, therefore, the clamor for the respect of human rights becomes a popular lingo among human rights activists, and serves as rallying cry for those who suffer from victimization in their politico-economic, religio-social and cultural systems. Generally, the complaint of human rights infringements by collectivities is intended to bring pressure to bear on the polity to change legally or politically those vices that tend to marginalize the group in the system so that in the final analysis, the call for human rights by the "victims" may be unnecessary. Thus, the possibility of realizing such a condition could only further the legitimacy of the state, which is one of the primary objectives of the custodians of the nation-state.

Conceptually, the basic discourse regarding the issue of human rights rests on the "character" of a human being: That is to say, philosophically, what does it imply to be an individual or a human being? Are all persons in society "equal" and therefore must *a priori* enjoy equal rights? Moralists may argue, theoretically, for such a utopia insisting that this might be the only way to create an ideal polity capable of promoting democracy and legitimacy. Realists, on the other hand, may argue that such a vision is only plausible on paper and contend that the argument on human equality is not only hollow, but also hogwash. Besides, given the competitive economic and political claims of human beings on a society, there are bound to be anomalies in the apportionment of goods and services which, invariably, may impact on the social stratification of any society (Udogu, 2001, p. 90).

Moreover, Jack Donnelly has argued that "an anthropological approach that seeks to ground human rights on cross-cultural consensus faces equally serious problems. History is replete with societies based on hierarchies of birth, gender, wealth, or power. … American history is marked by systematic torture and execution of religious deviants (witches); enslavement of and then legal discrimination against African Americans; … denial of political participation, property rights, and even legal personality to women; and repression of political dissidents (especially communists)" (Donnelly, 1998, pp. 20–21).

Additionally, the above thesis is furthered by an argument that has been propounded elsewhere that in most societies there can only be rich folks if there are poor folks to admire them for their wealth (Udogu, 1994, 161). Therefore, the desire of the wealthy to perpetuate the status-quo social order remains attractive and salient. Indeed, it is the perception of what Ted Robert Gurr termed relative deprivation (Couloumbis and Wolfe, 1990, 205), especially in segmented or divided societies that has not only sharpened, but also made the outcry for the practice of human rights universally reach its highest pitch at the dawn of the 21st century and after 50 years of the signing of the 1948 Universal Declaration of Human Rights. Historically, this whole matter of human rights is complicated and wrapped up in an enigma. Take for example:

> Classical Greeks considered themselves inherently superior to barbarians (non-Greeks), who were not entitled to the same treatment as Greeks. The American notion of manifest destiny or the British colonial ideology of the white man's burden justified barbarous treatment of non white peoples on the grounds of the superior virtue or moral development of Americans and Englishmen. Nazi Germany provides an even more extreme version of the denial of rights to "inferior races" on grounds of moral and political superiority (Donnelly, 1998, p. 22) …

Such political and socio-cultural treatment of human beings is endemic in many societies – untouchables in India, pygmies or Twas in Rwanda, blacks in apartheid South Africa, religious minorities in Egypt and elsewhere. These are incandescent examples and reminders of the problematic nature of human rights practices and issues. In fact, not even the views of naturalist scholars (in legal terms) that human rights were given to human beings by God appears to have currency, even among some of its ardent proponents, because of the political and social complexities of different societies. For example, one of the preambles in the American declaration of independence states that:

> We hold these truths to be self-evident, that all men are created equal, that they are endowed by their Creator with certain unalienable rights, that among these are Life, Liberty, and the pursuit of Happiness. That to secure these rights, Governments are instituted among Men, deriving their just powers from the consent of the governed. That whenever any Form of Government becomes destructive of these ends, it is the Right of the People to alter or to abolish it, and to institute new Government, laying its foundation on such principles and organizing its powers in such a form, as to them shall seem most likely to effect their Safety and Happiness (Ladd, 1985, p. A1) ...

This declaration does not allude to women and certainly African and Native Americans. Nevertheless, to fully grasp the character of the tone of this document one must situate it within its historic context (Udogu, 2001, 91). That notwithstanding, in contemporary political discourse, women and minorities are not still fully enjoying their human rights worldwide. For instance, some Muslim countries in connivance with the Vatican have remained steadfast in their denial of women certain human rights at women conferences based on theological grounds and interpretations of the role of women in the society. Asian countries emphasize the primacy of their values vis-à-vis human rights, and American and British conservatives contend that "economic, social and cultural rights are not really human rights" (Donnelly, 1998, p. 24).

Relativist scholars argue that moral values and, in fact, human rights issues should be based on the historicity and specificity of a given milieu. Therefore one's views, comprehension and analysis of human rights should be visualized within this framework. Further, they contend, Western democracies tend to stress civil and political rights and the right to private property, whereas the communists accentuate economic and social rights. Developing nations, on the other hand, are more concerned with self-determination and economic development. In light of the above conjectures, the interpretations of the concept of human rights could be conflictual on the basis of these different schools of thought (and their empiricisms). In general, this is the case even though the Vienna World Conference on Human Rights recognized and acknowledged the relativity of human rights (Udogu, 2001, p. 91).

Universalist scholars contend that human rights values are universal and are not subject to cultural manipulations and specificity. There are no historical differences and therefore rights apply everywhere – i.e., universally. These contending views, among others, have made the issue and observance of human rights problematical because of the various explications concerning its validity and relevance in different polities.

But what are some prevailing theories of human rights? Jack Donnelly (1998, pp. 28–29) provides three competing typologies: statist, cosmopolitan and internationalist models. The traditional statist model examines the issue of human rights within the context of the organic theory of the state or from the sovereign character of the state. In this framework, the supposition is that the juridical interpretation of human rights must flow from within the sovereign nation-state. It is thus outside the purview of the international community. In fact, any meddling in the internal affairs of the sovereign nation-state in the manner in which it handles or treats its citizens may even be considered as a violation of international law, specifically Article 2, paragraphs 4 and 7 of the UN Charter:

- All Members shall refrain in their international relations from the threat or use of force against the territorial integrity or political independence of any state, or in any other manner inconsistent with the purpose of the United Nations (paragraph 4).
- Nothing contained in the present Charter shall authorize the United Nations to intervene in matters which are essentially within the domestic jurisdiction of any state or shall require the Members to submit such matters to settlement under the present Charter (paragraph 7) (Charter of the United Nations) …

The cosmopolitan model sees the state as an impediment in the political calculus and conceptual analysis of human rights. This model stresses the significance of the individual rather than the state. It sees the state being assailed and sandwiched from below by influential individuals and powerful non-governmental organizations (NGOs) and from the top by the global community. The state having been 'squashed' in this model by two powerful forces becomes weak and therefore less confrontational toward external challenges on issues relating to human rights (Donnelly, 1998, pp. 28–29).

The internationalist model suggests the amalgamation and cooperation of the state (as represented by the activities of agents of the state) and the different informed publics including individuals with clout and NGOs to further human rights. The hypothesis is that human rights activity works within the context of the rules and norms established by the international community (Donnelly, 1998, pp. 28–29). Indeed, Article 28 of the Universal Declaration of Human Rights gives intergovernmental organizations (IGOs), NGOs and governments the mandate to intervene in the internal affairs of nation-states on behalf of human rights. Moreover, various regional organizations, for example, the Organization of American States, the African Union and the European Union with their various declarations and covenants on human rights support the above thesis.

At best, though, the aforementioned opinions are fundamentally descriptive. They explain what are theoretically sound, but are not always practical because of conflicting interests. In short, when it comes to the nitty-gritty of international relations, the state's national interest tends to trump ideologies and human rights proclamations. Witness, for instance, US granting of the most favored trading nation status to China despite the latter's dismal and problematic human rights record. The same argument could be made of the US violation of Article 5 of the UDHR that states: No one shall be subjected to torture or to cruel or inhuman or degrading treatment or punishment. These stated US infractions of the above Article, by human rights organizations, are in relations to the "War on Terror." In sum, the foregoing analyses are intended to provide the substructure for the conceptual, theoretical and even conflictive analysis of the perplexing issue of human rights. Indeed, because of its interpretative antinomies (sometimes based on national security/interest), it cannot be fully explained given the unique political, social and cultural norms of the various societies which make up our contemporary global system. Be that as it may, it is within the preceding prepositions that I raise, in brief, the human rights issues in Africa.

The debate on the question of human rights in Africa since independence is confounding. In fact, Issa G. Shivji's conceptualization and analysis is quite instructive especially as it applies to Africa. His intriguing discussion on the universality of the concept of human rights is provocative. Epistemologically and ontologically, human rights as a universal concept did not exist in pre-colonial Africa. So, "what are usually put forward as African human rights conceptions by its proponents are nothing more than notions of human dignity and worth which existed in all societies" (Shivji, 1989, p. 10). In this vein, some scholars have stated:

> There is no specifically African concept of human rights. The argument for such concept is based on a philosophical confusion of human dignity with human rights, and on an inadequate understanding of structural organization and social changes in African society. Underlying this inadequate understanding, a number of assumptions regarding the meaning of culture are used to buttress the reliance on the assertion of "cultural relativity," in order to argue that the allegedly "Western" concept of human rights cannot be applied to Africa (Howard, 1986, p. 23).

The conceptual debate aside, the fact that African countries wittingly endorsed human rights instruments within the United Nations and developed its own covenant, The African Charter on Human and Peoples' Rights, lend support to the universal validity and applicability of human rights ideas. Indeed, it is this view that informs my proceeding analysis.

Africa and the Human Rights Issue: A Concise Analysis

The African [Banjul] Charter on Human and Peoples' Rights (ACHPR), adopted on June 27, 1981, which was entered into force on October 21, 1986, represents the superstructure of African Convention on Human Rights (Banjul 1982). The covenant states, *inter alia,* that:

> This convention of the Organization of African Unity, which stipulates that freedom, equality, justice and dignity are essential objectives for the achievement of the legitimate aspirations of the African people (OAU Charter 1982, 7) ... and the Universal Declaration of Human Rights; Taking into consideration the virtues of their historical tradition and the values of African civilization which should inspire and characterize their reflection on the concept of human and peoples' rights; ... Convinced that it is henceforth essential to pay a particular attention to the right to development and that civil and political rights cannot be dissociated from economic, social and cultural rights [as] a guarantee for the enjoyment of civil and political rights; ... Undertaking to dismantle all forms of discrimination, particularly those based on race, ethnic group, color, sex, language, religion or political opinion; ... Firmly convinced of their duty to promote and protect human and peoples' rights and freedoms taking into account the importance traditionally attached to these rights and freedoms in Africa (Banjul Charter, 1982).

This synopsis of the preamble was immediately followed by an appeal to member states to adhere to the spirit of the charter in Articles 1 and 2. In particular, Article 1 states that: "The Member states of the [African Union], parties to the present Charter shall recognize the rights, duties and freedoms enshrined in this Charter and shall undertake to adopt legislative or other measures to give effect to them" (Udogu, 2004, p. 87).

This convention was designed for the protection of individual as well as group rights, as stated in Article 12, Section 5 of the ACHPR. But how efficacious an agreement could be depends on the interpretation and successful application of the tenets of the instrument. In other words, political entrepreneurs in African nation-states are charged to design legislation that are intended to enforce the spirit of the Charter, but how effective they have been in doing so is another matter. The tenets in the African Charter on Human and Peoples' Rights stress the individuality of rights more than they do group or collective rights despite the fact that the charter alludes repeatedly to "every individual" and "all peoples". In a real sense, this fine document does not clarify the rights, for instance, of collectivities. Indeed, it is the lack of respect for individual's human rights in spite of this Charter that prompted groups to converge in order to augment their influence in the quest and purpose of asserting their rights. This strategy was considered a more effective way of bringing pressure to bear on the state regarding the violation of their rights (Udogu, 2001, pp. 95–96)

For example, it was the inability of the Nigerian state to respect the individual rights of some of its minority groups that prompted the formation of the Ethnic Minority Rights of Africa (EMIROAF) to do battle with the state. The concern of the group was economic and political marginalization which it pursued within the framework of the ACHPR and Part 1, Article 1, of the International Convention on Civil and Political Rights. This Article states: "All peoples have the right of self-determination. By virtue of the right to freely determine their political status and freely pursue their economic, social and cultural development" (GA. Res. 2200A, 1996).

In a broader context, though, the human rights question, in spite of the concern raised by some scholars and members of the informed public, is wrapped up in an enigma. It is a confusion which Shadrack B. O. Gutto, in his in-depth analysis of "Human and Peoples' Rights in Africa," attempted to elucidate (Gutto, 1991, pp. 5–22). Indeed, human rights violations in Africa are so rampant that it has become imperative to undertake a critical examination of their impact on ordinary Africans – the masses that these rights were intended to protect.

The intellectual conversation on this topic at the international level is one that is occasionally troublesome, especially from certain African political apologists, nurtured by the Euro-centric view that human rights issues are in the main, or essentially, European. Therefore, as the argument goes, Africa and other emerging nations needed to understand this "truism" and attempt to imbibe the culture of human rights in existence in Europe. This view was necessary because the respect for human rights was imperative for the pollination and fertilization of democracy in Third World polities. Some political analysts argue that since human rights claims in Africa tend to assail the privileges of the governing elites, they blame their impact on colonial and specifically imperialist strategies to undermine their influence and power base in Africa. This view, contended Gutto, is not supported within the historical context of Africa (Gutto, 1991, p. 6). Nevertheless, though, there exist certain fundamental and immutable dimensions that impact on human rights issue in Africa. These are social class structures and relations; the inherited colonial culture; the depth of cultural and linguistic heterogeneity in virtually all African countries; the local and external forces, including social and economic models; authoritarian political systems; gender relations; wars and environmental conditions, *inter alia* (Gutto, 1991, p. 6). Moreover, the above factors are aggravated in the daily lives of a majority of Africans by the following:

> Police raids and repression, denial of the right to access to fair judicial processes in the adjudication of private and public legal disputes, the denial of the freedom of association and organization, the curtailment of the right to free participation in the choice of leaders through secret ballot, high infant mortality rates due to lack of food and proper medical care and housing, injuries sustained from women-beaters, inadequate income from hard labor ... (Gutto, 1991, p. 6; Odunsi, 2005, pp. 185–205).

These conditions are real in Africa despite the fact that African states were signatories to two vital international covenants on human rights, viz.: International Covenant on Economic, Social and Cultural Rights (U.N GAOR, 1996) and International Covenant on Civil and Political Rights which were entered into force in 1976. Whereas a review of the African Charter on Human and Peoples' Rights suggests that the covenant within the framework of human rights is on paper more inclusive than most other instruments (Nzongola-Ntalaja, 1994, p. 9), the actual implementation of its tenets leaves much to be desired. Indeed, from Nigeria to Kenya and from the Sudan to Zimbabwe, the above analysis brings into sharp focus the problem of apprehending the contradictions in the continent's practice (or lack thereof) of human rights provisions. In Africa, the infractions of the human rights of individuals and groups are problematic because of the area's political and economic instability. Yet, the respect for human rights is a *sine qua non* for the promotion of democracy, political stability and economic revitalization in the continent.

The "New Globalization" and Human Rights in Africa

Theodore A. Couloumbis and James H. Wolfe have summed up the UN 1948 Universal Declaration of Human Rights thus:

> The right to life, liberty, and security of person; the right to freedom of thought, speech and communication of information and ideas; freedom of assembly and religion; the right to government through free elections; the right to free movement within the state and free exit from it, the right to asylum in another state; the right to nationality; freedom from arbitrary arrest and interference with the privacy of home and family; and the prohibition of slavery and torture; ... The right to work, to protection against unemployment, and to join trade unions; the right to a standard of living adequate for health and well-being; the right to education; and the right to rest and leisure (Couloumbis and Wolfe, 1990, p. 29).

These rights are essential for the furtherance of harmony and stability in any polity. The key issue, though, is how to attain these laudable declarations in a world in which there exist numerous competing and conflicting social, economic and political interests? Moreover, the concept of human rights subsumes so many dimensions under its rubric, some of which conflict with many national and regional cultures. The major thrust of the following discussion relates to the instrumentalities for addressing human rights questions. Put another way, the concern is on how to encourage the existing organizations to pursue their work of promoting human rights with great vigor and rigor in Africa.

In the region, at this juncture of the continent's political history, it has been difficult for most regimes to implement the human rights instruments. This is the situation because they are, in the words of Gunnar Myrdal, soft states unable to enforce their laws. Moreover, in a number of cases the government itself is the major problem in the infractions of the human rights of its citizens (Wiseberg, 1994, p. 3 4). Human Rights Watch/ Africa and other non-governmental organizations have been vocal in calling the attention of governments to these issues. Their voices, however, have nearly always fallen "on deaf ears" of some of the despotic leaders in the continent. For example, the late Moshood Abiola, the presidential candidate, who was believed to have won the 1993 Nigerian Presidential Election, died in government detention charged with treason without trial, after he declared himself president of the country in 1994. The same is true of many human rights activists and advocates, particularly journalists and lawyers who expose human rights infringements. Given this prognosis, how might African nations and human rights organizations function effectively in advancing the respect for human rights in the continent?

The African Commission on Human and People's Rights

In Africa, the Organization of African Unity (now the African Union) established an African Commission on Human and Peoples' Rights whose *raison d'être* was to safeguard the human rights tenets contained in the African Charter on Human and Peoples' Rights. Indeed, the mandate of the Commission is stated in Article 45 thus:

- To promote Human and Peoples' Rights and in particular: (a) to collect documents, undertake studies and researches on African problems in the field of human and peoples' rights, organize seminars, symposia and conferences, disseminate information, encourage national and local institutions concerned with human and peoples' rights, and should the case arise, give its views or make recommendations to governments. (b) to formulate and lay down, principles and rules aimed at solving legal problems relating to human and peoples' rights and fundamental freedoms upon which African governments may base their legislation. (c) cooperate with other African and international institutions concerned with the promotion and protection of human and peoples' rights.
- Ensure the protection of human and peoples' rights under conditions laid down by the present Charter.
- Interpret all the provisions of the present Charter at the request of a State party, an institution of the OAU or an African Organization recognized by the OAU.
- Perform any other tasks which may be entrusted to it by the Assembly of Heads of State and Government.

Although the Commission is made up of elected members for six year terms, critics charge that they are often beholden to national governments and their meetings are generally mired by rules and secrecy and, therefore, are too slow in addressing human rights problems (Wiseberg, 1994, p. 3). Moreover, the African Commission does not have a supranational mechanism and power to enforce human rights infractions. The latter is significant to the extent that it could empower the Commission to deal more effectively with human rights issues in the continent.

National Constitutions

Most national constitutions address the issue of human rights, but African states appear not to enforce human rights breaches with enthusiasm. For instance, the following articles in Chapter IV of Nigeria's 1979 and 1999 Constitutions on Fundamental Rights state:

> 30-(1) Every person has a right to life, and no one shall be deprived intentionally of his [her] life …

31-(1) Every individual is entitled to respect for the dignity of his persons, and accordingly:

(a) no person shall be subjected to torture or to inhuman or degrading treatment;
(b) no person shall be held in slavery or servitude; and
(c) no person shall be required to perform forced or compulsory labor …

33-(1) In the determination of his[her] civil rights and obligations, including any question or determination by or against any government or authority, a person shall be entitled to a fair hearing within a reasonable time by a court or other tribunal established by law and constituted in such manner as to secure its independence and impartiality …

36-(1) Every person shall be entitled to freedom of expression, including freedom to hold opinions and to receive and impart ideas and information without interference (i.e., Right to freedom of the press and expression) (Nigerian Constitution 1979, 21-29)...

The South African constitution is very clear on human rights issues as contained in Chapter three on Fundamental Rights. In fact, it states in the Bill of Rights under

Section 9: Equality

1. Everyone is equal before the law and has the right to equal protection and benefit of the law…
3. The state may not unfairly discriminate directly or indirectly against anyone on one or more grounds, including race, gender, sex, ethnic or social origin, color, sexual orientation, age, disability, religion, conscience, pregnancy, marital status, language and birth…

Section 10: Human Dignity

1. Everyone has inherent dignity and the right to have their dignity respected and protected.

Section 12: Freedom and Security of the Person

1. Everyone has the right to freedom and security of the person, which includes the right

a. not to be deprived of freedom arbitrarily or without just cause
b. not to be detained without trial
c. to be free from all forms of violence from either public or private sources
d. not to be tortured in any way, and
e. not to be treated or punished in a cruel, inhuman or degrading way.

Section 16: Freedom of Expression

1. Everyone has the right to freedom of expression, which includes

a. freedom of the press and other media
b. freedom to receive and impart information and ideas
c. freedom of artistic creativity and
d. academic freedom and freedom of scientific research

Section 17: Assembly, Demonstration, Picket and Petition

> *a.* Everyone has the right, peacefully and unarmed, to assemble, to demonstrate, to picket, and to present petitions (S.A Constitution, Ch. 2, Bill of Rights: 1996)...

The Rwandan Constitution, under Title 11, Public Liberties, contains several Articles. For example, specific sections dealing with human rights are discussed in Article 12: Human Dignity and Personal Freedom:

> *Section* 1: The human being shall be sacred.
> *Section* 2: The liberty of the human being shall be inviolable ...
> *Section* 4: Any person shall be presumed innocent of the charges as long as a definite conviction has not taken place...

Article 16: Citizen Equality

> 1. All citizens shall be equal in the eyes of the law, without any discrimination, especially in respect to race, color, origin, ethnic background, clan, sex, opinion, religion or social status ... (Rwanda Constitution, 1991).

In general, in spite of Nigeria's 1979 Constitution (and Chapter 4 of the 1999 Constitution), intended to protect the human rights of all Nigerians, successive governments since the promulgation of this constitution have systematically violated the intents of this document. Indeed, human rights violations during the military regimes assumed an epidemic proportion in light of the number of journalists incarcerated across the country, and the clandestine killings of individuals who opposed the regimes. The situation since the rebirth of democracy in 1999 in the country has improved, but the human rights infringements of citizens in the oil-producing Niger Delta area are vexing to human rights advocates.

The U.S. Department of State's report on human rights in South Africa for 1995 was relatively good. It, however, noted that the cases of deaths in police custody in the country are serious problems for the republic. Indeed, the Human Rights Commission (HRC) reported that political violence resulted in 970 deaths in the first 11 months of 1996, compared with 1,296 for the same period in 1995. Moreover, in spite of the tenets of the constitution against torture, some members of the police use excessive force and torture and tend to abuse suspects and detainees. Perhaps there is no area of human rights violation in the country that is nearly as disturbing as that of the treatment of women. Indeed, there is a high rate of violence against women. It is reported that every 6 days a women is killed by her husband or boyfriend. The figures put out by the NGO, People Opposing Women Abuse, attest to this dilemma and similar violation of women's right in the Republic of South Africa (U.S. Dept. of State, 1996).

A similar report for Rwanda, after the 1994 genocidal civil war, presented an improving condition of human rights breaches in the country. In spite of this amelioration, however, the government continues to be responsible for major human right abuses. The Rwandan Patriotic Army (RPA) was involved in the killing of many Rwandan citizens both for political reasons and the acts of revenge. Over 80,000 prisoners are held in over-crowded jails, with serious sanitation problems, without trial. Official agents of the government harass journalists whose news items are considered to be antagonistic to that of the government's views. Newspapers are sometimes temporarily closed and so were journalists detained by security operatives or forces (U.S. Dept. of State: Rwanda, 1996).

There is no doubting the fact that the provisions in this selected number of national constitutions are commendable. It is, unfortunately, clear from what happens on the ground that it is one thing to promulgate human rights regimes and quite another to implement them. The human rights violations in Rwanda, Burundi, Algeria, Cameroon, Kenya, Egypt and elsewhere in Africa leave much to be desired. How, then, are human rights issues to be tackled in the new millennium? Some scholars have reiterated the significance of education on human rights issues in African schools (Aka and Browne, 1999, p. 432; Udogu, 2003, p. 121). These academics argue, and rightly so, that by sensitizing students to the importance of human rights issues in their lives and polities, these future leaders are likely to become true pioneers in the advancement of human rights practices in the area. It is to this important dimension that I center the proceeding analysis.

Education as a Tool for the Promotion of Human Rights in Africa

The assumption here is clear. Education on human rights provides individuals with the knowledge that could help them protect their rights and those of others not familiar with these rights. In fact, it has been argued that it might be hollow to catalogue the fundamental rights of individuals and groups in national constitutions or in global human rights instruments if those for whom these rights are guaranteed are ignorant that the protections exist (Aka and Browne, 1999, pp. 432–433). In short, education augments public knowledge about human rights. Thus, the centrality of this contention is that education should provide the people with the appreciation and right to know and consequently to act upon such rights when they are violated. Little wonder, then, that the United Nations Educational, Scientific, and Cultural Organization (UNESCO) convoked the International Congress on Education for Human Rights and Democracy held in Montreal, Canada, on March 8–11, 1993. The Conference adopted the World Plan of Action on Education for Human Rights and Democracy by noting that such an education was itself human right, and a *sine qua non* for the actualization of human rights, democracy, and social justice (U.N., 1995). Probably, it was the assumption that education on human rights was likely to promote its understanding and respect in different societies that the United Nations declared January 1995 to January 2005 the U.N. Decade for Human Rights Education (Aka and Browne, 1999, p. 439). With the percentage of educated Africans still very low in the continent (HDR, 1999, pp. 140-141), this objective requires immediate action.

But in much of Africa, and other developing countries, the political actors contend that they are more concerned with "nation-building" and "development", and do not wish to be "bothered" by group or individual human rights of those presumed to be trouble makers; this is especially so with groups seeking "special" concessions from any regime (e.g., the Sudan, South Africa, Ethiopia, Kenya, Cameroon, Algeria, Nigerian, Egypt, and so on) in the continent.

It has been suggested, however, that if human rights organizations are to be effective, they must build their support from the grassroots, especially since the present top down approach is not working (Matua, 1994, p. 30). But above all, the populace must be educated on the virtues of human rights. In this respect, the objective of Nigeria in 1997, on the eve of the 50th anniversary of the Universal Declaration of Human Rights, to introduce the subject for study in secondary schools in Nigeria is refreshing (Ejime, 1997). If adequately carried out, it should serve as an important step in attempts at ameliorating the human rights problems in post-military Nigeria and possibly serve as a framework or model for other African countries facing similar human rights crisis.

In sum, since the African Commission is relatively weak in enforcing human rights issues at this juncture, its functions should be augmented by NGOs. To this end, the insightful observation and remarks of Laurie Wiseberg (1994, p. 39) are worth considering:

> If there is any hope for progress in the human rights area, responsibility for promoting and maintaining human rights must reside with non-governmental organizations and sensitized pressure groups. It is largely through such groups and groupings, particularly if they act in coalition with each other and with those statesmen who, for whatever reasons, are willing to champion specific human rights causes, that state behavior can be surveyed, violations denounced, pressure … mobilized and applied on government, so that some progress may be made toward a more humane social order.

The activities of the Committee for the Defense of Human Rights (CDHR) in pressuring the Nigerian government to release political detainees under the infamous Decree (No. 2) which permitted government agents to arrest any "suspected" citizen without charge is a good case in point (Nigerian Vanguard, 1999) and should retained in civilian administrations. Furthermore, the activity of NGOs, such as Amnesty International (AI), in educating the public on human rights issues is laudable. It has fought relentlessly on behalf of prisoners of conscience throughout the world – a gesture which, among other factors, won the group the Nobel Prize for Peace in 1977.

These above mentioned achievements notwithstanding, the troublesome issue of human rights violations in Africa is going to be with us for a long time to come. This is so given the clash between some African traditional cultures, norms, values, religious beliefs on the one hand, and human rights demands, on the other. The above situations are aggravated by social and political marginalization of groups who lack numerical clout in national politics. Frustrations from exclusionary policies pursued by the dominant groups in power have in some instances led to the migration out of the continent of extremely qualified Africans. This condition creates problems for African development. But, it is possible that through education on human rights issues and the watchful eyes and legitimization of the activities of genuine and committed NGOs on human rights infringements, human rights problems could be mitigated. In this way, the visions of the UN 1948 Universal Declaration of Human Rights, African [Banjul) Charter on Human and Peoples' Rights, and other similar instruments for the promotion of peace and stability might be furthered in Africa and the contemporary global village.

Conclusion

I have in this disquisition discussed some of the critical issues relating to the state of human rights in Africa in the context of the new globalization. In 1981, African states adopted the African Charter on Human and Peoples' Rights as the superstructure of the African human rights regime. Among other things, the charter delineates the contours of the continent's human rights framework. However, the repository of evidence clearly indicates that there is a large gap between the provisions of the human rights regime and practice. Against the backdrop of the human rights crisis on the continent, three major suggestions are made as ways of addressing the problems.

First, the African Human Rights Commission needs to be strengthened. This should include, but not limited to, granting the commission a supranational power to enforce the provisions that are enshrined in the Banjul Charter. The commission's enforcement powers would need to be constructed on its capacity to collect data on human rights violations in various African states. So, this would mean that the commission's resource base would need to be expanded.

Second, there is a need to both strengthen and broaden the ambit of human rights education on the continent. Although some African states have human rights commissions that are mandated, among other things, to design and implement programs that are designed to educate the citizenry about their rights, much still needs to be done.

Finally, human rights-based non-governmental organizations on the continent would need to expand the scope of their educational programs from the urban to the rural areas. This is because rural dwellers constitute the most vulnerable group in terms of the violation of human rights. For example, it is quite common for even agents of a state to go to the rural areas and engaged in activities that violate the human rights of these citizens – a move that often impedes the advancement of the legitimacy and atomization of the multi-national and multi-lingual polity.

References

African [Banjul] Charter on Human and Peoples' Rights (1981), June 27. *OAU Doc. CAB/LEG/67/3 Rev. 5, 21 I.L.M 58 1982.*

Aka, Phillip C. and Browne, Gloria J (1999), "Education, Human Rights, and the Post-Cold War Era", *New York Law School Journal of Human Rights*, Vol. XV, Part 3, pp. 421–448.

Charter of the United Nations <http://www.un.org/aboutun/charter>

Constitution of the Federal Republic of Nigeria (1999), Abuja: Federal Ministry of Information and National Orientation.

Constitution of the Federal Republic of Nigeria (1979), *Daily Times Publication* (Lagos, Nigeria).

Coulumbis, Theodore A and Wolfe, James H. (1990), *Introduction to International Relations: Power and Justice* (Englewood, NJ: Prentice-Hall).

Donnelly Jack (1998), *International Human Rights* (Boulder, CO: Westview Press).

Ejime, Paul (1997), "Nigeria to Introduce Human Rights Studies in Schools", Panafrica-News Agency <http://www.africanews.org/west/Nigeria/stories/1997.html>.

General Assembly Resolution 2200A (XXI) 21, U.N. GAOR (No. 16) at 52, U.N. Doc A/6316 (1996).

Gutto, Shadrack B. O. (1991), "Human and Peoples' Right in Africa: Myths, Realities and Prospects", *Current African Issues*, Vol. 12, pp. 5–22.

Howard, Rhoda E. (1986), *Human Rights in Commonwealth Africa* (NJ: Rowan and Littlefield).

Human Development Report (1999), (New York: Oxford University Press).

International Covenant on Economic, Social and Cultural Rights, G.A Res. 2200A (XXI), 21, UN GAOR Supp. (No. 16) at 49, UN Doc. A/6316 (1966).

Ladd, Everett C. (1985), *The American Polity: The People and Their Government*,(New York: W. S. Norton & Company, Inc.).

Matua, Wa Matua (1994), "Domestic Human Rights Organizations in Africa: Problems and Perspectives", *Issue: A Journal of Opinion*, Vol. 22, No. 2, pp. 32–33.

Nigeria Vanguard (1999), March 16, '39 still held under Decree 2, says CDHR." <http://www.afbis.com/vanguard/F2170399.html>.

Nzongola-Ntalaja, Georges (1994), "Violation of Democratic Rights in Zaire", *Issue: The Journal of Opinion*, Vol. 22, No. 2, pp. 9–12.

OAU Charter and Rules of Procedure (1982), Published by the Division of Press and Information: Addis Ababa, Ethiopia.

Odunsi, Bennett (2005), "The Police and Human Rights Infractions: The Need of Reform", in E. Ike Udogu (ed.), *Nigeria in the Twenty-First Century: Strategies for Political Stability and Peaceful Coexistence* (Trenton, NJ: African World Press).

Riemer, Neal and Simon, Douglas W. (1997), *The New World of Politics: An Introduction to Political Science 4th edition*, (San Diego, CA; Collegiate Press).

Rwanda Constitution (1991), <http://www.oefre.unibe.ch/law/ic1/rw00000_.html>.

Shivji, Issa G. (1989), *The Concept of Human Rights in Africa*, (London: CODESRIA Books).

South African Constitution (1996), Chapter 2, The Bill of Rights, <http://www.gov.za/constitution/1996/96cons2.htm>.

Udogu, E. Ike (2004), "Human Rights and Minorities: A Theoretical Overview", in Paul T. Zeleza and Philip J. McConnaughay (eds), *Human Rights, The Rule of Law, and Development in Africa* (Philadelphia, PA: University of Pennsylvania Press).

Udogu, E. Ike (2003), "National Constitutions and Human Rights Issues in Africa", *African and Asian Studies*, Vol. 2, No. 2, pp. 101–123.

Udogu, E. Ike (2001), "Human Rights and Minorities in Africa: A Theoretical and Conceptual Overview", *Journal of Third World Studies*, Vol. 18, No. 1, 87–104.

Udogu, E. Ike (2000), "An Examination of Minority Groups and Human Rights Issues in Europe and Africa", *Journal of Political Science*, Vol. 28, pp. 21–43.

Udogu, E. Ike (1994), "The Allurement of Ethnonationalism in Nigerian Politics: The Contemporary Debate", *Journal of Asian and African Studies*, Vol. 29, Nos. 3–4, pp. 159–171.

United Nations Decade for Human Rights Education (1995), U.N GAOR, 49th Session, Agenda Item 100 (b), at 2, U.N. Doc. A/RES/49/184.

US Department of State: South Africa Country Report on Human Rights Practices (1996), *Bureau of Democracy, Human Rights, and Labor (January 30, 1997)* <http://www.state.gov/www/global/human_rights/1996_hrp_report/southafr.html>.

US Department of State: Rwanda Country Report on Human Rights Practices (1996).

Bureau of Democracy, Human Rights, and Labor (January 30, 1997), <http://www.state.gov/www/global/human_rights/1996_hrp_report/rwanda.html>.

Vance, Cyrus (1979), "Law Day Address on Human Rights", in , Donald P. Kommers and Gilbert D Loescher (eds), *Human Rights and American Foreign Policy* (Notre Dame, IN: University of Notre Dame Press).

Wiseberg, Laurie S. (1994), "The African Commission on Human and Peoples' Rights", *Issue: A Journal of Opinion*, Vol. 22, No. 2, pp. 34–36.

Chapter 5

The Norms of Displacement: NGOs, Globalization and the State in Africa

P.L.E. Idahosa

"Most NGOs in Africa are purely functional, whether they are working in the area of welfare, development, refugees, debt or human rights. There are only very few that might be considered as 'thinking' NGOs, organizations that sit back and reflect on what they are doing and how their particular activity is related to the broader issues related to state, society and development in the present international conjuncture. Unthinkingly, thus, many purely functional NGOs act as mere palliatives to reduce the effects of the deteriorating social and economic conditions in Africa. In recent years many large international NGOs that used to undertake 'development' work in Africa have now shifted their resources to welfare and refugee work. Many of them are doing 'good work' in these fields, no doubt, and yet they unwittingly help perpetuate the very conditions that they seek to alleviate" *Yash Tandon* (1995).

> "I have to have my own. To have my own NGO, I can achieve so much; but first I have to get someone to sponsor me". – Private correspondence

Introduction

Globalization takes many different forms; and the increasing role played by Non-Governmental Organizations (NGOs) in development is one of them. Globalization certainly lies in the compulsion of adopting practices that are issued from forces in places and processes that diminish the capacity of states to act autonomously. It also lies in an imperative of being required to converge at some point around an assumed consensus and having the terms of reference defined by that consensus, especially in relation to what one might call the norms of development. Debates about development and NGOs are one such example of this course of action.

Since the early 1980s, one can characterize many of the development norms about and within Africa by their relationship to the ongoing experiences of the "Washington Consensus". This is the "New Policy Agenda", with its post-Cold War triumphalism of adjustment and stabilization, and more recently of so-called new political and developmental paradigms of governance, civil society, participation and capacity building (see Hulme and Edwards, 1997, pp. 6–7). Indeed, even those that would claim to move beyond the consensus (see Mkandawire and Soludo, 1999), and who argue for a perspective for African initiatives and ownership, are "hemmed in" to having to come to terms with them. Moreover, those who might claim through their activities to be against the consensus, or those against most Western-engendered development models, often reinforce it, whether by default or design. Ironically, this is especially true with NGOs in Africa.

NGOs represent a number of interesting trends in the globalization of development in Africa. Especially interesting, of course, is a shift away from state-centred forms of governance to the dual process of a more decentralized, but also transnational forms of authority, all of which locate resources and authority in places other than the state. Consonant with globalization, NGOs also represent a proliferation of dependencies, through, that is, the redistribution of the agencies of authority by way of institutions that are themselves incapable of directly carrying out these functions, but which act as catalysts for these agents and institutional actors and structures. Whether local or expatriate, NGOs are often highly reliant upon agents outside and above the state within which they operate; and in so becoming, they turn into a form of authority often accountable not to the state, but rather to donors and their own constituencies. They form part of this dual direction towards the diffusion of and centralization of agencies in a globalized world, where powers, rights and duties, once the domain of the sovereign state, have become progressively more pooled among other institutions and agents such as multilateral agencies, international human rights and environmental organizations, as well as powerful states in the industrialized world. However, what they also form a part of is a coincidence not just about the direction of development, but also of presumed values that are meant to undergird and to guide it. NGOs are playing a central role in this process of shaping a global discourse on, as well as practice in, development.

It is important, then, to see that much of the debate about whether the continent is to grow and supposedly regain its place in a world of growth and prosperity is not just about the nature of adjustment in Africa, but more exactly, about the value-laden and practical character of the normatively prescriptive political-economic policy choices available. To be sure, at the nucleus of these prescriptions is the status of the accords with international financial institutions, where access to loans are subject to the rules of conditionality, requiring market reforms for various forms of development assistance. However, the problem for many Africans policy-makers and academics does not alone lie in the orthodox macroeconomic policy supervision of economic liberalism contained in adjustment – trade liberalization, various degrees of privatization and deregulation, and the move to increased reliance on market forces through both competitive domestic and global markets.[1] Nor does the concern with economic liberalism lie alone in whether the policies have been or can be effective. Rather the concern also resides in adjustments that would involve far-reaching transfers in governance away from the post-war, and nationalist conceit of relative national economic sovereignty, to a shift towards further integration into the world economy, and towards a decentering of economic decision-making, over which there appears little choice. The centralizing, or integrating of markets through

1 I say this, despite the present talk at the World Bank, which indicates some linguistic move away from the clear language of conditionality to the more euphemistic language of "selectivity", or an implied conditionality that stresses borrower participation – that is "ownership". See Nelson (1996, pp. 1551–59).

mulilaterism, is, as we shall see, entirely consonant with the rise of NGOs as part of the apparent shifting balance of power between national states, international bodies of economic governance and transnational forms of "civil society", of which NGOs are often said to be a part. Indeed, it is part of the argument of this chapter that NGOs are meant, both practically and *normatively*, to actively undermine the role of the state in Africa.

Thus, what I am interested in is not just the new political and economic trilateralism as development, but also in the practical justification and the normative, or moral, status for these new interventions given the ubiquity of NGOs in Africa's development process, and indeed in much of the political landscape. Why is it until very recently, outside some of the self-serving and often authoritarian attempts at circumscribing them by African governments, have NGOs received so very little normative attention and appraisal in discussions, not only of globalization, but also its older, if smaller, cousin, development? There is now a burgeoning literature, not just on NGOs, which is itself huge,[2] but also a critical literature as to their role in development, how they got there, and, to a much lesser extent, what the values are which inform their practice. However, despite the extraordinary expansion of the activities of NGOs in development, and the exponential growth of substantive, descriptive, and analytical literature on NGOs, there is little by way of an analysis of their *intentions* in terms of normative analysis, and how these norms are linked to the aims of neo-liberalism.

Non-Governmental Organizations (NGOs)

Background

There have been many attempts at refining analytically and taxonomically the bewildering types and indeed typologies of NGOs, with their equally confusing array of acronyms. While recognizing that the typologies for them have become increasingly elaborate, I will follow Hulme and Edward and others' nomenclature (1992; cf. Fowler et al, 1996; ODI, 1995, Wellard and Copestake, 1993; World Bank, 1997) and Vakil's (1997) and especially Ball and Dunn's (1996) analytical distinctions, which have identified thirty-one possible types of organizations. They either overlap, or can be identified with NGOs, whether private voluntary organizations (PVO) or a community-based Organization (CBO); from a voluntary development organization (VDO) to a people's organization (PO), which may or may not be a non-profit organization or a not-for-profit organization; to a grassroots organization to a community co-operative, which may be a registered charity. Here we are only discussing the status of those explicitly *engaged in development*, or

2 The World Bank (1999) published a 127 page selected Bibliography on Civil Society over the last twenty years (much of it complied by the prolific writer on NGOs, Alan Fowler, e.g 1988; 1997). There were no less than two hundred and seventy articles on NGOs. A similar, although less extensive bibliography has also been provided by CIDA (1998).

Non-Governmental Development Organizations (NGDOs), which we will generally use synonymously with NGOs.[3]

Finally, we are not talking primarily about advocacy NGOs, although some development NGOs have become more vociferously advocates.[4] Moreover, as we point out below, since some NGOs play/ed an important role in mobilizing opposition to authoritarian forms of rule and in organizing constituencies that suffered directly, this adds directly to their normative-participatory identity. We also acknowledge that there are different forms of organizational mechanisms for NGOs. The two principal forms are those controlled privately and independently by their founders or their nominees (i.e. management boards, committees or trustees), and those that are participatory, which are more democratic in organization, in that they are managed by elected bodies, or otherwise representative of their membership. Since 1983, the World Bank has been monitoring the evolution of NGOs, as it has with its relationship to them, and it even has a NGO Unit (see Shihata, 1995; World Bank, 1997a).

For our purposes, which seek to identify the foundations for claims or development NGOs, from this distillation, whether they are donor/Northern NGOs or indigenous ones, in the main they have the four following characteristics. First, they are formed *voluntarily*, and voluntary participation will be intrinsic to the organization. Second, they are *independent,* in that those who have formed them, run them. Third they are *not-for-profit*, not being for private personal gain or profit. Fourth, they do not have self-serving aims or related values. Through various forms of action, NGOs intend, often altruistically, to increase the well being and capabilities of *disadvantaged* people who are unable to realize their potential and/or achieve their full rights in society, rather than organizations engaged in the self-interests of its members. This fourth, attribute that we are interested in, identifies NGOs as having particular *values and goals*. It is these values and goals that mark them off from other organizations (Ball and Dunn, 1995 ch. 5 *passim*), sometimes tacitly claimed, often times overtly asserted, are the foundations of NGOs' claim for *legitimacy.*

Broadly, these values can be seen in terms of the objectives of alleviating poverty, being effective in increasing incomes and consumption and in improving the position and morale of the poor. However, that they have expertise in, and are therefore

---

3 A very useful collection, edited by Eve Sandberg (Sandberg, 1994) specifically on Africa, contains an excellent introduction with an analytical framework that sets out a five-fold descriptive-prescriptive typology of relationships between the state and NGOs in Africa – informal and ad hoc, state co-ordination, sector-specific coordination, local-decentralized coordination; and her own prescriptive "stratified, multifocused, institutional arrangement" (1994a, p. 15) model, where the state and NGOs collaborate and coordinate activities at different political administrative levels within different regions. While the framework is not always relevant to the purpose set out here, in that it primarily focuses on state or institutional relations with NGOs, who may or may not be development NGOs, the framework and some of the case studies that inform the typology, will be drawn upon throughout this chapter.

4 Some claim that this is what NGOs do best and on what they should concentrate their efforts, especially Northern ones, particularly when they are part of a wider, global network and are linked to Southern constituencies, (see, for example, Korten, 1990). Not everyone believes this in part because of the conflict over multiple aims and constituencies (see Nelson, 1997).

effective in carrying out tasks assigned to them, is not enough. In addition, according to Nelson (see Nelson, 1997; cf. Attack, 1999), Northern or international NGOs have especially had to construct grounds for their legitimacy, or the justification for their participation in development; and they have done so by locating their legitimacy within being in partnership with Southern NGOs and representing Southern views. Nelson identifies two other forms of NGO legitimation: they have a domestic political constituency, and they are granted a designation – that is, when an NGO takes part in an officially (e.g. multilateral or bilateral) sanctioned committee or gathering. I think that he is right on when he says that these aims are inherently unstable, even though many NGOs see them as complementary items in package of values.[5]

It is important to acknowledge these characteristics of NGOs as bases for legitimacy, as Tvedt (1998, pp. 35–37), in a major and important book on the role of – primarily Norwegian – NGOs, claims that classifying NGOs according to their value orientation, unlike services supplied, cannot provide adequate grounds for commensurability between them. He argues that criteria around such values as self-reliance, participation, voluntaryness, and so on, are likely to result in too many subjective appraisals in contrast to the more "objective" claims of efficiency and effectiveness. However, not to take these values into account would also be remiss since so many NGOs use them to justify themselves, but who, by their own admission, so often fail on these grounds. Even the highly contested notion of participation, so central to NGOs *raison d'être*, can be used as a subject of evaluation, precisely because of the competing standpoints held by parties with divergent, political, ideological and economic interests. If we are assessing and evaluating development and identifying which agents and institutions have a right to intervene, we have to engage in some value discourse when pointing to its aims, its various means and its consequences, as well as its subjects and its agents. Development ethics, a sub-field of development inquiry that began in the mid-1970s to evaluate change that presumes to improve people's lives asserts the need to seek out, explore, reveal and test the moral values, stated or unstated, implicit or explicit, in the prescriptive goals of development theory and practice. Although we cannot explore here the different kinds of ethical approaches (see Goulet, 1995; cf. Crocker, 1991 and Qizilbash, 1996, for a summaries), there are some questions that might be asked of any approach to or practice of development, and where NGOs and their embedded principles might lie within them.

Can we identify and criticize or commend development practices based on some set of values held, like participation? What are development norms that justify the values held, and, as Goulet would say, the alternative futures of development envisaged of which some development practitioners and theorists claim to have

5 One of the most extraordinary developments in recent years has been both the language and practice of "stakeholding". It is often assumed that because they are there, or because they have been invited, or because they have global rights based upon issues of sustainability there, that Northern NGOs have sovereignty and an equality of voice with those whom they are acting on behalf of. This position has been particularly true in the environmental field, especially since Rio (see Roe, 1999, p. 11, and Derman, 1995). The tension in such a position should be obvious.

knowledge (Goulet, 1995, pp. 7–10)? The language of NGOs and those who support them is real, has normative effect, and needs to be evaluated as such, especially where the values proclaimed often fail in practice or come into conflict with those whom they depend upon, even where, as with participation, they appear to be talking about the same thing.

Despite their often specific and varied programs and agendas, then, NGOs consistently have some common values – at least as evinced through their documents and mission statements from the 1980s and early 1990s (see Tvedt, 1997, pp. 78–79; cf. Nelson, 1997) – and which tend to endorse and sustain the values of accountability, participation, sustainability, and equity. NGOs on this account are therefore necessarily about increasing autonomy, in that they seek to increase peoples' independence. They are also altruistic in that they seek to contribute to people's well being without expectation of anything above the (opportunity) costs involved in the expending of resources on the communities or people with whom they work.

Finally, NGOs are redistributive, in that they seek to shift resources from one group to another. In short, they are for self-determination, the collective good, and equal sharing. We will return to some of these characterizations in section five when we discuss the gaps between the function of NGOs, what is claimed for them, and what they actually do.

NGOs in fact appear to fit the image of recent conceptions of *human* development. These ideas demand that subjects in development be viewed as the ends rather than the means of development. Here, development is conceived of in terms of an improvement in the quality of human lives, "is equitable (within and across generations) and consistent with the non-violation of rights" (see Qizilbash, 1996, p. 145). Regardless of the inherent theoretical tensions contained in this notion, with too few exceptions, however, we do not know, beyond *intending* rather than *doing good* (Fisher, 1997, pp. 439–42), what good NGOs actually engage in for their subjects. It is the contention of this chapter that as trustees of a certain kind of development, for NGOs in Africa to do good they must depend upon a political economy that, despite best intentions, is compatible with neo-liberalism, and despite, and even because, of these intentions they are "normatively primitive" (Gasper, 1994, p. 167). In what follows, I will try to outline the reasons for these claims, pointing in particular to the normative role that NGOs play in consolidating neo-liberalism, but also identifying why many NGOs are a species of simple ethics of aid – a global discourse of liberal cosmopolitanism's commitment to humanitarian intervention. I will also suggest that Western NGOs often end up speaking for or in the name of other's development, despite the claim to sometimes being part of the alternative, or post-development thinking, and despite the apparent move away from NGOs being providers *of aid* to being apparent agents *of co-operation* (see Padron, 1987; cf. Korten, 1987).

NGOs and Development AID

That NGOs now play a primary role in the politics, the activities of humanitarian assistance and development, most especially, but not only in Africa, is not an issue for debate. NGOs are now a principal part of any discussion about contemporary notions of development, whether as theory, policy and/or practice, whether by those claiming to do "alternative" development or by those who claim to bring more efficiency through the market. As the World Bank has put it, the extent of the influence of NGOs is evident in the fact that

> [O]ver the past several decades, NGOs have become major players in the field of international development. Since the mid-1970s, the NGO sector in both developed and developing countries has experienced exponential growth. From 1970 to 1985 total development aid disbursed by international NGOs increased ten-fold. In 1992, international NGOs channelled over $7.6 billion of aid to developing countries. It is now estimated that over 15 percent of total overseas development aid is channelled through NGOs. While statistics about global numbers of NGOs are notoriously incomplete, it is currently estimated that there is somewhere between 6,000 and 30,000 national NGOs in developing countries, while CBOs across the developing world number in the hundreds of thousands (World Bank, 1997a).

In fact, it appears that no one has come up with an absolute or even an approximate number of how many indigenous or expatriate NGOs there are operating in Africa.[6] One figure, by Streeton (1998, p. 194) has it that there are twenty-five thousand voluntary women's organizations in Kenya alone, although, as we have suggested, in the strictest of senses, voluntarianism is only one criterion of being an NGO.

If, however, first-hand impressions along with second hand reports are sufficient evidence, one would have to say that Africa has a population explosion of NGOs, which anyone who has visited any number of different parts of the continent over the last 10 years can bear witness to. The population has, indeed, according to Marcussen (1996), and others, mushroomed exponentially since the 1980s, evidently corresponding to Africa's economic crises. From being a relatively insignificant and marginal player in the development industry, they have come to be major players in intergovernmental affairs, and have become mainstreamed into the provisioning of so many development services, between, within and for multilateral and bilateral agencies, which for their part have solicited their input as to affect their own policies.

In addition to the Bank figures, the most recent global figures for NGOs show just how remarkable the increase in how aid is channelled through them. Between 1983 and 1991, the amount going to NGOs throughout the third world literally doubled, while the rate of growth in the 1980s alone surpassed fivefold the rate of growth of official ODA. Africa alone in per capita terms accounting for nearly an eight-fold increase. Indeed, this has been one of the most discernible indicators of the growing influence of NGOs – the change in the quantity of funds official aid agencies direct

---

6 Welch (1998, pp. 45 and 48) cites contradictory surveys. One claims that at present there are "between 18,000 and 20,000" NGOs in Africa, another that in 1993 in South Africa alone, there were 54,000. Such figures are neither accurate nor helpful either in and of themselves (how many are there, even in the four countries he addresses, Ethiopia, Nigeria, Senegal, and Namibia?), or as useful measures of *types* of NGOs (he is talking about human rights). Nevertheless, however exaggerated or underestimated his estimates are, he is right about two things: their growing numbers in all fields, especially in human rights and humanitarian intervention, and foreign funders' often enormous sway over the direction and policies of NGOs.

to and through NGOs in general for their *development* activities. Figures from the Organization for Economic Cooperation and Development (OECD) show that the total amount of official aid going to NGOs for development in 1992/93 was US$2.2bn, while data from the World Bank put the 1992 figure at $2.5bn. OECD data suggest that in aggregate about 5% of all official aid is now directed to NGOs. As The Overseas Development Institute of the United Kingdom has pointed out, "Not only are these figures an underestimate, but they fail to capture wide variation among different donors in the share of official aid going to and through NGOs. For single donors, the ratio ranges from less than 1% for some donors to up to 30%. (ODI, 1995). Estimates by the World Bank show that in the early 1970s about 1.5% of total NGO income came from donor sources, whereas by the mid-1990s this share had risen to about 30%. Such figures, too, disguise wide disparity between donor countries, ranging from about 10% of total NGO income to 80% or more (for Scandinavian countries). Also of importance has been the rate at which donors have increased the funds they channel to NGOs. For instance, in the ten years to 1993/94, the United Kingdom increased its official funding of NGOs by almost 400% to £68.7m, raising the share of total aid channelled to NGOs from 1.4% to 3.6%. In the same period, Australia increased its official funding of NGOs from A$20m to A$71m, raising the share of total aid going to NGOs from 1% to 6%. From the early 1980s to the early 1990s, comparable growth took place in the case of Canada, Finland, Norway, and Sweden. The amounts going from governments to NGOs vary from as high as 25% of development assistance in Switzerland, to as low as 3% in France. The World Bank, itself, between 1987–1994 gave the equivalent of 55% of its allocations for credits and loans in Africa through NGOs; by 1997, 61% of all project aid approved in Africa went through NGOs (compared to 84 percent of South Asian projects and 60 percent in Latin America and the Caribbean); and in general global terms, NGOs get about 50% of all of their revenues from governments (see World Bank, 1997; cf. Tvedt, 1998; Hume and Edwards, 1997; Wallace, 1997; Stewart, 1997; Streeton, 1997). However, many NGOs, of whatever type there might be, their increased role in development for the near future is unquestionable.

Yet, what accounts for this shift in funding and why have NGOs suddenly become to be accepted as a principal conduit through which development assistance should be channelled? As the World Bank (1997) itself asked, "What do NGOs – often small, inefficient, technically inadequate, and dependent on the voluntary commitments of staff and private donors – have to offer?"

NGOs: The Pessimism of Afro-Development and the New Norms of Development

One early view from the late 1980s, and one which has been repeated extensively in official literature, is that the shift in funding was a mixture of the ostensible failure of governments to promote development, the apparently demonstrated effectiveness of NGO responses to recent famines throughout Africa, and donors' preference for private sector development (Drabek 1987; Borghese, 1987; OECD, 1988). NGOs became to be considered as useful partners of governments and of development agencies, able to deliver certain types of programs more effectively than others because of their capacities for reaching the poor, or for mobilizing people "at the grass roots" and for encouraging participation, or, more simply, because they were thought to be able to do things cheaply. It is because of these beliefs that NGOs have become increasingly important channels for the funds of official development agencies. There were other factors, however.

As the hard rock of poverty, inequality and declining, or stagnant economic growth through world recessions in the 1970s and 1980s persisted, the state was often viewed as a major source and cause of development's uncertainty and/or decline. The distinct, and now very familiar charge of this period, whether because of various forms of adaptive modernization theory through development planning, the attempts at redistribution with growth, or basic needs, was the failure of the 1960s and 1970s state-dominated economic development and regulation. As the World Bank (1997, p. 23) characteristically put it, "government failure, including the failure of publicly owned firms, seemed everywhere glaringly evident". There have been a number of intriguing correspondences at a time when the first wave of optimism about development gave way to an acute decline in economic growth coupled with the sneaking realization of Africa's diminished role in the international division of labor, as a first hint at global forces beyond her control became evident. Given the increasing impoverishment of many of Africa's poorest people, the increasing authoritarianism and centralization of power, along with various civil conflicts within many African states, a development melancholy about both the prospects for participatory politics, let alone progress in increasing peoples' material well was understandable. It is also no wonder that the diminution of the ideological authority of the activist and prescriptive role for the state in development would coincide with the coming into focus of development ethics. As we said, development ethics would begin to provide normative criteria to evaluate the prospects, practices and malaise of development; it would also be part of its redefinition in light of the dissatisfaction with the view that development is an expansion in material prosperity within states. With their own moralism and critiques of the lack of intervention in human disaster relief and, in many cases, their own critical assessment of development, it would be no accident that NGOs came into their own during this time.[7]

That human disaster relief efforts throughout the world by NGOs, especially in Africa, did play a role in the consequent and causal expansion of a pre-eminent role for NGOs in development is not in dispute (cf. Duffield 1993, World Bank, 1998). Indeed, many major Northern NGOs (e.g. OXFAM, Save the Children, PLAN International and World Vision) came out of ventures in disaster relief or distress over the prospects and well being of children in circumstances of acute deprivation.[8]

7 Perhaps also not coincidentally, there were other movements that would mushroom at this time, many of them through NGOs: women, environmentalism and human rights, to mention a few.

8 Tvedt (op.cit. p.34) has made the interesting observation that many traditional development NGOs have moved into or back to humanitarian assistance because they realize "that there are official funds easily available in this area", a view borne out by Donald Brandt (1997), a senior researcher with World Vision International, who sees no operational distinction between humanitarian aid and development assistance.

However, we should distinguish here between the failure or the inability of the African governments to respond, and the successes and failures of outside organizations in bringing help. Part of the moral claim for interventions should not lie in interventions, but rather the success when carrying them out. The services provided by disaster relief interventions are important; however, they do not necessarily support, increase, or sustain local capabilities for development. Indeed, the afforded assistance might well produce or reinforce dependency on external resources. What is often not mentioned is how unsuccessful much of this assistance was, both in actually helping those in need of it, and also because of the longer term impacts that it did have. There was a very mixed record throughout northeastern and southern Africa in circumstances of drought and civil war in the 1980s and early 1990s. This was especially true for the problematic consequences of intervention for the longer-term sustainability brought about because of the introduction of and dependence upon food aid, which often went through NGOs (see Macrae and Zwi 1994; cf. Duffield, 1994), and which was also linked to the problems of accountability to recipients and a lack of professional standards of relief workers, which, according to Duffield, created a "markedly deregulated" aid market (cited in Brandt, 1995, p. 22). There are two further interrelated issues concerning what NGOs do or have engendered in circumstances of humanitarian assistance that need to be flagged for their relevance to reviewing their role in development.

David Smock cites Mary Anderson, from the NGO, Collaborative for Development Action, in saying that NGOs' transfer of resources sometimes "contribute to and reinforce violent conflicts pre-existing in the societies where they work" (in Smock, 1997). Resources under the authority of one or another warring party, often unintentionally, assist in bolstering the authority and legitimacy of that warring faction. Frequently, "intergroup tensions are also reinforced when NGOs provide external resources to some groups and not to others." For instance, when "NGOs hire people from certain groups and not others", and when "NGOs have more funds than local governments, that creates an imbalance between external resources and domestic resources, making it difficult for local institutions to build for peace, [and where] NGOs hire away much of the best talent from domestic agencies" (in Smock, 1997). Perhaps more important is the *ethical message conveyed* by the provision of assistance, when NGOs confer legitimacy on one group as opposed to another. Here we have both inequality of recognition, between the particular group and community, and also in resources supplied. While some of this might be inevitable in circumstances of conflict, it is nevertheless something that is mirrored in conditions of doing development. NGOs, as we shall see, at times reinforce inequalities, while people come to depend upon the resources they provide, and where it is, therefore, the NGO *not the state* that is seen to be the source of praise and recognition. Thus, although we are not here primarily concerned with the practical issues raised by, or the moral implications of, international intervention in deadly civil conflicts, we can see how these "complex humanitarian emergencies", make, as Hoffman says, "the contemporary challenge to sovereignty … much more profound" because "the distinction between domestic and international politics is crumbling" (Hoffman, 1996, p. 13). Indeed so; however, the issue is also to see what the practical and normative mechanisms for this disintegration are. If the erosion of the post-war model of sovereignty and the diminished capacity of some states to protect their citizens, suggests, according to Hoffman, a practical ethics that justifies and "allows for collective intervention when a state's condition or behavior results in grave threats to other states' and peoples' peace and security" (Hoffman, 1996, p. 13; see also Deng et al, 1996), it is one that implies a global disposition (i.e. a superpower), or global institutions (e.g. the U.N.) for carrying it out. The most compelling normative and globalizing political model that undergirds this position, and which is inclusive of the role of NGOs in the guise of civil society, has been described and set out by Held (1993) as the challenge of developing a model of "cosmopolitan democracy." Held argues that in order to assist the emerging "international form and structure of politics and civil society", a number of the bases of democratic thought and practice need to be reshaped, three of which are particularly relevant to any discussion of the conduits of development assistance through NGOs. The first requirement is "territorial boundaries of systems of accountability" being put in place to contend with "those issues which escape the control of the nation-state." Second, is the need to reconsider "the role and place of regional and global regulatory and functional agencies" so that they become more constructively engaged in "public affairs." Finally, there must be the insurance that relations with political institutions are genuinely re-evaluated, and that significant groups within "*international civil society*" should be allowed to become part of the procedural democratic process (Held, 1993, pp. 39–40, my emphasis). Three of the principal multilateral organizations from which so much African "donor" assistance comes, various agencies in the UN, the World Bank and the E.U., as well as the OECD and numerous bilateral agencies, most especially USAID, have all committed themselves to "listen to" and take into account the views of such groups, especially endorsing and supporting the role of international NGOs and civic organizations in both the North and the South.[9]

Here is a globalizing political theory, built upon notions of humanitarian assistance, and a conception of rights linked to and threaded by a of civil society perspective that is practically and conceptually in opposition to the state. This theory merges with the issue of the limits of sovereignty and/or the legitimacy of states to act in their own self-interest. A drastic and unfortunate true-life expression of these limits can be found in Hanlon's (1997) apposite and valuable depiction of post-civil war Mozambique. Hanlon claims that Mozambique is held in thrall by an acute dependence on all forms of international assistance, whether international NGOs or the IMF, as both have, in effect, became substitute states. The former having the liberty to move wherever they wanted to, in part because of the freedom of movement granted at the end of the war and also because of the diminished authority of government; and the latter because of its ability to impose

9 As an Overseas Development Institute (1995) report stated, "A direct effect of the growing influence of the reverse agenda [between NGOs and aid agencies] has been to increase the common ground between donors and NGOs. No longer is it easy to talk of distinct differences between NGO and donor approaches to development." See the various references cited above in section II, but see especially the UN's (1999) document on NGOs, where, notwithstanding the difficulties of operationalizing the idea in practice, the "right to participate" is enshrined (see also Smillie, Douxchamps, Sholes and Covey, 1995).

adjustment and stabilization policies upon the Mozambican state. The point is that non-state actors are viewed not as substitutes for global institutions, but as parallel and complementary to them.

This matching of functions has been coincidental with a second factor in the causality of NGOs – the growth and political activity of local "civil societies" before the development of liberalizing and pluralistic formal democratic party politics in Africa. To Stephen Ndegwa (1994, 1996), this link has been associated with important challenges against authoritarian governments and with fundamental political change in African countries. He claims that this link is an important correlation that allows for theorizing about the capacity for political influence among associational groups and non-state actors, and NGOs in particular. For example, in focusing on particular conflicts between NGOs in Kenya and the Kenyan government, he attributes a combination of factors that enabled NGOs to effectively counteract state control of their development activities. In particular, he identifies the availability of political opportunity to articulate dissent; the combined resources of NGOs and the degree of their collective organization; but especially important was the NGO alliance with international donor agencies and a coalition between NGOs and other oppositional forces in civil society.[10] NGOs were identified with political liberalization *and* economic liberalization and with a donor agenda, or at least donor support. The net result of this, in Bratton's language, federated structure of the linked, external partners, was to promote the perception of NGOs in Africa as having greater legitimacy (see Bratton, 1990).

Joseph Stiglitz (1999), the former Senior Vice President, and Chief Economist of the World Bank, retrospectively summed up the motivation of the Bank in its support of political liberalization and civil society by turning a kind of practice of groups in opposition to the state into a political theory of and for practice:

> There is a second prong to the strategy [of participation]: strengthening the "checks" on abuses of this power and influence. This prescription encompasses at least three elements. The first is to strengthen civil society, as a source of countervailing power – from political parties, to unions, to consumer groups, to think tanks, and to a variety of other NGOs. In the parlance of modern economics, ensuring participatory processes, and promoting the public good more broadly, is itself a public good. As with other public goods, there will be too little provision of such participatory processes in the absence of public support. A strong civil society is an important element in a strategy of implementing meaningful democratic reforms (<http://www.worldbank.org/html/extdr/extm/is-022799>).

However, Ndegwa's analysis, like Stiglitz's post hoc liberal appraisal of the role and function of NGOs and civil society, is partial. It is only one side of the from-below

---

10 They fall, as do most civil society groups, into a number of overlapping categories: those concerned with supporting political liberalization, those concerned with promoting economic liberalization, and those furthering the rights and political participation of particular socially excluded groups, such as rural women or the urban poor. Even if it is true that many NGOs and many development practitioners remain hostile to the approaches of neo-liberalism (e.g. Oxfam), their intentions are in a sense only part of the point.

story of a forged nexus of local NGOs, civil society and international agencies arrayed against the African developmental state. An alternative, or at least an amended, explanation can be found elsewhere in the opposition to the duress of adjustment and the authoritarian state, as both often went hand-in-had in the 1980s and 1990s (see Gibbon et al, 1993, Mkandawire, 1994 and Nyang'oro, 1993). In the case of Tanzania, ordinary people in groups within the informal economy developed various autonomous and resistive strategies politically and economically to the overarching state; ordinary people also came to have just as an important impact upon the state as the elites and the international agencies through the networks that they had created, both because of, but also in spite of adjustment (see Tripp, 1994). In contrast, Anang (1994) showed in the case of Ghana that the various relationships and strategies available to NGOs were constrained by the centralizing Rawlings state, and that all NGOs, indigenous and international, had to operate through a specific ministry which sought to control their activities. To be sure, in other cases there was conflict and confrontation; but in others there was also rank opportunism and cooptation as well (see Gary, 1996). Finally, in several other instances, many local and international NGOs and advocacy groups came together as global networks, and sometimes as loose coalitions, to variously demand a greater say in the adjustment process, to insist on greater poverty alleviation, to demand more project lending, and, in some instances, to abort the process altogether (see Nelson, 1997). In short, responses to the state by NGOs are frequently complex, as are the local and international forces and groups that have engaged them.

Regardless of the perspective one may hold on the origins of political liberalization, or about the specific and particular relationship they might have with the state, NGOs have regularly been deemed to represent the best that personifies the effectiveness of local development, and that they have come to embody a large part of development as "civil society". The positive agendas and values of superior economic efficiencies and greater political participation are believed to result in a shift in power away from the state and the powerful to the less powerful. Indeed, their proliferation is seen as a part of an "associational revolution" (Clarke, 1998). NGOs belong to intermediary, "mediating" institutions, which relate to everyday lives in ways in which the abstract (and sometimes oppressive) state cannot do. In the de Toquevillian sense, they supposedly provide "schools for democracy"; and for others – simplistically in my view – NGOs provide a third force set against both state and market. NGOs are part of an "associative democracy", which has put in a new set of political actors between the people and the government, which would take over certain services of the state while staying embedded in civil society (Robinson and Riddell et al, 1995; Clarke, 1998; cf. Fowler, 1997). Unlike central government, the problems that people face would be known intimately by internal and/or external associative groups, who would be able to gather the appropriate information about the communities that are the subject of development and be capable of realizing and executing more effective public policy. NGOs, therefore, can be considered good associates, even partners of governments and of development agencies, able to deliver particular kinds of programs more effectively than the traditional providers – the state. Much of this third force identity can be self-serving. As Streeton says (1997, p. 205), citing Judith Tendler, "NGOs often derive their identity by defining themselves in contrast and opposition to government, which is said to be large, rigid, inflexible, bureaucratic, hierarchical, and incapable of reaching the poor. In spite of this rhetoric, the relations between NGOs and government are often complex, rich, and intricate."

Nevertheless, from a normative standpoint, it is easy enough to see how this thinking, like the call for cosmopolitan democracy, could also be entirely compatible with the so-called "paradigm shift" in development thinking. This was a shift in philosophy which stressed "participation in … decision-making by the clientele group, [and] building the capacity of individuals and institutions in the development process" (Blunt and Warren, 1996, p. xiii; cf. Chambers, 1997; Nelson and Wright, 1995). As we earlier suggested, among development practitioners and institutional donors, as well as many academics, this change led to a growing concern with trying to accommodate the perspectives and the voices of the subjects of development. There, was, for example, an insistence upon utilizing "the nature of indigenous or local-level community-based knowledge and how it provided the basis for both individual and community-level decision-making" (Blunt and Warren, 1996, p. xiii.), while emphasising a requirement that communities and grassroots groups be involved in policy discussions and implementation, stressing participatory planning, implementation, monitoring and evaluation techniques. Denis Goulet claims, for example, that experience with development processes indicates that those most likely to be able to carry out projects within the guidelines of the Participatory Rural Appraisal (PRA) research model are NGOs, or grassroots development groups. They are, he declares, most likely to be able to provide the native populace with control over the process of value change and creation of authentic choices. Obviously, one can contest this claim on empirical grounds in general, which we will do in the next section. However, notice how this is a good example of the overlap of the usage of the term NGO with grassroots, one that compounds a kind of populist moralism: NGOs = local = community = grassroots = good.

An interesting example of the uses to which this kind of discourse has been put can be found in the way that principles of preliminary community consultations, research and expected outcomes inform a number of ventures that use NGOs as media of development. Take, for example, the following communitarian spirit, framed within a participative, self-determining wish list, written by a consultant group for a mining company that wishes to appropriate land in central Ghana with the assistance of Foreign AID, a Northern and a local NGO.[11] According to the framework,

> The main goal was the Participative Rural Appraisal (PRA) as endorsed by the Amansie Resources Limited was to secure the necessary socio-economic information on 16 selected communities to serve as the basis for drawing up a plan to be executed under the *community livelihoods project* to be jointly sponsored by the Amansie Resources Limited (ARL) and other *stakeholders* within the company's concession area. It is hoped that the implementation of the recommendations which reflect the *people's* own interpretation of their problems, needs and aspirations will be able to transform the rural economy and create

11 Amansie Resources is a joint venture between the government of Ghana and The Resolute Group, an Australian "natural resource" – that is, mining – company. Resolute owns 90% of Amansie, while the Government of Ghana has a carried interest of 10%.

> the necessary atmosphere needed by ARL and the people living around its concession to work as partners in development (Asare and Boateng, 1998, p. 9 my emphases.)

This arch of moral decentralized cooperation can be replicated repeatedly, whether from major organizations doing the funding or by the extraneous NGOs whom they do it through. Typically, because, this is a discourse of meeting local needs, one involving partnerships, and because there appears to the decentralization of economic and civic decision-making, it can be presumed to be good in both the intrinsic moral sense and in the consequentialist sense of providing efficiently and effectively what other, namely government, forms of organization cannot.

However coincidental, then, there is certainly an appropriation of the alternative development models of participatory development, especially when, as in the case of Stiglitz, it is couched in a language directed towards vindicating a neo-liberal model of the state. If these conjunctural shifts in development thinking and practice are not all causal, their parallelisms are not entirely coincidental either. The growing significance of NGOs in part lies in the actual declining power and importance of African governments, primarily, although not only, because of the constraints on their economic capacity through instruments of structural adjustment and stabilization policies and the impact of privatizing economic policy. This weakening of the African state has further re-enforced the complementarities of non-state actors like NGOs, who have made themselves attractive to global institutions because they appear to be able to fill policy and practical lacunas created by ineffectual, impecunious and financially indebted governments and "their" programs. This has been as much a factor in the multilateral and other, bi-lateral donor appeal to NGOs, as has been their inclination to support the development of liberal democratic democratization. It has also come about, however, because of the reality and the perception of the failure of markets, and the inability of the weakened state to compensate for their deficiencies in the face of the problems created by market adjustments. That is, NGOs are viewed as being able to carry out primarily project-based tasks that neither the state nor the market can achieve; they are the "result of disillusionment with government, combined with a reluctance to hand over all activities to private profit-seeking enterprises" (Streeton, 1997, p. 195). Perhaps so, but disenchantment with the state has also led to a contracting out of services.

NGOs have often taken on what Robinson (1997) has called "public service contractors." Hulme and Edwards (1997, p. 6) are quite explicit that for many donors, NGOs "are seen as the preferred channel for service provision in deliberate substitution for the state", often against the interests and wishes of host countries themselves, authoritarian or multiparty. The preference for NGOs as a conduit for development and services is in part, again, because there is the belief that they, rather than the local state, can engage in good governance. The state's engagement with NGOs, both indigenous and external is so much so, that even some analysts and NGO practitioners have worried about their own complicity in the process. They are concerned that they would be used to substitute for government in ways which they believe to be damaging to democratic development and even the provision of efficient social (i.e. health and education) services, and where international donor agencies must recognize that "good government" does not mean "less government".

Indeed, Fowler has put it quite starkly when he says that the proliferation of NGOs throughout Africa has become part of the new colonialism (cited in Hearn, 1997, p. 89). Another observer has called the proliferation of NGOs in Kenya, the NGO-ization of Society (Hearn, 1997), all of which lends itself to the practices of NGOs making it even easier for state authorities to pass on problems and discharge themselves of the responsibility of their actions, or inaction, and to as it were pass the buck to others, while diminishing the authority and presence of the state.

The delegitimating of the African state corresponded to, and has even been part cause of, the moral emboldenment for the voluntary sector, one piece of which are NGOs who have become partial policymakers and who have come of age in a neo-liberal world. As we have seen, they and their institutional supporters have prescribed a moral *ought* as much as a practical *should*; and they have contributed to a process of practical imperatives becoming moral norms.

Development Practices and Development Values

What, then, about the very global and indeed, globalizing claims of NGOs, or those who would make claims on their behalf? What about the values that *they* hold or the values that are implicit in their aims and actions that we identified above, and that give them the claim to legitimacy? Nothing we have said thus far undervalues their status normatively; only that their operational and sometimes value disposition and placement makes them attractive to institutions that are by their very nature global and globalizing and which many claim have undermined the capacity of Africa states to sustain their normative claim upon development. How are we to evaluate these practices as values or values in practice?

There is an easy way, which could question them in terms of their outcomes and consequences, where evaluations would be in terms of their practices, a policy-outcomes approach which views effectiveness and efficiencies as the measurement of success. Such "supply-side" analyses have and will continue to be done as part of any project appraisal, as the results of many of NGOs activities are being monitored and appraised by those who provide the funds, as well as those in the field themselves. It is beyond the scope or capabilities of this chapter to attempt a summary of the literature concerning Africa. However, what we know points to a very uneven record. There have been very few overview-like surveys of these results. Many deal with specific activities of NGOs in Africa, such as government-NGO relationships (Sandberg, 1994) or those relationships over specific areas, such as agriculture (see Wellard and Copestake, 1994). There are others that deal with specific projects and their effectiveness; others that address the effectiveness of aid in general through case specific examples, where NGOs play a role (see Carlsson et al, 1997); and others that deal with Africa in comparative perspective (see Tvedt, 1997; Robinson, 1997 and Riddell et al, 1995). Nevertheless, there is little doubt that the results have been irregular, to say the least.

Marcussen (1996) provides the most comprehensive critique of NGO claims and a skeptical view of their effectiveness in Africa. In his survey of a number of declarations for or by NGOs, he argues that by traditional development administration criteria of efficiency, effectiveness, and economy, they may not necessarily be as competent as the claims might appear to make them. In fact, in many instances in West African countries as different as Ghana and Burkina Faso, but also in Uganda, Kenya and Tanzania, NGO-related development projects have shown no better design and implementation process nor have been any more successful in achieving their aims any better than many state initiatives. NGOs have often experienced cost overruns, not because of corruption, but through simple inexperience and inefficiencies. (cf. ODI, 1996a). He provides evidence of an inability to deal with the recurrent costs involved in major projects, and in particular, owing to inappropriate scale in a number of projects, the lack of demonstrated cost efficiencies that were supposed to be generated from NGOs comparative advantages. In short, many of these claims about efficiency are overstated (cf. Carlsson, 1997, pp. 220–221).

Even among the most successful of projects, there are several problems. A fascinating, and probably one of the most meticulous and careful set of comparative studies of the work of NGOs between regions in Africa and South Asia was carried out by Robinson and Riddell (1995) for the British Overseas Development Institute. This study focused specifically on sixteen poverty alleviation projects in four countries – Uganda and Zimbabwe, Bangladesh and India. It sought to establish whether projects had been successful in achieving their stated goals: whether the economic circumstances of the aid recipients had improved and why; appraising whether improvements had been disbursed equitably; and the nature of the effect of non-project determinants, about the relations of costs to benefits, and about the prospects for both reproducing and sustaining the projects. Crucial to the studies of the operation and impact of the projects, through the evaluations of donors, recipients, non-recipients and other local people, was understanding what factors were important in contributing to the relief of poverty. Participation was an essential component in the success of alleviating poverty, in increasing incomes and consumption, and in improving the standing and self-assurance of the poor in seventy-five percent (or 12/16) of the projects that were studied.[12] However, and not surprisingly, class and gender mattered profoundly, as "Almost without exception the poor benefited to a greater extent than the poorest, and men to a greater extent than women, by virtue of having prior access to land and other assets" (Robertson and Riddell, 1995, p. 65). While the latter circumstances are more prominent in the South Asian cases, the African case studies also provide ample evidence of widespread inequality.

Brett (1997, p. 332) has alleged,

> National and local agencies often fail to produce adequate results, so many smaller and less capital-intensive projects have been entrusted to NGOs. Too much reliance on NGOs *weakens state capacity* and encourages a *piecemeal and non-universalistic approach to service delivery.* The use of non-traditional agencies is encouraging experimentation and diversity, but has led to wide inequalities in access and quality. These serious weaknesses

---

12 Project performance was related to a number of different influences, none of which in isolation was sufficient to determine success or failure. Three factors in particular stood out: (1) the participation of the beneficiaries in different cycles of the project; (2) strong and effective NGO management and institutional capability; and (3) the calibre of project staff, their commitment to overall project objectives, their skills and the degree of empathy with the intended beneficiaries.

> are inevitable given the complexity of the poverty problem, the atomization of the donor community and the weakness of state and local NGOs, *but they impose a very heavy tax on the poor* (my emphases).

Paul Streeton's extensive experience in both Africa and South Asia, has led him to acknowledge the qualities of NGOs that are commonly not avowed – that they are, for example, generally adaptable and suited to promoting self-reliance. However, he too has come to question the assumption that NGOs are normally good at the activities they claim as their merit. In particular, they rarely reach the poorest, they depend in many ways on government support, and they are often *not* participatory.

> [A]mong the drawbacks of NGOs are objectives that are sometimes vague: management problems; lack of sustainability; low replicability; and, because NGOs are small, reaching few people … The NGOs do not reach the poorest of the poor, partly because groups of poor people often are not keen to have themselves included, or because they are difficult to form into groups, partly because they are often dispersed, live in remote regions, and are difficult to reach. Optimistically speaking, NGOs today reach 250 million poor people in developing countries. They fail to reach over 80 percent of the 1.3 billion estimated to be living in extreme poverty. … However fast the growth of NGO activities in the coming decade, their impact will not be substantially increased (Streeton, 1997, p. 200).

Even the local and the indigenous NGOs have not always been especially successful either on the more high-minded principles of participation and representativeness. To be sure, the inability to found reliable forms of participation owes much to the context of their operation and, where available, of accords reached between NGOs and the somewhat centralized and often authoritarian governments, with top-down decision-making processes that do not easily convert into effective grassroots participation (see Anang, 1994). Even so, it is not authoritarian governments per se that are the only problem. As Warren Nyamugasira (1998) has recently said, despite the widespread belief that indigenous, or local and African NGOs represent the authentic voices of the poor in general, and women, and children in particular, their dis-enfranchisement continues despite the advocacy on their part.[13] There is often insufficient attention paid to conflict and differentiation within both civil society and the NGOs. As well, there is inadequate recognition of interests and differences amongst the various agencies and agents engaged in the particular project/s NGOs are involved in, even where there is an acknowledgement that the impact of a development policy, in class and gender terms may have obvious differential effects.

Moreover, the association between NGOs and participation has often been used more as an exhortary catchphrase than a thought-out guiding principle and is frequently undergirded by the globalizing civil society discourse that is on occasion, at the very least, dense. For example, Clarke's (1998) positive views of NGOs and his stance suggesting new political vistas around popular sovereignty that both political scientists and political theorists have hitherto not envisaged are understandable, but neither original nor unproblematic. Cohen and Rogers (1995,

13 Actually and ironically, he calls for a joint relationship between indigenous and expatriate NGOs to resolve this in terms of the effectiveness of actions, political and economic.

p. 35), for example, in their commitment to notions of associative democracy in the developed, industrialized world, have provided a prescriptively theoretical position on civil society groups, and non-governmental social groups, especially labor unions and work groups in particular, which they see as the practical foundation for "popular sovereignty, political equality, distributive equity, civic consciousness, good economic performance and state competence." Similarly, in the African context, Ake's (1993, p. 1996) later work called for the need to rethink the forms and locations of sovereignty, and to approach African democracy through it being rooted in the local and through its identification with the activities and aspirations of non-state actors, including NGOs.

As important morally as such participatory and egalitarian injunctions are, however, they rarely – typical of much of the writing on NGOs and civil society in general – put any cogent conception of *power* at the center of their discourse. Paraphrasing Paul Hirst's (1995) critique of Cohen and Rogers, we might ask why would the current dominant interests in government and civil society in Africa (or anywhere for that matter) allow the egalitarian shift in power and representation beyond the affirmation of a liberal democratic franchise? Indeed, there is every reason to believe that under associative democracy previously privileged socio-economic groups would be strongly placed to advance their economic resources and political control. In fact, one might ask the question how much participation and over what and by whom?

Even, if the points made by Streeton and others about areas of NGOs ineffectiveness were *not* true, one can question in some way a fundamental value that many NGOs make for themselves for doing things differently. In this regard, the question about the role of NGOs in Africa once more becomes salient. Take some neo-liberal examples again. What is their role in assisting certain neo-liberal policies, such as the privatizing of health care by user fees, or through the establishment of micro-credit schemes for women, or again, by supporting educational projects that end up asking for user fees? These are a few of the more elaborated polices currently taking place throughout many parts of Africa where adjustment policies are ongoing and, also, where NGOs have played a role (see Hearn, 1997; Watanabe and Takahashi, 1997). Clearly, here would be a case where one might ask if these policies undermine some basic principle of equality, and where there can be anticipated unequal outcomes because of differential access and because of the limited available choices through any other mechanisms than the market, which while in principle provide, or offer the hope of more welfare, might also produce less equality? To put it starkly, the very nature of such polices might (and they might not) lead to more efficiency, but they may well lead to more inequality.[14] Under the guise of alleviating poverty, or increasing access to some, are many NGOs indifferent to inequality? Regardless of the intention, have NGOs

14 Again, either way, it is difficult to know on empirical grounds, how. One of the most recent attempts, a World Bank sponsored study (Sahn et al, 1997), gives an overall assessment of market and financial adjustments on poverty, general welfare, and gender poverty. While not concluding that its impact of adjustment has generally been effective, it argues that doing otherwise would lead, not so much to less inequality, but to *more* poverty. However,

become complicit in a process of furthering inequality? This is the sense in which I mean they are normatively primitive, and have a simple redistributive ethics of aid.

There are further issues here, however. As interceding associations, NGOs will make it easier for governmental authorities to shift the blame and evade responsibility for their own actions and inactions. They will give the state an excuse to leave its basic public tasks in the hands of impecunious and over-extended local governments that often do not have the capacity to sustain themselves, and whose functions are progressively being taken over by internationally funded NGOs (see Wallace, 1997; cf. Ndulu 1997).[15] Besides, if through foreign donors NGOs increasingly provide grants and loans for community development, infrastructure, and clinics, etc., and if, as Collier (1995) suggests, this shift in the character of aid means that outsiders will effectively finance the development budgets of many African countries, will it be the donors that gain the goodwill that projects bring, and what will be left for which the governments can claim credit? In the face of the overwhelming presence of others who do what states have traditionally done, this diminution of state power further reduces the ability of the state to play normatively relevant role in the lives of its nominal citizens.

Conclusion: New Angels of Merciful Development?

It would be easy and in many cases unfair to argue that the real source of NGOs' recent and proliferating engagement in development is a kind of supply-side *realpolitque*, most especially through the AID regime, which dispenses resources to them (Tvedt, 1997). However, it has become increasingly evident that regardless of the various motivations that inform their intent to assist development in Africa, NGOs have become part of globalizing process. NGOs, we said at the outset, have become a part of globalization as much because of the values they have begun to inscribe as their ubiquity in the policy process of affirming Africa's sustained dependence on outside assistance. Much of the continent's perilous economic and political status throughout the eighties and nineties created a space not just for the presumption of such values, but also practices that, to many, have become consonant with a political economy of economic practices and institutions that displaces the role of the state – the de-stating of Africa, as Clapham (1996) has called it – as more efficient providers of welfare to people and communities in the development process. In the absence of the state with capacities to deliver services and resources, especially to the poorest and most vulnerable, other agents, instruments or institutions must be positioned to supply

the significant point here is that inequality, remains a desideratum, even where NGOs are committed to it.

15 Ndulu's (1997) point has less to do with NGOs as such, but rather the broader network into which local actors have to fit: the broader policymaking that depends upon research that local actors are incapable of fulfilling. Still, other research across civic communities, parliaments and NGOs, for their part, have minimal capacity for policy analysis and economic research, which further reinforces the point that dependence is all the more likely on outsiders.

people with the capabilities that increase the range of opportunities that they cannot provide themselves. That this may or may not be true appears not to be the point, for, as we have identified, and Fowler has affirmed (1995), support for emphasizing the role of NGOs rests on ideological grounds rather than empirical confirmation. NGOs have become part of the ideological reconfiguring of the relationship between state and society, civil or otherwise, that until recently was once presumed to be given in the various models of development that characterized the post-colonial state up until the late seventies and the recent adjustment processes, most African political economies have undergone in the name of a new development paradigm.[16]

If development, by its very nature, implies a disposition that is in need of improvement, where those who are the subject of it cannot do it by themselves, then in fewer places does the need for guided trusteeship appear be clearer than in Africa? However, the history of development is littered with moralistically paternalistic accounts of some people having been entrusted to manage others' well-being or development, until such time as they can do so themselves (see Rist, 1997). Even the nominally technical arguments for development connected to issues of efficacy or efficiency, have always tended to be inextricably linked to the paternalistic and the normative. The more explicitly moral justifications are rooted in some presupposed, given, or foundationally evaluative criteria of *why* it is better that this or that approach to development and change (or their absence) should be enacted, or why this or that group ought to be legitimately authorized with intervention for improvement. Like all agents of development, NGOs have doctrines of development (Cowen and Shenton, 1996), wherein they have mapped out a moral space for themselves. NGOs have combined the claim (the intention) to develop with the declaration for doing it through procedures that are moral in their apparent altruistic localism, their seeming distributive proximity to the "people" – a kind of associational redistribution – and a participatory ethos and practice, all of which give many NGOs their moral force and confers on them a degree of legitimacy above and beyond their tangible effectiveness in actual delivery.

Without throwing out the baby with proverbial bathwater, and while also acknowledging the doing good that many NGOs do, we might nevertheless want to periodically question their claims on their own implicit or explicit normative principles, and the political space that they operate within; we might want to ask

---

16 There is no suggestion here that African governments *were* necessarily always acting out these policies, only that they were part of a development discourse inherited from the legacy of nationalism. As Robert Tignor has put it in his survey of government-business relations within the framework of nationalism and decolonization in Africa, both domestic capital and entrepreneurship were central to the early nationalist visions of most parts of Africa. There was, he claims, uniformity about what had become in most parts of Africa at the close of World War II a consensual view of economic development. "The main tenet of what would soon be called development economics stressed the role as the creator of the infrastructural and legislative environment for private investment, the importance of entrepreneurship … Much of the literature focused upon *the place of state planning and even in the mobilization of investment capital*" (1997, p. 395; my italics). The intellectual history of development and public sector organization is one which it took for granted a major role for the state as a manager and as a principal agent in the economy (see Toye, 1993, pp. 56–62).

more concretely when needs are met through NGOs, and in what ways they assist in the process of development? With NGOs playing such a central role throughout the world, and with their playing a pre-eminent role in Africa, it is time to look and scrutinize more acutely, not just their role, but their reasons for their roles to see whether indeed the language about delivery, about participation, and so on is actually effected? What appears certain, however, is that given the inevitably contradictory interest and outcomes of NGO activities identified in the context of the neo-liberal agenda of contemporary development, many African communities and states will, for good or ill, remain at the mercy of their significant assistance for some time to come.

References

Ake, Claude (1993), "The Unique Case of African Democracy" *International Affairs*, Vol. 69. No.2, pp. 239–244.

Ake, Claude (1996), *Democracy and Development* (Washington D.C.: The Brookings Institution).

Anheier, H. (1994), "Non-Governmental Organizations and Institutional Development in Africa: A Comparative Analysis", in E., Sandberg (ed.), *The Changing Politics of Non-Governmental Organizations and African State (*Westport, CT: Praeger), pp. 101–120.

Asare, A. B., and Boateng, Kyereh (1998), A *Socio-Economic Profile and Development Strategies The Case Of Communities On Amansie Resources Concession Area.* Report Commissioned for Amansie.

Ball, Colin, and Dunn, Leith (1996), *Non-governmental Organizations: Guidelines for Good Policy and Practice* (London: The Commonwealth Foundation).

Barnes, Sam (1998), "NGOs in Peace-Keeping Operations: Their role in Mozambique", *Development in Practice,* Vol. 8. No. 3, pp. 309–322.

Beckman, David (1991), "Recent Experience and Emerging Trends", in Samuel Paul, and A. Israel (eds), *Nongovernmental Organizations and the World Bank: Cooperation for Development* (Washington, D.C.: World Bank) pp. 135–137.

Blunt, Peter and Warren, Michael D. (1996), "Introduction.", in P. Blunt and D .M. Warren (eds), *Indigenous Organizations and Development* (London: Intermediate Technology Publications), pp. i–xxii.

Borghese, Elena (1987), "Third World Development: The Role of Non-Governmental Organizations", *OECD Observer*, April–May.

Brandt, Donald P (1997), "Relief as Development, But Development as Relief?" *Journal of Humanitarian Intervention,* posted July 1997 <http:/www.jha.sps.cam.ac.uk/a/a005.htm>

Brandt, Donald (1995), "War Work: Humanitarian Assistance in Complex Human Emergencies" *Journal of Humanitarian Assistance,* posted 23 October 1995 <http://www-jha.sps.cam.ac.uk/jcontent.htm>

Bratton, Michael (1990), "Non-governmental Organizations in Africa: Can They Influence Public Policy?", *Development and Change,* Vol. 21. No.1, pp. 87–118.

Carlsson, Jerker, Somolekae, Gloria and Van de Walle, Nicholas (eds) (1997), *Foreign Aid in Africa: Learning from Country Experience* (Uppsala: AfrikaNordiska Afrikainstituetet).

Chambers, Robert (1995), "Paradigm Shift and the Practice of Participatory Research and Development" in N. Nici and S Wright (eds), *Power and Participatory. Development: Theory and Practice* (London: Intermediate Technology Publications), pp. 30–42.

Chambers, Robert (1995), "The Primacy of the Personal", in M.Edwards and D. Hulme (eds), *Beyond the Magic Bullet: NGO Performance and Accountability in the Post-Cold War World* (London: Earthscan and West Hartford, CT: Kumarian Press), pp. 241–253.

Clark, John (1995), "The State, Popular Participation, and the Voluntary Sector" *World Development*, Vol. 23. No. 4, pp. 593–601 (Reprinted in Hulme and Edwards, op. cit, pp. 43–58).

Clarke, Gerard (1998), "Non-governmental Organizations and Politics in the Developing World", *Political Studies*, Vol. 46. No.1, pp. 36–52.

Clapham, Christopher (1996), *Africa and the International System: The Politics of State Survival* (New York: Cambridge University Press).

Cohen, Joshua and Rogers, Joel (1995), "A Proposal for Reconstructing Democratic Institutions: Secondary Associations and Democratic Governance", in J.Cohen and J. Rogers (eds), *Associations and Democracy* (New York: Verso), pp. 7–13

Collier, Paul (1995), "The Marginalization of Africa", *International Labor Review,* July–Oct., Vol.34. Nos. 4 & 5, pp. 541–557.

Covey, Jane G. (1992), "Accountability and Effectiveness in NGO Policy Alliances", in M. Edwards, and D. Hulme (eds), *Making a Difference: NGOs and Development in a Changing World* (London: Earthscan Publications), pp. 167–181.

Crocker, David A. (1991), "Toward Development Ethics: The Need for an Ethic of Third World Development", *World Development*, Vol. 19. No. 5, pp. 457 – 83.

Deng, Francis M., Kimaro, Sadikiel, Lyons, Terrence, Rothchild, Donald and Zartman, William I. (1996), *Sovereignty as Responsibility: Conflict Management in Africa* (Washington D.C.: The Brookings Institution).

Derman, Bill (1995), "Environmental NGOs, Dispossession, and the State: The Ideology and Praxis of African Nature and Development", *Human Ecology: An Interdisciplinary Journal*, Vol. 23. No. 2, pp. 199–216.

Duffield, M. (1992), "The Emergence of Two-tier Welfare in Africa: Marginalization or an Opportunity for Reform?", *Public Administration and Development*, Vol. 12. No. 2, pp. 139–154.

Duffield, M. (1993), "NGOs, Disaster Relief and Asset Transfer in the Horn: Political Survival in a Permanent Emergency", *Development and Change*, Vol. 24. No. 3, pp. 131–51.

Edwards, Michael and Hulme, David (eds) (1992), *Making a Difference: NGOs and Development in a Changing World* (London: Earthscan Publications).

Edwards, Michael (1994), "Profile of International Non-Governmental Organizations, 'Good Government' and the 'New Policy Agenda': Lessons of Experience at the Program Level 1990s", *Democratization,* Vol. 1. No. 3, pp. 504–515.

Farrington, John and Bebbington, Anthony, Wellard, Kate and Lewis David J. (eds) (1993), *Reluctant Partners: Non-governmental Organizations, the State, and Sustainable Agricultural Development* (London: Routledge).

Fisher, William F. (1997), "Doing good? The Politics and Anti-politics of NGO Practices", *Annual Review of Anthropology Annual*, Vol. 26. No. 4, pp. 439–464.

Fowler, Alan (1988), *Non-governmental Organizations in Africa: Achieving Comparative Advantage in Relief and Micro-Development*, IDS Paper No. 249. (Brighton: Institute of Development Studies).

Fowler, Alan (1991), The Role of NGOs in Changing State-Society Relations: Perspectives from East and Southern Africa", *Development Policy Review*, Vol. 9. No.2, pp.53–84.

Fowler, Alan (1993), "Too Close for Comfort? The Impact of Official Non-governmental Organizations", *World Development*, Vol. 24, No 6, (in D. Hulme and M. Edwards (eds) (1997), *NGOs, States and Donors: Too Close for Comfort?* (Basingstoke/ London: Macmillan in association with Save the Children), pp. 961–973.

Fowler, Alan (1997), *Striking a Balance: A Guide to Enhancing the Effectiveness of Non-Governmental Organizations in International Development* (London: Earthscan).

Gary, I. (1996), "Confrontation, Co-operation or Co-optation: NGOs and the Ghanaian State during Structural Adjustment", *Review of African Political Economy*, Vol. 23. Issue 68, pp.149–68.

Gibbon, Peter, Bangura, Yusuf, and Ofstad, Arve (eds) (1993), *Authoritarianism, Democracy and Adjustment: The Politics of Economic Reform in Africa* (Uppsala: AfrikaNordiska Afrikainstituetet).

Goulet, Denis (1995), *Development Ethics: A Guide to Theory and Practice* (New York: Apex Press).

Joseph, Hanlon (1997), The IMF in Mozambique, Peace Without Profit (London: James Currey).

Hearn, Julie (1998), "The 'NGO-ization' of Kenyan Society: USAID & the Restructuring of Health care", *Review of African Political Economy*, Vol. 25. Issue 75, pp. 89–100.

Held, David (1993), "From City-States to a Cosmopolitan Order?", in D. Held, (ed.), *Prospects for Democracy: North, South, East, West* (Cambridge: Polity Press) pp.13–52.

Hirst, Paul Q. (1995), Comments on "Secondary Associations and Democratic Governance", (response to Joshua Cohen and Joel Rogers) in J. Cohen and J. Rogers (eds), *Associations and Democracy* (New York: Verso), pp. 101–113.

Hoffman, Stanley (ed.) (1996), *The Ethics and Politics of Humanitarian Intervention* (Notre Dame, IN: University of Notre Dame Press).

Hulme, D. and Edwards, M. (1997), "NGOs, States and Donors: An Overview", in D. Hulme and M. Edwards (eds) (1997), *NGOs, States and Donors: Too Close for Comfort?* (Basingstoke/London: Macmillan in association with Save the Children), pp. 3–22.

Korten, David C. (1987), "Third Generation NGO Strategies: A Key to People-centered Development", *World Development*, Vol. 15, No. 4, pp. 145–159.

Korten, David (1990), *Getting to the 21st Century: Voluntary Action and the Global Agenda* (West Hartford, CT: Kumarian Press).

Macrae J. and Zwi, A. (eds) (1994), *Rethinking International Responses to Complex Emergencie* (London: Zed Books).

Marcussen, Henrik, S. (1996), "NGOs, the State and Civil Society" *Review of African Political Economy*. Vol. 23. Issue 69, pp. 405–423

Mkandawire, P. Thandika (1994), "Adjustment, Political Conditionality and Democratization in Africa" , in Giovanni Cornea and G. K. Helleiner (eds), *From Adjustment to Development in Africa: Conflict, Controversy, Convergence, Consensus?* (London: Macmillan), pp. 155–73.

Mkandawire, P. Thandika and Charles C. Soludo (1999), "Introduction", in Thandika Mkandawire and Charles C. Soludo (eds), *Our Continent, Our Future: African Perspectives on Structural Adjustment* (New Jersey: Africa World Press), pp. 1–13.

Mozaffar, Qizilbash (1996), "Capabilities, Well-being and Human Development: A Survey", *Journal of Development Studies,* Vol. 33, No. 2, pp. 143–162.

Ndegwa, Stephen N. (1994), "Civil Society and Political Change in Africa: The Case of Non-governmental Organizations in Kenya." *International Journal of Comparative* Sociology. Vol. 35, Nos. 1–2, pp. 19–36.

Ndegwa, Stephen (1996), *The Two Faces of Civil Society: NGOS and Politics in Africa* (West Hartford, CT: Kumarian Press).

Nelson, Joan M. (1996), "Promoting Policy Reforms: The Twilight of Conditionality?" *World Development*, Vol. 24. No. 4, pp. 1551–1559.

Nelson, N., and Wright, S. (eds) (1995), *Power and Participatory Development: Theory and Practice* (London: Intermediate Technology Publications).

Nelson, N. and Wright, S. (1997), "Conflict, Legitimacy and Effectiveness: Who Speaks for Whom in Transnational NGO Networks Lobbying the World Bank?" *Nonprofit and Voluntary Sector Quarterly*, Vol. 26. No. 4, pp. 421– 441.

Nyamugasira, Warren (1998), "NGOs and Advocacy: How well are the Poor Represented?", *Development in Practice*, Vol. 8. No. 3, pp. 297–308.

Nyang'oro, Julius E. (1993), "Development, Democracy and NGOs in Africa" *Scandinavian Journal of Development Alternatives*, Vol.12. Nos. 2–3, pp. 277–291.

OECD (1988), *Voluntary Aid for Development: the Role of Non-Governmental Organizations*, Paris.

Overseas Development Institute (1995), "NGOs" <http://www.oneworld.org.odi>

Overseas Development Institute (1996), "The Impact of NGO Development Projects" Briefing Papers. No. 2, pp. 1–4.

Padron, Mario (1987), "Non-governmental Development Organizations: From Development Aid to Development Cooperation", *World Development*, Vol. 15. No. 3. (Supplement), pp. 67–77.

Petras, James (1997), "Imperialism and NGOs in Latin America", *Monthly Review*, December, pp.10–27.

Riddell, Roger C. and Robinson, Mark with de Coninck, John, Muir, Ann and White, Sarah (1995), *Non-governmental Organizations and Rural Poverty Alleviation* (Oxford: Clarendon Press; and New York: Oxford University Press, in association with Overseas Development Institute, London).

Rist, Gilbert (1997), *The History of Development: From Western Origins to Global Faith* (London: Zed Books).

Robinson, M. (1997), "Privatizing the Voluntary Sector: NGOs as Public Service Contractors?", in D Hulme and M. Edwards (eds), *NGOs, States and Donors: Too Close for Comfort?* (London/Basingstoke: Macmillan in association with Save the Children), pp. 59–78.

Shihata Ibrahim F. I. (1995), "The World Bank and NGOs", in *the World Bank in a Changing World*, Vol. 2. Washington D.C: World Bank, pp. 54–62.

Smillie Ian, Douxchamps, Francis and Sholes, Rebecca/Covey, Jane (1995), *Partners or Contractors? Official Donor Agencies and Direct Funding Mechanisms: Three Northern Case Studies – CIDA, EU and USAID* (London: Interact).

Smock, David R. (1997), "Humanitarian Assistance and Conflict in Africa" *Journal of Humanitarian Assistance*, posted, July 1997 at <http://www-jha.sps.cam.ac.uk/a/a016.htm>.

Streeton, Paul (1997), "Non-governmental Organizations and Development", *The Annals of the American Academy of Political and Social Science*,Vol. 55. No. 4, pp. 193–211.

Stewart, Sheila (1997), "Happy Ever After in the Marketplace: Non-government Organizations and Uncivil Society", *Review of African Political Economy*, Vol. 24. Issue 71, pp. 11–34.

Stiglitz, Joseph (1999), *Participation and Development: Perspectives from the Comprehensive Development Paradigm* (Remarks at the International Conference on Democracy, Market Economy and Development) Seoul, Korea, 27 February, 1999 <http://www.worldbank.org/html/extdr/extme/js-022799/>.

Tandon, Yash (1995), *Reclaiming Africa's Agenda: Good Governance and the Role of NGOs in the African Context*, Paper presented at the Conference on Good Governance for Africa: Whose Governance? University of Limburg and ECDPM, Maastricht, 23–24, November.

Turner, Mark and Hulme, David (eds) (1997), *Governance, Administration and Development: Making the State Work* (Houndsmills, Basingstoke: Macmillan).

Tignor, Robert L. (1998), *Capitalism and Nationalism at the End of Empire: State and Business in Decolonizing Egypt, Nigeria, and Kenya, 1945–1963* (Princeton: Princeton University Press).

United Nations (1999), NGOs and the United Nations: Comments for the Report of the Secretary General, *Global Policy Forum,* June, 1999 <http://www.globalpolicy.org/ngos/docs99/gpfrep2.htm#17>.

Vakil, Annac (1997), "Confronting the Classification Problem: Toward a Taxonomy of NGOs", *World Development*, Vol.25. No. 12, pp. 2057–2070.

Wallace, Tina (1997), New Developments Agendas: Changes in U.K. Policies and Procedures", *Review of African Political Economy*, Vol. 24. Issue 71, pp. 35–55.

Watanabe, Michio and Takahashi, Mokoi (1997), "The Effectiveness of Donor Aid in Kenya's Health Sector", in Jerker Carlsson, Gloria Somolekae and Nicholas Van de Walle (eds) (1997), *Foreign Aid in Africa: Learning from Country Experience* (Uppsala: AfrikaNordiska Afrikainstituetet), pp. 112–127.

Welch Claude E. (1996), *Protecting Human Rights in Africa: Strategies and Roles of Non-governmental Organizations*, (Philadelphia: University of Pennsylvania Press).

Wood, Geoff (1997), "States Without Citizens: The Problems of the Franchise State", in D. Hulme and M. Edwards (eds) *NGOs, States and Donors: Too Close for Comfort?* (Basingstoke, London: Macmillan in association with Save the Children), pp.79–92.

World Bank (1994), *The World Bank and Participation.* (Washington D.C.: Operations Policy Department)

World Bank (1996), *Ethics and Spiritual Values: Promoting Environmentally Sustainable Development* (Washington D.C: World Bank)

World Bank (1997), World *Development Report, 1997: The State in a Changing World* (New York: Oxford University Press).

World Banks (1997a), *Relevant Literature on Civil Society* <http://wbln0018.worldbank.org/ external/lac/lac.nsf/>.

World Bank (1997b), *Handbook on Good Practices for Laws Relating to Non-Governmental Organizations* (Discussion Draft). Prepared for the World Bank by The International Center for Not-for-Profit Law, at <http://wbln0018.worldbank.org/ essd/kb.nsf/ec168cc2ef09fc248525668700496 1cd/>.

Chapter 6

State Sovereignty and the New Globalization in Africa

Jacques Mangala

Introduction

The current research agenda on globalization has brought the issue of state sovereignty at the center of theoretical and analytical considerations in international relations and international law. Debate among realist, liberal interdependence, and critical theorists has rescued the concept of sovereignty from its abstract, arcane and sterile treatment in the fields of international law and political philosophy and infused it with new meaning, theoretical significance, and practical relevance in today's increasingly globalized world (Walker, 1988).

State sovereignty has, for the past several hundred years, been a defining principle of interstate relations and a foundation of world order. Traditionally, sovereignty has been defined in reference to the Westphalian order as it emerged from the Treaty of Westphalia in 1648, which ended the Thirty Years War and gave its name to the modern international system. The traditional meaning of sovereignty, as it relates to the Wesphalian order, encompasses comprehensive, supreme, unqualified, and exclusive control of the state over its designated territorial domain. The concept is normally used to include all matters in which each state is permitted by international law to decide and act without intrusions from other sovereign states. The matters include the choice of political, economic, social, and cultural systems and the formulation of foreign policy.

This traditional understanding of sovereignty is being challenged by globalization which, despite its complexities, is widely regarded as "the integration of economies throughout the world through trade, financial flows, the exchange of technology and information, and the movement of people"(Ouattara, 1997, p. 1).

But what are the challenges that globalization poses to the nation-state? What is the meaning of state sovereign in today's world? How is sovereignty being impacted and redefined by globalization? Is the core Wesphalian norm of sovereignty still operative today? An abundant literature has been produced which analyzes the nexus between the phenomenon of globalization and the concept of state sovereignty. However, the impact of the former on the latter has received divergent interpretations in the doctrine. While some have argued the end of sovereignty (Camilleri and Falk, 1992), others have stressed only its erosion (Chopra and Thomas, 1992.) or evolving nature (Krasner, 1999; Schrijver, 2000; Krasner, 2001). The image of a powerless state presented by some scholars (Evans, 1997) has been treated as a myth by others

(Weiss, 1999). If these studies offer deep insights and useful theoretical constructs that capture the nexus between globalization and state sovereignty, they have overall reserved only a peripheral attention to Africa as a unit of analysis. It seems as if globalization, along with the study of its impact on state sovereignty, has bypassed Africa (Ottaway, 1999).

Africa represents a special locus from which to assess the impact of the new globalization on state sovereignty. Under colonization, which constituted one dimension of the "old globalization", Africa was essentially treated as an object of international relations whose interests and destiny were decided by foreign powers. With a few exceptions, the post-colonial state inherited only a nominal sovereignty, which gave its plain measure during the Cold War and the subsequent ideological struggle as it was played on the continent. Since the end of the Cold War and the emergence of what has been called the "new globalization", what qualitative change has state sovereignty undergone in Africa? In what ways is the new globalization different from the old one which witnessed the "scramble for Africa"[1] and the penetration of the international capital in the continent?

My major points are two. First, I contend that, with a few exceptions, African states never enjoyed all dimensions of sovereignty and that there is a need for a dialectical approach, which deals with the core issue of power, in understanding Africa's role in history, especially in the era of the "new globalization". Second, I argue that the only way for Africa to move from heteronomy to autonomy and weigh on its own destiny is through the formulation of a coherent alternative regional response and the redefinition of the sovereignty concept in order to cope with the pressures and challenges of the "new globalization".

To demonstrate these points and answer the fundamental questions before us, the present chapter will be divided in three sections. The first offers a broad conceptual and theoretical framework of state sovereignty and globalization. It reviews key scholarly works that focus on state sovereignty and globalization, with a special emphasis on works that link theoretically and analytically the two concepts. After this theoretical and conceptual exploration of the nexus between globalization and state sovereignty, the second section will adopt a more analytical approach in assessing globalization's challenges to state sovereignty in Africa. It is aimed at discussing, *in concreto*, the constraints imposed on state sovereignty in Africa under conditions of new globalization and their significance for the evolution of the African state. Against the background of developments in the second section, the third and final section discusses possible arrangements and responses to globalization challenges and constraints on state sovereignty in Africa. It calls for a pooled sovereignty, which seeks an autonomous regionalism and uses power allocation analysis as core operating principle in the pursuit of African development.

---

1 "Scramble for Africa" is borrowed from the title of the documentary series on Africa's history produced by Dr. Basil Davidson.

State Sovereignty and Globalization: A Conceptual and Theoretical Overview

State sovereignty has, for the past several hundred years, been a defining principle of interstate relations and a foundation of world order. The concept lies at the heart of both customary international law and the United Nations Charter and remains both an essential component of the maintenance of international peace and security and a defense of weak states against the strong.[2] Easier to enounce than define, the concept of state sovereignty remains a complex notion. It has generated an enormous and contentious literature. As summarized by Schrijver (2000, pp. 69–70):

> Few subjects in international law and international relations are as sensitive as the notion of sovereignty. Steinberger refers to it in the *Encyclopedia of Public International Law* as "the most glittering and controversial notion in the history, doctrine and practice of international law." On the other hand, Henkin seeks to banish it from out vocabulary and Lauterpacth calls it a "word which has an emotive quality lacking meaningful specific content," while Verzij notes that any discussion on this subject risks degenerating into a Tower of Babel. More affirmatively, Brownlie sees sovereignty as "the basic constitutional doctrine of the law of nations" and Alan James sees it as "the one and only organizing principle in respect of the dry surface of the globe, all that surface now…being divided among single entities of a sovereign, or constitutionally independent kind." As noted by Falk, "There is little neutral ground when it comes to sovereignty."

Before we venture further into theoretical considerations and doctrinal controversies, it is worth, at this point of the study, that we explore the various meanings and dimensions of state sovereignty. Krasner (2001) distinguishes between four meanings of sovereignty: interdependence sovereignty, domestic sovereignty, Westphalian or Vattelian sovereignty, and international legal sovereignty. Interdependence sovereignty refers to "the ability of states to control movement across their borders." Domestic sovereignty refers to "authority structures within states and the ability of these structures to effectively regulate behavior" (Krasner, 2001, p. 231). Authority structures can take many different forms including monarchies, republics, democracies, unified systems, and federal systems. According to Krasner, the loss of interdependence sovereignty, which is purely a matter of control, would also imply some loss of domestic sovereignty, at least domestic sovereignty understood as control since, as he puts it "if a state cannot regulate movements across its borders, such as the flow of illegal drugs, it is not likely to be able to control activities within its borders, such as the use of drugs" (Krasner, 2001, p. 232).

Westphalian or Vattelian sovereignty deals with the exclusion of external sources of authority both *de jure* and *de facto* which means that, within its own boundaries, the state has a monopoly over authoritative decision-making. This notion of sovereignty forms the basis of the cardinal principle of non-intervention in the internal affairs of other states. Finally, international legal sovereignty refers to mutual recognition

---

2 This sentiment was captured by Algerian President Boueteflika who, as President of the Organization for African Unity (OAU), addressed the UN General Assembly in 1999, immediately after the Secretary-General, and called sovereignty "our final defense against the rules of an unjust world."

which, in the international practice, is accorded to "juridically independent territorial entities … capable of entering into voluntary contractual agreements" (Krasner, 2001, p. 233). These four meanings of sovereignty emphasize five key concepts or dimensions in the notion of sovereignty which require further considerations, especially in relation to the post-colonial African state.

First is the recognition dimension of sovereignty. It has been argued that "sovereignty is not an attribute of the state but is attributed to the state by other states or rulers (Ashley, 1984, pp. 239, 259, 269, 272; Miller, 1984, 1986). Jackson (1990) has persuasively demonstrated the state's dependence on other states for its authority. In the modern state system, members recognize one another as equal authority claimants, who are juridically equal and have the final and exclusive authority to use coercion within their respective borders. External recognition plays a crucial role in constituting state sovereignty. The recognition dimension of sovereignty entails an important empirical question as to what an entity must do to be recognized as a sovereign state. By claiming that the state "decides for itself how it will cope with its internal and external problems, Waltz (1979, p. 96) seems to suggest that capabilities are central to our understanding of sovereignty. Building on the work of Jackson and Rosberg (1982) and Jackson (1990), Thomson (1995, p. 220) answers the above empirical question as follows:

> States are recognize as sovereign when they present a fact of sovereignty; that is, states recognize another's sovereignty when the latter has achieved the capability to defend its authority against domestic and international challenges. European history largely supports this argument but the post-World War II period of decolonization does not. By no stretch of the imagination is it possible to explain the existence of the vast majority of today's sovereign states in terms of their empirical power capabilities. Most cannot defend against either external or internal challenges (…) Power capabilities are equally as or more important than outside recognition. It may (…) that sovereignty is limited to those who possess the material resources to defend it while the less powerful are nominally sovereign but in fact are subject to heteronomy.

Second is the state dimension of sovereignty. International relations theory is based on the assumption that sovereignty resides with the state. This assumption is the product of European history, which witnessed the emergence of the modern national state only after long and bloody struggles in which "society" strenuously and often violently resisted state-builders' efforts to monopolize authority and violence (Tilly, 1975). For Giddens (1985, p. 121), it is only when the state monopolizes coercion both internally and externally that the national state, in which the state is equivalent to the polity, emerges. State-building literature provides historically grounded bases for theorizing about the state, depository of sovereignty in modern international system, as the product of a series of bargains between state-builders and wealth-producers in European history, as "a product of both internal and external competition, of conflict and cooperation" (Thomson, 1995, p. 221). This excursus into the historical formation of the modern nation-state is of particular interest in order to take full measure of the sovereignty challenges and pressures its faces from substate actors in this era of globalization, especially in Africa where the post-colonial state came into existence under different historical and social circumstances.

Third is the authority dimension of sovereignty. Thomson (1995, p. 222) has framed sovereignty as the authority to define the political, "political being what is subject to state coercion." She contends that, in examining sovereignty, our focus should be on the state's meta-political authority claims rather than on control. Authority and control are analytically separable but their empirical relationship is of crucial importance in understanding and measuring sovereignty. Authority is contingent on recognition; control depends on concrete capabilities to monitor and enforce compliance with the rules that are made under that authority. Using this distinction, Jackson and Rosberg (1982) assert that, although not empirically sovereign, the new African states are still sovereign by virtue of the interstate system's recognition of their claims to sovereignty.[3] Understanding the relationship between authority and control appears thus central to defining and measuring sovereignty.

Fourth is the coercion dimension of sovereignty. Coercion as a hallmark of the state is defined as "a monopoly on the major, organized forces of violence" (Weber, 1964, p. 154). The ability to "effectively-patrolled the territory" is considered a prerequisite for recognition as a sovereign state (Ashley, 1984, p. 272). Coercion is key to sovereignty because, ultimately, the exercise of authority depends on it (Blau, 1963, p. 313). The monopolization of coercion by the state was historically achieved by the late nineteenth century. The disarming and pacification of nonstate actors is a product of three centuries of state-building and interstate interaction. With a few exceptions, the same cannot be said for post-colonial African states, still engaged in state-building and where control over coercion, as an expression of state sovereignty, is being eroded and challenged by internal (warlords, private armies and militia) and external (foreign military interventions) actors (Cornwell, 1999).

Fifth is the territoriality dimension of sovereignty. There is a general agreement that sovereignty provides the central organizing principle of world politics by connecting territory with political authority, which is vested in "a set of administrative, policing, and military organizations headed, and more or less well coordinated by an executive authority" (Skocpol, 1979, p. 29) – the state. Thomson (1995, p. 227) stresses that sovereignty delineates authority not according to function but to geography and that this dimension of sovereignty is what separates sovereignty from heteronomy. The territorial basis of sovereignty is regarded as inherently Euro-centric by some scholars who contend that sovereignty has been extended to non-European areas so that global politics now evolved around sovereignty, which has been given-at least juridically – even to political authorities lacking the empirical hallmarks of European state sovereignty (Bull and Watson, 1982, pp. 2 and 123; Miller, 1984, p. 285; Strang, 1991a, 1991b). This movement corresponds to what some have called the "globalization of sovereignty" (Thomson, 1995, p. 227).

Despite the formal extension of sovereignty to countries in the global South, the sovereignty of non-European states in the contemporary system has been seriously questioned. It has been suggested that sovereignty applies only in the northern tier

3 Indeed, capabilities may be supplied by other states or international organizations, as in the case of Somalia or the earlier case of the Congo, where international intervention is aimed at building the state's power capabilities, especially the security and police forces

of states; politics between the north and the south is characterized by heteronomy (Wendt and Barnett, 1993, p. 335; Onuf and Klink, 1989, pp. 164–170).

The territorial dimension of sovereignty is of particular interest in the study of the African state, still engaged in the double process of state and nation-building. Thomson (1995, p. 227) has succinctly presented the problem:

> At one level, territory is simply a geographic space whose limits are defined by physical borders-lines on a map. With sovereignty, however, states mutually recognize one another's exclusive authority over what is contained in that space. The essence of the state-building process has been the state's drive to penetrate, exploit, and mobilize those resources for interstate competition and war. One of those resources, of course, is the people who live within the state's borders, and part of the state-building process – still incomplete in most of the world – entails creating a "society" or nation out of these people; that is, forging their loyalty to and identification with the state. So the territorial dimension of sovereignty entails not just the defense of geographic boundaries but tight linkages between the state and people.

Can states that are still at an early stage of state and nation-building processes exhibit sovereignty as defined in its territorial dimension? To what degree is the territoriality of African states, as a dimension of sovereignty, real? More research is needed but it is clear that there is a need to deconstruct the concept of sovereignty as it applies to global politics in general and to African states in particular.

A large body of literature is very critical of the notion of "sovereignty" as it has generally been known and presented. Krasner (1999) has referred to the sovereignty concept as "organized hypocrisy", while Flower and Bunck (1995, p. 21) see it as being "of more value for purposes of oratory and persuasion than of science and law." Other authors have attempted to reconstruct the concept of sovereignty, which they frame as a "social construct" with no particular inherent characteristics and whose nature depends very much on the customs and practices of nation-states and international systems, which practices could change over time (Weber and Biersteker, 1996, p. 278). This analysis is echoed by Schermers (2002, pp. 185, 192) who writes:

> Sovereignty has many different aspects and none of these aspects is stable. The content of the notion of "sovereignty" is continuously changing, especially in recent years (…) From the above we may conclude that under international law the sovereignty of states must be reduced. International co-operation requires that all states be bound by some minimum requirements of international law without being entitled to claim that their sovereignty allows them to reject basic international regulations.[4] Thirdly, we may conclude that the world community takes over sovereignty of territories where national governments completely fail and that therefore national sovereignty has disappeared in those territories. The world community by now has sufficient means to step in with the help of existing states and has therefore the obligation to rule those territories where the governments fail.

---

4 There are important and widely accepted limits to state sovereignty and to domestic jurisdiction in international law, which come either from customary international law or treaty obligations – e.g. Chapter VII, UN Charter. Also Articles 1(2) and 2(7).

Criticisms offered by these authors are part of a larger scholarly movement of contestation and deconstruction of the sovereignty concept, which has been intensified by the "new globalization". The contestation of sovereignty gained intellectual momentum in the literature in reaction to the state-centric approach of international relations.

State-centric theories, which have dominated international relations, are built on the assumption that states are, by definition, sovereign. What is meant by this is that, at a minimum, states are territorial units with juridical independence; are not formally subject to some external authority; and have *de facto* autonomy (Krasner, 2001, p. 230). While rationalist theories of international relations (realism and liberalism institutionalism) see in state sovereign the genetic material of the international system (Waltz, 1979; Keohane, 1984), constructivists contend that the system of sovereign states is no more than the expression of an intersubjective shared understanding (Ruggie, 1998).

The state-centric approach to international relations was challenged in the 1970s and early 1980s by liberal independence theorists who argued that state sovereignty was being eroded by economic interdependence, global-scale technologies, and democratic politics (Cooper, 1972; Keohane and Nye, 1972; Morse, 1976; Rosecrance, 1986). They fundamentally contended that states can no longer control their borders. Modern technology empowers nonstate and substate actors to evade state efforts to control the flow of goods, people, money, and information across territorial boundaries. Capital, especially, can flow to another state or another currency to escape state fiscal and monetary policies (Cooper, 1972). Efforts to defend cultural values or bar subversive ideas are stymied by computer and telecommunications technologies in the hands of other states and substate and nonstate actors (Rosecrance, 1986). Challenges to state sovereignty identified by these authors have been exacerbated since the end of the Cold War, which led to the "new globalization". How does the "new globalization" impact state sovereignty? Does the "new globalization" represent any qualitative break from the past? What does "sovereignty", as practically used today, signify? What is the future of the nation-state, and the international system as a whole given the challenges posed by the "new globalization"? General answers and approaches to these central questions express contending views about the magnitude of the impact of the "new globalization" on state sovereignty.

Many scholars of globalization have suggested that the "new globalization" poses a clear threat to state sovereignty in that it is eroding state control over certain activities. Some have contended that current challenges, pressures and changes coming from, among others, the activities and expansion of international organizations (the United Nations, the International Monetary Fund, the World Bank, the World Trade Organization), the spread of democracy and technology, the activities of transnational non-governmental organizations, and the criminal opportunities and malicious activities associated with the cyberspace, could lead not only to the erosion of the state control, but also to dramatic changes in the structures of state authority itself. Studies that follow under this view have successively stressed the "fragmentation" of the state, its "eclipse", or the emergence of a "powerless state" (Evans, 1997; Kreijn et al., 2002).

This lecture of the current dynamic has been contested by other authors who have argued that such interpretation lacks historical perspective and overstates the magnitude of current changes and challenges and their impact on state sovereignty. By comparing current to past international capital flows, capital integration, international migration, international trade and other global processes, they argue that there is nothing fundamentally or qualitatively "new" with current global flows. Even new challenges posed by the activities of international organizations and transnational non-governmental organizations, the spread of democracy and technological evolution, and the cyberspace, are ultimately denied their ability to "displace sovereignty", whose resilience has been stated as "stricking" by Krasner (2001, pp 234 and 236):

> States … have always operated in an interdependent environment. They have never been able to perfectly regulate transborder flows… It is not that globalization has had no control on state control, but rather those controlling transborder movements, not to speak of developments within a state's boundaries, has always been a challenge. The problems for states have become more acute in some areas, but less so in others. There is no evidence that globalization systematically undermine state control; indeed, the clearest relationship between globalization and state activity is that they have increased hand-in-hand, and in some arenas states are more capable than they have been in the past.[5]

Although there is disagreement over the extent of the impact of globalization on state sovereignty, the dominant view in the doctrine emphasizes, however, the "evolving nature" of sovereignty under conditions of globalization. Rather than declaring the "end of sovereignty", many scholars and policy-makers have proposed new conceptualizations and ways of defining, approaching and thinking through sovereignty, which underline the complexity and adaptability of the sovereignty concept. New conceptualizations have emerged along different lines, which correspond to various challenges to traditional state sovereignty. One such challenge comes from the changing balance between states and people as the source of legitimacy and authority. The older version state-centered rule of law is being tempered by the rule of law based on the rights of individuals. And a broader concept of sovereignty, encompassing both the rights and responsibilities of states, is now being more widely advocated in policy-making circles.

In 1999, the UN Secretary General Kofi Annan introduced his annual report to the General Assembly by noting that "post-war institutions were built for an international world, but we now live in a global world". Kofi Annan (1999) then expressed impatience with traditional notions of sovereignty:

> A global era requires global engagement …. If states bent on criminal behavior know that frontiers are not the absolute defense; if they know that the Security Council will take action to halt crimes against humanity, then they will not embark on such a course of action in expectation of sovereign impunity …. If the collective conscience of humanity – a conscience which abhors cruelty, renounces injustice and seeks peace for all peoples – cannot find in the United Nations its greatest tribune, there is a grave danger that it will look elsewhere for peace and for justice … Any such evolution in our understanding of

5 For similar view, see also Waltz (1970); Thomson and Krasner (1989).

> State sovereignty and individual sovereignty will, in some quarters, be met with distrust, skepticism, even hostility. But it is an evolution that we should welcome.

The Secretary General would later formulate his conceptualization of sovereignty in a widely cited article in *The Economist* on the "two concepts of sovereignty", which helped launch an intense debate on the legitimacy of intervention on humanitarian grounds. Kofi Annan argued that one concept of sovereignty is oriented around states and the other around people:

> State sovereignty, in its most basic sense, is being redefined – not least by the forces of globalization and international co-operation. States are now widely understood to be the instruments at the service of their peoples, and not vice versa. At the same time individual sovereignty – by which I mean the fundamental freedom of each individual, enshrined in the Charter of the UN and subsequent international treaties – has been enhanced by the renewed and spreading consciousness of individual rights. When we read the Charter today, we are more than ever conscious that its aim is to protect individual human beings, not to protect those who abuse them.[6]

For Kofi Annan and others, although sovereignty remains the cardinal principle of international affairs, it must however be understood as "the peoples' sovereignty rather than the sovereign's sovereignty."

Stemming from the same challenge is the notion of "sovereignty as responsibility", most explicitly formulated by Deng (1993), the Representative of the Secretary- General for Internally Displaced Persons. At the heart of this doctrine is the idea that when states are unable to provide life-supporting protection and assistance for their citizens, they are expected to request and accept outside offers of aid. Should they refuse or deliberately obstruct access to their displaced or other affected populations and thereby put large numbers at risk, there is an international responsibility to respond. Sovereignty then means accountability to two separate constituencies: internally, to one's own population; and internationally, to the community of responsible states and in the form of compliance with human rights and humanitarian agreements. This doctrine stresses the contingent nature of sovereignty and the legality of its suspension for gross violations of human rights and international humanitarian law.

From academic and scholarly circles have emerged a number of new conceptualizations, notions and analytic tools, which are based on the idea that earlier conceptions of sovereignty do not suffice to explain current events in international relations. Recent conceptions of "pooled", "complex" or "unbundled" sovereignty have attempted to trace the contours of contemporary political challenges and changes across the globe, while further fortifying and legitimating various legal orders: international, municipal, and otherwise. Central to these conceptions is the concern about the practicality of sovereignty and its meaning in today's world. Thomson (1999) argues that, under conditions of globalization, sovereignty is best approached and understood as authority rather than control. She goes on to suggest

6 Kofi Annan, "Two Concepts of Sovereignty", *The Economist* 352 (September 18, 1999), pp. 1–2.

that, in assessing the current status and future prospects of sovereignty, attention be (re-) directed to the issue of rule-making and enforcement. She writes (1995, p. 230):

> … the bottom line is not whether or not states can pursue autonomous economic, human rights or environmental policies in an interdependent world, but if and how interdependent (or anything else) is affecting the states' recognized claim to monopolize the coercive and policing function upon which their meta-political authority rests.

After confronting sovereignty "fictions" as expressed in its "antiquated" definition, Jackson (2003, p. 790) contends that, in current policy debates, sovereignty is better conceptualized in terms of allocation of power or government decision-making power. The practicality of sovereignty rests upon the resolution of the question on which level (domestic or international) should decisions be made as a matter of good governmental policy. To answer this central question to the "evolving" understanding of sovereignty concept, Jackson develops an analytic tool, the power allocation analysis, which centers on many values or policy objectives (coordination benefits, factor mobility, global commons, subsidiarity principle, accountability, substance of an issue, misuse of power, and the so-called "rule of orientation") that could influence consideration of the appropriate level or other (horizontal) distribution of power within a landscape of governmental and nongovernmental institutions. Jackson (2003, p. 800) asserts:

> …the power allocation analysis, when explored more profoundly, can help overcome some of the "hypocrisy" and "thought-destructive mantras" surrounding these concepts so that policymakers can focus on real problems rather than myths. This analysis can thus help policymakers weigh and balance the various factors to reach better decisions … Such an analysis recognizes that there are desiderata in sovereignty concepts other than the "core" power allocation issues, and that even as regards the core issues there are clearly cases that the world must resolve by explicit (or well-recognized implicit) departures from traditional sovereignty concepts.

This conceptual departure from the historical and discredited Westphalian concept of sovereignty and other current versions of sovereignty is called "sovereignty-modern", whose power allocation analysis is supposed to introduce an element of dynamism in an otherwise "frozen-in-time" concept. To cope with the many challenges of globalization, the "sovereignty-modern" power allocation analysis suggests moving the discussions of sovereignty from sterile concepts to the domain of state decision-making power. The essence of sovereignty and its practical meaning is that the nation-state retains the ability to decide in each case, for itself, whether it is willing to allocate "its own sovereign power" either up the scale or downward; in other words, to decide, for itself, at which level decisions will be taken and to which actors it may allocate power in order to better confront globalization's challenges. Have African states developed such ability? How is sovereignty, so understood, being expressed and challenged under conditions of the "new globalization" in Africa?

Before answering these questions in the second part of the study, I would like to close the first by surveying some conceptual and empirical analyses of globalization that are of particular interest in the study of its impacts on state sovereignty in Africa in particular, and in the developing world in general. The majority of studies on globalization does not place the phenomenon within a dialectical and historical framework which exposes issues of power and exploitation and give sense to contradictory processes. Advocates of globalization point to the emergence of the "middle-class" in developing countries, economic growth within peripheral economies, and the continued expansion of global stock markets, democratization and the emergence of a "global culture" as indicators of the benefits of the process. We are led to forget, as Professor Herman (1999, p. 1) puts it, that "globalization is also an ideology, whose function is to reduce any resistance to the process by making it seem both highly beneficent and unstoppable ... Globalization is just one of an array of concepts and arguing points that have been mobilized to advance the corporate agenda." From the perspective of post-colonial states, a critical and historical framework helps to take globalization for what it is and not attribute to it an aura of virtue, like free trade and other similar social and intellectual constructs.

In his seminal study, *What is the Concept of Globalization Good for? An African Historian's Perspective*, Professor Cooper (2001) has superbly argued the inadequacy of the concept of globalization from an African history standpoint. He writes (p. 189):

> In contrasting a present of flows with a past of structures, it [the concept of globalization] misreads the ways in which a 400-year-long process defined both Africa and the Atlantic-centered capitalist economy. In regard to both past and present, it draws attention to the specific mechanisms by which long-distance connections were forged and the limits of those mechanisms. Like modernization theory in the 1950s and 1960s, globalization talk is influential – and deeply misleading – for assuming coherence and direction instead of probing causes and processes.

Cooper contends that the concept of globalization emphasizes change over time but remains ahistorical. He calls on Africanists to be particularly sensitive to the time-depth of cross-territorial processes, "for the very notion of 'Africa' has itself been shaped for centuries by linkages within the continent and across oceans and deserts... The concept (globalization) cannot be salvaged by pushing it backwards in time, for the histories of the slave trade, colonizing, and colonization, as well as the travails of the era of structural adjustment fit poorly any narrative of globalization – unless one so dilutes the term that it becomes meaningless. To study Africa is to appreciate the long-term importance of the exercise of power across space, but also the limitations of such power" (Cooper, 2001, pp. 190–191).

In addition to the historical approach, globalization and its implications for developing countries are better understood within the framework of imperialism and class conflict. Petras and Veltmeyer (2001) contend that globalization is little more than imperialism in a new form. They argue that the inevitability of globalization and the adjustment of peoples all over the world to free market capitalism depend on the capacity of the dominant and ruling classes to bend people to their will and convince people that their interests are the people's interests. A key element in theorizing about globalization, they assert, is the understanding that, as has always been the case with imperialism, globalization is being propagated to advance the interests of those who already enjoy power and privilege. To analyze and understand some of the seemingly contradictory processes of the global political economy, Ramsaran and Price (2003, p. 4) suggest a critical framework which contends that the economic, political and cultural (or ideological) dynamics of globalization reflect a dialectical relationship between and within suprastatal, statal, and intrastatal sectors, which represent "the hegemonic structure through which struggles of globalization occurs". Within this dialectical framework, the suprastatal sector encompasses global institutional forces such as the International Monetary Find, the World Bank, the World Trade Organization, and the United Nations, which are directly or indirectly controlled by, and represent the interests of, international elite who promote liberalization, comparative advantage and free market-oriented economies. The statal sector encompasses the power and role of governments to negotiate treaties and to coordinate political and economic activity between nations. The intrastate sector is represented by the varied struggles between different groups and institutions within nations over state activities and the distribution of economic resources. In order to enhance the transformative potential embedded in the processes of globalization, argue Ramsaran and Price (2003, p. 3), it is necessary to expose the latent tendencies of globalization, which reflect the hierarchies of power within the global political economy.

By focusing on questions of power, inequality, unevenness and injustice embodied in the "new globalization", the above historical and critical analyses depart from the dominant neo-liberal discourse on globalization, which overemphasize the "time-space compression", "shrinking world", new technologies, integrated markets, global interdependence and global flows. It is within this broad theoretical and conceptual framework that I shall now assess and reflect on globalization's challenges to state sovereignty in Africa.

The "New Globalization" and Challenges to State Sovereignty in Africa

Before discussing the "new globalization's" challenges to state sovereignty, I intend first to take the measure of globalization's penetration in Africa and briefly comment on the key features of the African state. When we talk about globalization in Africa, it is worth putting this discourse into some perspective. By any standard, globalization is bypassing Africa. African states remain largely marginal to all global trends. The basic economic indicators are discouraging. With over 10 percent of the world population, sub-Saharan Africa accounts for only 1.5 percent of world trade. It receives less than .6 percent of foreign direct investment, while portfolio investment is essentially nonexistent, except for South Africa. Sub-Saharan Africa has only 15 telephone mainlines per every 1,000 people, compared with a worldwide average of 133 per every 1,000 people. While some trends look promising – foreign direct investment more than doubled in the 1990s – the continent is, to say the least, economically, socially, and culturally marginalized (Ottaway, 1999, pp. 19–20). Examining the continent' marginalization and "survival", Ihonvbere (2001, p. 4) asks:

> Was Africa prepared for this new "revolution"? Are there institutions and structures on ground to receive, mediate, resist, or recompose the products of ongoing changes? What are the ideological platforms on which Africa will be participating in the new globalization and engaging the powerful forces of monopoly capitalism? Finally, how will the plethora of contradictions, conflicts and suspicions all over the region, within and between nations, condition Africa's location and role in the emerging order? One would be really stretching the limits of generosity to claim that Africa was ready for the numerous developments within the continent, much less in other parts of the world ... Beyond these, the new globalization is marked by other critical features that further demonstrate the weakness and vulnerability of the African economy.

The continent's economic marginalization is why, in most of the ongoing discussions about the "new globalization", Africa is accorded only a peripheral attention, "despite the encouraging progress made in transforming sub-Saharan Africa, and the far-reaching socio-economic and political reforms that governments have been forced to adopt to please lenders, donors and international pressure groups" (Ihonvbere, 2001, p. 6).

Globalization challenges are being handled by an African state which, for the most part, has been conceptually and analytically defined as "soft" and "collapsed" (Zartman, 1995), "failed" (Holsti, 1996), "fractured" (Young, 1994), "weak" (Claphan, 1996), "irrelevant" (Ihonvbere, 1994),"illegitimate" (Englebert, 2000), "pseudo" (Cornwell, 1999), "criminal" (Bayart et al., 1999), or even "rogue" (Rubin, 1993) in some extreme instances. These characterizations by such outstanding scholars imply that, in most cases, the African state hasn't exhibited some fundamental characteristics of the state which are directly related to core issues associated with sovereignty: the ability to patrol the territory, exercise authority and control, and embody legitimacy. It is within the reality of this double limitation (economic marginalization and limited state capacity), that globalization challenges on state sovereignty will now be addressed.

In a speech at a meeting of 15 developing countries in Cairo in 2000, Nigerian President Olusegun Obasanjo bravely conceded:

> Our societies are overwhelmed by the strident consequences of globalization and the phenomenon of trade liberalization. The options open to us have narrowed as our increasingly shrinking world imposes on our countries a choice of integration or the severe conditions of marginalization and stagnation[7]

Such frustration, expression of globalization's assaults on the ability of African states to make their own decisions, has been echoed by many political leaders, policy makers and academics, who have identified numerous challenges to state sovereignty under conditions of globalization in Africa. The following discussion will mainly focus on decision-making and policy-making as dimensions of state sovereignty. Many observers and professionals of African politics have indicated that globalization has contributed to the erosion of African states' autonomous decision–making power. Apolo Nsibambi (2001, p. 4), Uganda's Prime Minister, writes:

---

7 Cited by J. Matethia, "Africa and Globalization", *Nigerian Guardian*, August 15, 2000.

> Most African governments are finding themselves in a situation of "*fait accompli*" when it comes to making certain policies and decisions. International agencies such as the World Bank, IMF, the United Nations World Trade Organization, etc take decisions which are binding on countries. This could be looked at as eroding the sovereignty and power of the state … The poorer the country, the more chance of power erosion for the state.

Although it is true that all developing countries are increasingly facing the same pressures on their decision-making power, the situation has taken a particular relief in Africa. Trevor Manuel (2004, p. 2), South Africa's Minister of Finance, has attributed this further erosion of African states' decision-making capacity to the weakness of the apparatus of the state in many African countries.

The erosion of state sovereignty has been particularly evidenced in the formulation of social policies. According to Apolo Nsibambi (2001:4), it has made the task of poverty eradication more difficult. Here is how the Prime Minister of Uganda, one of the few African countries praised by financial international institutions and foreign donors, stresses African states' predicament:

> As global actors pressurize African governments to open up more and more to maximize foreign investment and capital flows, and as big multinationals and local enterprises utilize this environment to cater for their interests, the government is having less and less room to pay attention to the abject poverty among its poor people. Evidence that shows the widening gap between the poor and the rich in country and between countries is increasingly becoming abundant. The African State will have to be encouraged to pay more attention to the fate of its poor than to the fate of big global actors. The big global actors can talk for themselves with little problem. The issue is: who will talk for the poor?

Manuel (2004, p. 2) shares the same analysis: "… the globalization challenge can trip states in the wrong direction-away from good governance, effective regulation, and pro-growth policies and toward rent-seeking, the stifling of the private sector, and the further weakening of already inadequate social policies and institutions". This inability to formulate and implement a progressive social agenda is intimately linked to the ideology of globalization itself, which has become a new *Leviathan* in that it affects developmental thinking and actions of the developing polities and relegates ethical equity and social concerns behind market consideration and reduces the autonomy of the state.[8] According to Ohiorhenuan (1998), globalization challenges the meditative role of the state vis-à-vis external pressures. It threatens the discretion of the state everywhere. Furthermore, Tandon (1998, p. 3) argues that globalization encourages "decreasing national control and increasing control over the (internal) economy (of the state) by outside players… globalization has been elevated to the position of the absolute truth, a sort of *pensée unique* against which there is no

8 Speaking about the social and political effects of IMF's policies on Nigeria, Jeffrey Sachs writes in the London Financial Times of June 14, 2000: "Until now, the US and Europe have insisted on stringent International Monetary Fund-led measures, including massive debt servicing …, a denial of debt cancellation, crumbs of aid, and demands for the elimination of fuel subsidies that, as we have seen during the past days, are a guaranteed trigger of violence"

credible alternative." Akindele, Gidado and Olaopo (2002, pp. 7–8)) address the African continent's marginalization in more concrete terms:

> Globalization is an awesome and terrifying phenomenon for African countries (...) Its universalization of communication, mass production, market exchanges and redistribution, rather than engendering new ideas and developmental orientation in Africa, subverts its autonomy and powers of self-determination. It is rather by design than by accident that poverty has become a major institution in Africa despite this continent's stupendous resources...Nation-states in Africa today, rarely define the rules and regulations of their economy, production, credits and exchanges of goods and services due to the ramping menace of globalization. They are hardly now capable of volitionally managing their political, economic and socio-cultural development. Globalization has imposed heavy constraints on the internal management dynamics of most if not all polities in Africa... The reality is that globalization has made it difficult for governments to provide social insurance – one of their central functions and one that has helped many developed nations to maintain social cohesion and domestic political support.

The inability of most African states to pursue a progressive social agenda under conditions of globalization represents a central contributing factor to the current legitimacy crisis of the state itself, which has led to many civil conflicts. To sum up this point, it can convincingly be argued that by undermining the ability of African states – still at an early stage of their development – to freely decide for and undertake much needed social initiatives aimed at securing citizen loyalty and building national social cohesion, the forces of globalization have not only contributed to a significant lost of state sovereignty but also to the erosion of the *raison d'être* of the state itself, to which the people less and less look for solutions for their problems. For states that are still engaged in a nation-building process, loosing one of the means for fostering a sense of national cohesion represents a major setback in the quest for independence. This conclusion is shared by Ihonvbere (2001, p. 5) who writes:

> These reform packages, often imposed from abroad and supervised by multinational agencies and credit clubs, have served in no small measure to erode the autonomy and sovereignty of African states. The combination of externally designed, imposed, and supervised political and economic conditionalities...is part of the conditions determining Africa's integration into the emerging global order as a dependent, vulnerable, weak, dominated, and almost helpless, peripheral actor in the new divisions of labor and power.

In his study of the political economy of restructuring in South Africa, Carmody (2002) explains how the South African state is trying, with mixed results, to "negotiate globalization" and why major South African conglomerates have moved their headquarters to Britain. The author concludes his study by asserting that, as a result of the restructuring of globalization, the South African state is increasingly characterized by "negative autonomy" from domestic social forces and embeddedness with transnational capital, which undermine the potential for a national development project.[9] If South Africa, the state south of the Sahara with the most state capabilities, can hardly preserve its decision-making power and is increasingly moving toward negative autonomy, what can be said about other African states? South Africa's experience has important implications for globalization theory, which can inform praxis.

A third sovereignty challenge engendered by the new globalization is directly linked to the "fait accompli" situation, which undermines the democratization process. Kura (2005, p. 7) notes that globalization hampers democracy by obstructing the autonomy and sovereignty of states especially in terms of public policies that would positively affect its citizens and strengthen the democratization process. Amuwo (2001, pp. 5–6) observes that it is difficult to preach democracy, however understood, to countries at the mercy of a global financial system whose decision-making mechanisms are insulated from the general processes of democratic accountability. He goes as far as to attribute the lack of crucial resources for nation-building and economic development as well as the proliferation of intra and inter-state conflicts that this often engenders to crucial decisions taken in the inner recesses of IFSs (International financial institutions). Along the same lines, Uganda's Apolo Nsibambi (2004, p. 4) writes:

> While the democratization process would require that the people of the country in question get involved in the taking of decisions and policies that concern them, some of the big decisions affecting Africa today are more or less imposed by the globalization players .... This has been the case for example with the liberalization and privatization policies in Africa. This makes the people not trust the democratization rhetoric they hear from their leaders when they are confronted with this "fait accompli". There is a discrepancy between the rhetoric from these bodies (World Bank, IMF, WTO) concerning the need for democracy and the way the same bodies arrive at decisions of great consequences. It is not possible to be seen to be democratic by the people you govern when they do not see or get involved in the process of making the decisions and policies you follow to govern them. This is a big dilemma for African leaders.

This third globalization challenge to sovereignty brings into question the whole notion of "good governance" as aggressively promoted by globalizers of all boards in Africa, who tend to emphasize a technocratic/economic approach to good governance. According to this approach, all that is required from aid recipients is to balance their financial books, avoid balance of payments deficits, pursue trade liberalization, currency devaluation, subsidy withdrawal from agriculture and other social sectors, privatization of key sectors of the economy, all of which are supposed to bring the state into the global economy. Questioning this globalization's reform agenda, Amuwo (2001, p. 7) observes that the problem is that the people, the real beneficiaries of these reforms, are hardly factored in. It seems as if "the administration of things is prioritized above the greatest welfare for the greatest number of the people. Ends appear to justify the means. The whether of economic

9 In his study of South Africa's restructuring of its telecommunications sector, Cogburn (1998) has concluded that the South African government has exhibited a high degree of state autonomy despite pressures from the WTO and IMF.

development is deemed more important than how and for whom it is realized. Some dosages of authoritarianism not excluded from the equation."

To restore some intellectual sanity to the good governance discourse, it is essential to assert that good governance is primarily a political imperative grounded on the concept of legitimacy. Good governance is about not only a government duly put in place by the people, but which stays in close touch with the needs of people in the formulation and implementation of national policies. Good governance is not about the mechanics of policies but their ends. Good governance in this sense is intimately linked to the pursuit of a democratic agenda, which seeks "ownership" by the people of reform and development program enunciated by the state/government. Participatory democracy, decentralization of economic and political decision-making centers of power are central to this broad democratic agenda, which should constitute the measure of "good governance", especially when assessed against the background of state sovereignty.

A four challenge to state sovereignty identified in the literature and confirmed by African government officials is that globalization has overstretched state capacity to handle international and computer-based crime. The increase in computer-based crimes (especially fraud), for which the law and order forces were not well prepared in most countries, makes them look helpless, unhelpful and incapable. According to Nsibambi (2001, p. 4), this situation "tends to erode the confidence of the public in the state, thus weakening further its legitimacy". With relatively weak state capacity and eroding legitimacy due to the forces of globalization, how meaningful is African states' sovereignty? Does it make sense to talk about "sovereignty" when the state is loosing its legitimacy?

A fifth and final challenge deals with overstretched capacity to regulate and protect the environment under condition of globalization. Already constrained, the capacity of most African states to handle issues such as production of harmful chemicals, global warming, depletion of natural resources, destruction of organic agriculture, and dumping of nuclear waste, has been pushed to its limits by global corporate forces. Nsibambi (2001, p. 3) argues:

> …As global actors invest and expand their activities, especially related to industrial, agriculture, mining, forest exploitation and fishing, the regulatory capacity of public administration in African countries, which is already limited in many respects is becoming overstretched. The state is getting caught in the middle of its need to speed development through industrialization, agricultural modernization, exploitation of natural resources, etc. and the pressure of local and global environmentalist groups. Global forces in this respect, rather than putting too much pressure on governments to do what is beyond their capacity, should first and foremost concentrate on strengthening the capacity of these governments in relevant aspects.

Nsibambi's lecture on the situation is shared by many observers of African politics who have noted that, by putting too much pressure on already limited states' regulatory and institutional capacity, the forces of globalization have contributed in further weakening the state apparatus and thus substantially constraining the ability of states to control the activities of these global actors and protect the common good. A diminished regulatory and institutional capacity for states means a limited ability to make their own decisions, which in turn means less effective sovereignties. In short, for the most part, African states' sovereignty has retreated as globalization forces have expanded in the continent, creating a dangerous vacuum for the survival of the African state itself as a meaningful entity in the international polity. This situation calls for the reinvention of sovereignty in Africa around the concept and practice of pooled sovereignty, which seems to represent the only credible alternative if African states are to avoid being further relegated to the margins of history, where they would be deprived even from the formal sovereignty that many of them have inherited from the colonial era. A pooled sovereignty would require the emergence of an autonomous regionalism, qualitatively distinct from past and current attempts at regional integration, which have been dominated by excessive politicization, a lack of political will, and a misreading of African history and its relations with the West. This is a challenge that African states must take. The next section takes a prospective view into the future of state sovereignty in Africa, as global forces expand their reach and the "new globalization" seems, at least for now, unstoppable.

Towards a Pooled Sovereignty? Autonomous Regionalism in Africa and the "New Globalization"

African states have faced many challenges throughout their collective troubled history. To the anomalies of colonial rule and exploitation and the subsequent task of national liberation, they responded by embracing pan-Africanism, whose overall aim was to advance the cause of sovereignty and self-determination for Africans. A pan-Africanist ethos enveloped the relations between and among African states as they gained independence and formed the Organization of African Unity (OAU) on May 25, 1963. To the challenges of regional integration and development, they responded by transforming the OAU into the African Union (AU). Parallel to the regional integration, a subregional integration dynamic has seen the consolidation of a number of subregional institutions in response to the developmental particularities and challenges of specific regions. The Economic Community of West African States (ECOWAS), the Economic Community of the Great Lakes Countries (CEPGL), the Preferential Trade Area of Central Africa (PTA), and the Southern African Development Community (SADC) represent a few examples of subregional attempts at political, economic or military cooperation. This double regionalism (continental and subregional) has been both ideologically and practically challenged and transformed by the new wave of globalization, which poses new threats to state sovereignty and autonomy and exposes the fragilities and flaws in Africa's attempts to assert its place in the community of nations.

Many scholars and policy-makers have addressed the fragilities and flaws of African integration attempts, which remain largely symbolic and inefficient. Manuel (2004, p. 4), South Africa's Minister of Finance, points out the general aversion to regional institutions, which stems from the idea that collective action reduces sovereignty. Manboah-Rockson (2000, p. 58) notes that "As institutionalization is in its early stages, many sub-regional integration organizations in Africa are only mechanisms for organizing and servicing meetings and maintaining contacts, while others concentrate on national matters". In *Survival in Contemporary Africa*, Ihonvbere (2001, p. 16) draws a particularly negative picture of Africa's integration experience:

> If the developed economies are taking regionalism seriously, as evidenced in the establishment of the North American Free Trade Area (NAFTA) and the European Union, then Africa should take it even more seriously. To date, the record of regionalism in the region has been poor, characterized by excessive politicization, lack of political will, disrespect for protocols ... petty jealousies, colonial legacies, and pressures from conditions of underdevelopment and dependence.

Furthermore, all these regional integration schemes don't ideologically challenge the neo-liberal model of development embodied in the "new globalization". Calls to consolidate regional integration are usually aimed at advancing the dominant neo-liberal agenda. The fundamental parameters of current global processes are seldom questioned or put into perspective with Africa's own history. The erosion of sovereignty is often not mentioned or simply treated as a by-product of globalization, credited with the potential to unlock Africa's development. The case of the New Partnership for Africa's Development (NEPAD) offers a good illustration of the "new regionalism" lack of a robust intellectual and ideological response to forces and processes of globalization. Among its many objectives, NEPAD seeks to halt the growing and deepening poverty of Africans by working towards altering the basis of the relationship between the rich North and the poor South. The initiative seeks a new global partnership based on shared responsibility and mutual interest through the instrumentality of political democracy and economic development on the continent. It is also concerned to institute people-centered development via market-oriented economies capable of holding their own ground in the "global village". Finally, NEPAD proposes a frontal attack on the negative fall-outs of the continent's integration into the global system as extremely weak partner and peripheral player. Despite these broad objectives, the underlying thinking behind NEPAD doesn't seem to suggest that the Western paradigm of development, embodied in the "new globalization", is being challenged or contested. Amuwo (2001:1) offers a sharp rebuttal of NEPAD and its overall ambition:

> ... Since Africa's history of unequal relations with the developed world in the last three centuries or so is such that it has largely become a non-autonomous actor without the capacity to decide its own fate and future – by being essentially a-historical does not constitute an adequate response to the continent's underdevelopment. It needs to be replaced by a more African-centered economic action plan that takes the continent's history into account ...In NEPAD's attempt to grapple with that history, it seems to have treated the 'international community' with kid gloves. And, what is more, this has been done in a rather simplistic manner, in a A then B explicatory schema: If Africa puts its house in order, the continent's 'traditional' partners will fund its development. It is as if authors of NEPAD have turned the history of Africa's relations with the West on its head. It is as if contemporary globalization – particularly in the trade practices of the North in relation to the South – has no abiding hard lessons to teach Africa's political leaders.

How can African states effectively respond to erosion of sovereignty? How can they react, individually and collectively, to the lost of control over their decision-making power? Is there any credible alternative to the continent's marginalization and states' vanishing sovereignty? I argue that, to fully address "new globalization" challenges to state sovereignty, it is imperative that African states abandon an antiquated form and meaning of sovereignty – with no practical relevance – and fully embrace and commit themselves to a pooled sovereignty, which takes the region as a unit of analysis and operation. A pooled sovereignty is not a mere juxtaposition of individual sovereignties – largely in existence in any event. It is about moving the center of decision where both individual states and the region as a whole can better achieve growth, development, peace and stability. It requires a voluntary surrender of substantial degrees of sovereignty. This imperative is shared by Ihonvbere (2001, p. 17):

> In Europe, nation states have demonstrated some desire and resolve to give up a degree of sovereignty in order to enjoy the benefits of regionalism. It is amazing that African governments that willingly (or unwillingly) accepted economic, and later political conditionalities which were openly designed and supervised by foreign interests still spend much time protecting claims to absolute sovereignty. The truth is that with the embarrassing record of most African governments, they have practically no legitimate ground on which to exercise sovereign rule over their peoples.

If African states fail to exploit the current global momentum towards regionalism, the region's marginal location and role in the global order might just become permanent.[10] As Ihonvbere (2001, p. 18) writes:

> In the new globalization, with the rapid integration of information networks and the unprecedented improvements in communication, traditional notions of sovereignty, beyond its legal articulation to capture the sanctity of recognized boundaries, will mean very little. Africa must realize that only through the collective mobilization of resources, planning, design of viable and interconnected future, can the small, weak, distorted, and marginalized economies survive the ongoing competition in the global system.

But, so far, African states have largely responded to the "new globalization" by a corresponding "new regionalism", which promotes primarily the pursuit of a globalist and neo-liberal agenda at the regional level. To the new regionalism, which saw a substantial increase in the regionally based institutionalized co-operation among states during the 1990s (Hettne, Inotai, and Sunkel, 1999), African states must now

---

10 Many of the contemporary debate centers on the intriguing relationship between globalization and regionalism. There are many perceptions of, and opinions about both of these processes and how they relate to each other. There are no clear-cut answers as to what extent they mutually support and reinforce each other. According to deMelo and Panagariya and Fawcett and Hurrell, the relationship tends to be symbiotic rather than contradictory. While others emphasize a dialectic rather than a linear relationship among the processes of regionalism and globalization. See Hurrell, "Regionalism in World Politics: Regional Organization and International Order", in Fawcett and Hurrell, (eds), *Regionalism in Theoretical Perspective*, Oxford: Oxford University Press, 1995.

respond with what I call autonomous regionalism. Autonomous regionalism is not an autarchic project. It does not mean retreat behind protectionist walls or the utopia of Westphalian sovereignty. Autonomous regionalism seeks openness to the world and integration into the "global". But to fully benefit from the world, African states must learn from their individual and collective history and come together in formulating a development vision which takes into account their individual and collective interests first. Only then African countries might regain some control over their destiny. They might not be able to change reality, but they will create the conditions, within the constraints of the reality imposed upon them by the forces of globalization, to seek the best possible outcome and, over time, stand on their own. Autonomous regionalism is not an ideological project either. To the globalization challenges on state sovereignty, it suggests a pragmatic approach of decision-making guided by a power allocation analysis as analytic tool. It rests on the conviction that the final measure of sovereignty is the satisfaction of the people needs and the promotion of common good (Franck, 1992; Schermers, 2002).

Professor Jackson (2003) has outlined the key components of a power allocation analysis, which contributes to the emergence of what he calls "sovereignty-modern", an analytic and dynamic process of disaggregation and redefinition than a "frozen-in-time" concept or technique. Jackson suggests that a "sovereignty-modern" power allocation analysis takes into consideration the following values or policy objectives in deciding about the appropriate level or other (horizontal) distribution of power within a landscape of governmental and nongovernmental institutions. Among the reasons for preferring governmental action at the international (regional) level are coordination benefits and factor mobility. The former deals with situations in which, if governments each act in their own interest without coordination, the result will be damaging to everyone; whereas the latter refers to situations where governments find it difficult to regulate in an effective way (personal migration). The need for allocating power up the ladder is also justified with regard to some subject areas such as the environment or, more generally, issues pertaining to the protection of global commons. A power allocation down the ladder takes into consideration the values and policy objectives of subsidiarity and accountability. Some other policy goals and values seem to support the allocation of power either way. Among these is the substance of an issue. For example, national leaders will use the international level to pursue a policy that they feel is important to implement at their own level but is difficult to do because of the structure of their national constitution or political landscape. Values related to the misuse of power and policy goal that promotes "rule orientation" can also justified placing the level of decision or action either down or up the ladder. A power allocation analysis doesn't disregard sovereignty as a fundamental principle of international relations. Rather, it seeks to "disaggregate and to analyze: break down the complex array of "sovereignty" concepts and examine particular aspects in detail and with precision to understand what is actually at play" (Jackson, 2003, p. 801).

In the quest for autonomous regionalism, a power allocation analysis, with its pragmatic approach to sovereignty, could help African states focus on the real sovereignty challenges posed by the "new globalization" and not on the perpetuation of a mythical understanding of sovereignty which has, so far, impaired their ability to respond to those challenges in an effective and coherent way. The example of the Southern African Development Community (SADC) seems to suggest possible alternatives to marginalization. It indicates that, despite unprecedented pressures toward homogenization, a collective response to the forces of globalization, based on a common formulation of individual and collective interests within a regional framework, is possible. A certain level of independent decision-making power can be achieved or maintained when countries define they common interest and act upon it. Although limited, SADC's experience has lessons to offer other African countries and deserves further developments.[11]

To comprehend the relative success of SADC in formulating a regional response to globalization, it is important to understand the integration dynamic within the region's particular history of white-minority rule and apartheid. Just before the independence of Zimbabwe (April 1980), the Frontline states (Angola, Botswana, Mozambique, Tanzania, Zambia) established the Southern African Development Coordination Conference, a regional economic group, which would later become SADC. All majority-ruled countries were invited to join the organization, even those (e.g. Lesotho and Swaziland) who were too vulnerable politically and economically to criticize apartheid. The original idea was to offer a regional response and an economic alternative for those economies dependent on South Africa. Although Namibia, still ruled by South Africa, and the latter itself were excluded, delegations from South Africa and Namibia's liberation movements were invited to attend the meeting of the organization. An African National Congress (ANC) document stresses this regional solidarity:

> The region sustained us during our struggle and, with our own, its people's blood was spilled to end apartheid. Our destiny is intertwined with the region's; our people belong to each other…We are convinced that the long-term interests of South Africa economy will best be served by an approach to regional cooperation and integration which seeks to promote balanced growth and development.[12]

This history of common struggle is one of the factors which explain SADC countries' approach to regionalism. According to Thompson (2000), because of their history, sovereignty has long been viewed in a regional context, with, for example, every head of state stating that their own national security is inseparable from regional security. It is worth repeating too that such statements were not mere rhetoric, but were accompanied by economic, military and political support at high costs in terms of loss of life and delayed economic growth. Another factor is the ideological affinity of leaders in the region. From Namibia, Zimbabwe, Mozambique to South Africa, leaders who stood up and fought the forces of apartheid – actively supported by the West (USA, UK, Germany) as a bastion against 'communism' – were often, by necessity, of a socialist or leftist inspiration. Even though they have now converted

11 The remaining of the section largely draws on the excellent article of C. Thompson, Regional Challenges to Globalization: Perspectives from Southern Africa. *New Political Economy,* 5, 2000, pp. 41–57.

12 African National Congress, "New Foreign Policy for South Africa", mimeo (October 1993), pp. 9–10.

to free market economy, this ideological affinity is certainly instrumental in the way they approach their respective countries and the region's problems. A third factor, which sets apart SADC from other regional organizations in Africa, is the relative prosperity, state capacity and commitment of South Africa, the dominant country in the region and the driving force, in the quest for regional autonomy.

SADC's regionalism underlines a number of core concepts and principles. It is a multifaceted approach, which encompasses both political and economic dimensions. It also emphasizes the concept of "development integration" which highlights a more holistic vision of cooperation that goes beyond trade and economic growth and seeks to "enhance the quality of life... and support the socially disadvantaged through regional integration".[13] Another SADC's key concept is the rejection of integration by stages and the formulation of priorities by sectors important to the region, not to global transactions (Thompson, 2000). These historical, ideological and conceptual frameworks help understand SADC's attempts to cope with the forces of globalization and preserve some autonomous decision-making power, as we shall see in areas related to state agency and privatization, and regional environmental security.

Contrary to the dominant neo-liberal thinking advocated by the forces of globalization which seeks to remove the state as an important economic actor, SADC has promoted projects which retain state ownership, while encouraging private investment in the enterprise, rather than the reverse of state subsidizing corporations ('incentives'). This policy choice stems from the overall consensus, among SADC members, that "the market can be efficient, but it is not a planner, while governments, individually and collectively, can select and choose" (Thompson, 2000). The SADC's view on state role is more balanced than what is being promoted by then neo-liberal agenda, as expressed by Trevor Manuel (2004, p. 6), South Africa's Minister of Finance, " I do not subscribe to the idea that either the institution of the state or the institution of the market can or should do everything in economic development. There are simply too many examples of failures of systems of paternalistic states and uncontrolled markets for me to accept either as one-size-fits-all model for development". SADC's members have affirmed the centrality of the state in promoting and guiding regional integration.

The successful attraction of investment to the state-run Beira Corridor of port, rail, road and oil pipeline development for landlocked neighbors offers a clear illustration of SADC's innovative approach in maintaining state agency. In 1997, SADC members signed the Beira Development Corridor to encourage business to build along the road-rail line for easy access to the port of Beira in Mozambique. Although the development of the Beira Corridor attracted private investments, SADC countries successfully resisted pressures to surrender its control to private corporations. A number of key projects have been developed along the Corridor (the Beira Iron Project, the Zimbabwean citrus industry) which has also retained state ownership.[14] In contrast to the Beira Corridor, SADC members have adopted

13 Southern African Development Community, "Objectives" in "Declaration and Treaty", revised 17 August 1992, Windhoek, Namibia.

14 Beira Corridor Group, "Committed from the Top", *BCG Bulletin*, No. 52 (January 1997), pp. 7; 103; and "Building on Beira", *BCG Bulletin*, No. 51 (September 1996), pp. 1–4.

a different approach with the Maputo Corridor, which comprises road and railways from South Africa's Gauteng Province to the Mozambican port of Maputo. This project was mainly financed by the private sector. Governments are the lesser partners. These two cases show that SADC countries are less than enthusiastic about neoliberal demands for unregulated privatization and are developing a more pragmatic response to the forces of globalization.

The overall reluctance to privatize in the region is grounded on the commonly shared idea that it amounts to "selling off the family silver".[15] Since very few Mozambicans, Tanzanians or Zambians can afford to buy privatized companies, resistance has been building up, which has forced governments to seek alternatives or develop regional strategies. One such example is the decision of the Mozambican government to convert the national railways from a government authority into a public company, with the government as the sole shareholder, as a response to IMF/World Bank demands without surrendering state control of this transportation network of strategic importance to five landlocked SADC countries. It is fair to say, however, that resistance to neoliberal agenda under cover of Structural Adjustment Program (SAP) conditionalities has not always been successful. As a matter of fact, hundred of industries and companies have been privatized with overall negative results:

> Our experience of foreign investment in Africa is that it is minuscule in scale, concentrated in the extractive sectors, and ...it has many negative economic and environmental effects. The purported necessity to attract foreign investment is utilized by financial institutions and foreign governments as an instrument to impose their policies upon our governments.[16]

Another area where SADC states are resisting IMF and the World Bank's neo-liberal dictates has to do with selective protection and subsidies to help the most vulnerable. Despite pressure from those institutions, Zimbabwe and Malawi maintained, for years, free distribution of seed packets to small farmers in drought areas. Targeted for privatization under SAPs, Zimbabwe insisted in separating the commercial accounts of its state-owned Grain Marketing Board (GMB) from its social welfare accounts of storage and provision of grain during droughts. GMB has aided remote areas of Zimbabwe and other SADC countries during droughts. In contrast to Zimbabwe, Tanzania, Zambia and Mozambique abolished their state marketing boards under SAP conditionality. This abolition has resulted into a disruption of supply in remote areas in need, "for those remote areas are unprofitable for private transporters" (Thompson, 2000, p. 47). This experience has led SADC to formulate a regional response to grain reserves. Despite pressure to do so from the forces of globalization, SADC continues to refuse to enter the global grain market on a country-to-country

15 The expression was used by the ANC in 1989, when the apartheid government sold Iscor, the state steel corporation. This decision was largely regarded as selling to apartheid friends before a majority-ruled government.

16 United National Commission on Trade and Development (UNCTAD), "The market doesn't replace the need for development cooperation", NGO Declaration, IX International Meeting of UNCTAD, Midrand, South Africa, April 1996, p. 2.

basis. The same regional resistance to state disengagement can also be seen in the provision of primary education and primary health care, which had experienced a decline after imposition of fees under SAP conditionalities in the 1980s and 1990s.

Regional environmental security is another area where SADC's "development integration" and its pragmatic approach to sovereignty are being developed as a response to globalization's challenges. The regional sharing and protection of water resources is the top environmental priority for SADC countries. South Africa, for example, is dependent on other countries for its water supply. There are 13 international river basins, with 70 per cent of the regional surface water shared by two or more countries. This vital and strategic commodity is increasingly dealt with at the regional level as a common good. SADC has pursued an integrated water strategy, which has allowed its members to better respond to globalization's pressures on water resources – large-scale farms, increased irrigation for cash crops, industrialization, water pricing, and calls for privatization (Thompson, 2000, 51). Only by pooling their sovereignty in order to address, as a collectivity, issues surrounding water resources, that SADC countries have been able to develop an autonomous response to globalization forces, based on the organization's concept of "development integration" whose ultimate test is "to enhance the quality of life and support the socially disadvantaged". As stressed by Swatuk (1996, p. 31),

> What is needed… is an approach to River basin Management that does not in every case privilege the arguments of science and business… To ignore the needs of rural people in the hope of generating power for export or to increase irrigation crops is to sacrifice long-term ecological sustainability and human security for short-term, debt-driven gains.

The case of water resources management in SADC shows the road forward for a pragmatic and meaningful understanding of sovereignty in Africa.

Conclusion

The aim of this chapter was to discuss the "new globalization's" challenges to state sovereignty in Africa. To that end, I first presented a broad theoretical and conceptual framework of sovereignty and globalization, with a particular focus on works that address the dynamics between the two concepts. While the latter is relatively easy to grasp, the former is more complex and has several dimensions which mean different things to different peoples. From its Westphalian conception, sovereignty has undergone a conceptual mutation over time. While many agree that the new globalization poses tremendous and unprecedented challenges to state sovereignty, there is more disagreement as to the outcome of theses challenges and the future of state sovereignty. While some have argued the "end of sovereignty" and the "powerless of states", others have stressed sovereignty's resilience and don't see any qualitative change to current global processes. While some have addressed globalization processes in a liberal and ahistorical approach, others have proposed a historical and dialectic analysis which is of particular relevance for post-colonial states.

It is within the parameters of these theoretical and conceptual uncertainties and controversies that I have addressed, in the second part of the study, globalization's challenges to state sovereignty in Africa. An analysis of the post-colonial state in Africa shows that the forces of globalization are putting tremendous pressure on an actor which , by virtue of its historical conception and post-colonial trajectory, lacks, in most cases, state capacity and whose sovereignty remains, so far, essentially formal. The dominant neoliberal economic agenda executed through IMF's conditionalities, privatization and foreign investment penetration, has seriously eroded the ability of most African states to pursue an internally conceived, executed and directed development project. Given most African states' structural weaknesses and impediments, their already limited ability to make their own decisions has been seriously constrained under conditions of the "new globalization".

In the final and prospective part of the study, I have argued in favor of a pooled sovereignty as the only credible alternative to Africa's globalization predicament. I have laid down a rationale in two points. First, in pursuing a pooled sovereignty, African states must seek to establish an autonomous regionalism whose interests and goals are African centered. Second, in the definition and formulation of these common interests, which determine the extent of sovereignty surrender, African countries must be guided by a high degree of pragmatism – rather than ideology – based on a rigorous power allocation analysis. The example of SADC indicates that it is possible, using the region as a unit of analysis, to retain relative autonomous decision-making power in the face of globalization forces. The challenge for African countries is to either hang on an antiquated and largely mythical version of sovereignty – which they never enjoyed anyway – or rise above current challenges to reinvent sovereignty and craft their own destiny. Current global processes will lead either to Africa's further marginalization or to its revival. Within the limits of the reality imposed upon them, it is up to African states to resolutely choose the latter.

References

Akindele, S.T., Gidado, T.O., and Olaopo, O.R. (2002), "Globalization, Its Implications and Consequences for Africa", *Globalization*, Vol. 2. Issue 1, pp. 1–17.

Amuwo, K. (2001), "Globalization, NEPAD and the Governance Question in Africa", *African Studies Quarterly*, Vol. 6. No. 3, pp. 11–18.

Ashley, R. (1984), "The Poverty of Neo-realism", *International Organization*, Vol. 38. No. 2, pp. 225–286.

Bayart, J.F. et al. (1999), *The Criminalization of the State in Africa*, (Bloomington: Indiana University Press).

Beliaev, M. (2003), "Democracy and Globalization: Sources of Discontent", *Globalization*, Vol. 3, Issue 1, pp.1–12.

Blau, P.M. (1963), "Critical Remarks on Weber's Theory of Authority", *American Political Science Review*, Vol. 57. No. 2, pp. 305–316.

Bull, H. and Watson (eds) (1982), *The Expansion of International Society* (Oxford: Clarendon Press).

Camilleri, J.A. and Falk, J. (1992), *The End of Sovereignty? The Politics of a Shrinking and Fragmenting World* (Aldershot, UK: Edward Elgar).

Carmody, P. (2002), "Between Globalization and (Post) Apartheid: The Political Economy of Restructuring in South Africa", *Journal of Southern African Studies*. Vol. 28. No. 2, pp. 255–275.

Cerny, P.G. (1999), "Globalization and the Erosion of Democracy", *European Journal of Political Research*, Vol. 36. No. 1, pp. 1–26.

Chopra, J. and Thomas, G. W. (1992), "Sovereignty Is No Longer Sacrosanct: Codifying Humanitarian Intervention", *Ethics and International Affairs*, Vol. 6, No.1, pp. 95–117

Claphan, C. (1996), *Africa and the International System: The Politics of State Survival*, (Cambridge: Cambridge University Press).

Cogburn, D.L. (1998), "Globalization and State Autonomy in the Information Age: Telecommunications Sector Restructuring in South Africa", *Journal of International Affairs*. Vol. 51. No. 2, pp. 583–604.

Cooper, F. (2001), "What is the Concept of Globalization Good for? An African Historian Perspective", *African Affairs*, Vol. 100, No. 399, pp. 189–213.

Cooper, R. (1972), "Economic Independence and Foreign Policy in the Seventies", *World Politics*, Vol. No. 24, pp. 159–181.

Cornwell, R. (1999), "The End of the Post-Colonial State System in Africa?" *African Security Review*, Vol. 8, No. 2 <http://www.issafrica.org>

Devetak, R. and Higgott, R. (1999), "Justice Unbound? Globalization, States and the Transformation of the Social Bond", *International Affairs*, Vol. 75, No. 3, pp. 483–498.

Drezner, D.W. (2001), "Sovereignty for Sale", *Foreign Policy*, No. 126, pp. 76–77.

Englebert, P. (2000), *State Legitimacy and Development in Africa* (Boulder: Lynne Rienner).

Evans, P.B. (1997), "The Eclipse of the State: Reflections on Stateness in an Era of Globalization", *World Politics*, Vol. 50, No. 1, pp. 62–87.

Fowler, M.R. and Bunck, J.M. (1995), *Law, Power and State Sovereignty* (University Park, PA: Pennsylvania State University Press).

Geng, F. (1993), *Protecting the Dispossessed* (Washington, DC: Brookings Institution).

Gerhart, G. (2001), "Africa", *Foreign Affairs*, Vol. 80. No. 6, pp. 193–195.

Giddens, A. (1985), *The Nation-State and Violence*, (Berkley, CA: University of California Press).

Helman, B. and Ratner, S. (1993), "Saving Failed States", *Foreign Policy*, No. 89, pp. 3–20.

Herman, E.S. (1999), "The Threat of Globalization", *New Politics*, Vol. 7, No. 2, pp. 26–40.

Hettne, B., Inotai A. and Sunkel, O. (1994), *The New Regionalism: Implications for Global Development and International Security*, (Helsinki: UNU/WIDER), pp. 75–94.

Hettne, B. (1997), "Development, Security and World Order: A Regional Approach", in Kay, C. (ed.), *Globalization, Competitiveness and Human Security*, (London: Frank Cass).

Hinsley, F.H. (1986), *Sovereignty* (Cambridge: Cambridge University Press).

Hurrell, A. and Woods, N. (1995), "Globalization and Inequality", *Millennium: Journal of International Studies*, Vol. 24. No. 2, pp. 447–470.

Ihonvbere, J.O. (2001), *Survival in Contemporary Africa*, Paper Presented at the Symposium on the Challenges of Closer Global Integration. Online at <www.india-seminar.com>.

Ihonvbere, J.O. (1994), "The 'Irrelevant' State, Ethnicity and the Quest for Nationhood in Africa", *Ethnic and Racial Studies*, Vol. 17. No. 1, pp. 42–60.

Imade, L.O. (2003), "The Two Faces of Globalization: Impoverishment or Prosperity?", *Globalization*, Vol. 3. Issue 1, pp. 1–28.

Jackson, J.H. (2003), "Sovereignty-Modern: A New Approach to an Outdated Concept", *The American Journal of International Law*, Vol. 97. No. 4, pp. 782–802.

Jackson, R. (1990), *Quasi-States: Sovereignty, International Relations and the Third World* (Cambridge: Cambridge University Press).

Jackson, R. and Rosberg, C. (1982), "Why Africa's Weak States Persist: The Empirical and the Juridical in Statehood, *World Politics*. Vol. 35. No. 1, pp. 1–24.

Kaiser, K. (1972), "Transnational Relations as a Threat to the Democratic Process", in R. Keohane and J. Nye (eds), *Transnational Relations* (Cambridge, MA: Harvard University Press).

Kelvi, H. (1996), *The State, War and The State of War* (Cambridge: Cambridge University Press).

Keohane, R. and Nye, J. (eds) (1972), *Transnational Relations* (Cambridge, MA: Harvard University Press).

Keohane, R. (1984), *After Hegemony: Cooperation and Discord in the World Political Economy* (Princeton: Princeton University Press).

Kofi, A. (1999), "Two Concepts of Sovereignty", *The Economist*. No. 352, pp. 49–50.

Krasner, S. (1999), *Sovereignty: Organized Hypocrisy* (Princeton, NJ: Princeton University Press).

Krasner, S. (2001), "Abiding Sovereignty", *International Political Science Review*, Vol. 22. No. 3, pp. 229–251.

Kura, S.Y. (2005), "Globalization and Democracy: A Dialectical Framework for Understanding Democratization in Nigeria", *Globalization*, Vol. 5. Issue 1, pp. 1–18.

Lumumba-Kasongo, T. (2002), "Reconceptualizing the State as the Leading Agent of Development in the Context of Globalization in Africa", *African Journal of Political Science*, Vol. 7. No. 1, pp. 79–108.

Maiti, P. (2001), "Humpty Dumpty Had a Great Fall: Would Globalization Impact on States' Dissolution?", *Globalization*, Vol. 1. Issue 1, pp. 1–10

Manboah-Rockson, J. (2000), "Regionalism and Integration in Sub-Saharan Africa: A Review of Experiences, Issues and Realities at the Close of the Twentieth Century", *Innovations: A Journal of Politics*, Vol. 3. No. 1, pp. 47–68.

Manuel, T.A. (2004), *Globalization and Africa*, Inaugural Global Economic Governance Lecture, Oxford University, 8 March. Online at <www.southecentre.org>.

Mazrui, A. (2001), "From Slave Ship to Space Ship: Africa between Marginalization and Globalization", *African Studies Quarterly*, Vol.3, No.4. Online at <www.web.africa.ufl.edu>.

Miller, J. (1984), "The Sovereign State and Its Future", *International Journal*, No. 39, pp. 284–301.

Miller, J. (1986), "Sovereignty as a Source of Vitality for the State", *Review of International Studies*, Vol. 12. No. 2, pp. 79–89.

Morse, E. (1976), *Modernization and the Transformation of International Relations*, (New York: Free Press).

Munck, R. (2002), "Globalization and Democracy: A New 'Great Transformation'?" *Annals of the American Academy of Political and Social Science*, Vol. 581. No. 1, pp. 10–21.

Nkiwane, T.C. (2001), "Africa and International Relations: Regional Lessons for a Global Discourse", *International Political Science Review*, Vol. 22. No. 3, pp. 279–290.

Nsibambi, A. (2001), *The Effects of Globalization on the State in Africa: Harnessing the Benefits and Minimizing the Costs*. Paper presented at the UN General Assembly's Panel Discussion on Globalization and the State, 2 November, 2001.

O'Donnell, P.S. (2004), "Sovereignty Past and Present", *Globalization,* Vol. 4. Issue 1, pp. 1–9.

Ohiorhenuan, J.F. (1998), "The South in an Era of Globalization", *Cooperation South Journal*, Vol. 9. No. 2, pp. 6–15.

Ojo, B.A. (2004), "Africa's Triple Dilemma: The State, Democratization and the Challenges of Globalization", *Globalization*, Vol. 4. No. 2, pp. 1–14.

Onuf, N. and Klink, F. (1989), "Anarchy, Authority, Rule", *International Studies Quarterly*, Vol. 33. No. 2, pp. 149–173.

Ottaway, M. (1999). "Africa". Foreign Policy, No. 114, pp. 13–25.

Ouattara, A.D. *The Challenges of Globalization for Africa*. Address at the Southern Africa Economic Summit, Harare, May 21, 1997. Online at <www.imf.org>.

Petras, J. and Veltmeyer, H. (2001), *Globalization Unmasked – Imperialism in the 21st Century* (New Delhi, India: Madhyam Books).

Ramsaram, D. and Prive, D.V. (2003), "Globalization: A Critical Framework for Understanding Contemporary Social Processes", *Globalization*, Vol. 3. No. 2, pp. 1–21.

Rosecrance, R. (1986), *The Rise of the Trading State*, (New York: Basic Books).

Rubin, B. (1993), "US Foreign Policy and Rogue States", *Middle East Review of International Affairs*, Vol. 3. No.3.<http://meria.it.ac.il>.

Ruggie, J.G. (1998), "What Makes the World Hang Together? Neo-utilitarianism and the Social Constructivist", *International Organization*, Vol. 52. No. 4, pp. 855–885.

Rugumaru, S. (2001), *Globalization and Africa's Future: Towards Structural Stability, Integration and Sustainable Development*, (Harare: African Association of Political Science, Occasional Paper Series).

Ryan, C. (1997), "Sovereignty, Intervention, and the Law: A Tenuous Relationship of Competing Principles", *Millennium: Journal of International Studies*, Vol. 26. No. 1, p. 77–100.

Schermers, H. (2002), "Different Aspects of Sovereignty", in G. Kreijen et al. (eds). *State, Sovereignty, and International Governance* (Oxford: Oxford University Press).

Scholte, J.A. (1997), "Global Capitalism and the State", *International Affairs*, Vol. 73. No. 3, pp. 427–452.

Schrijver, N. (2000), "The Changing Nature of State Sovereignty", *The British Yearbook of International Law 1999* (Oxford: Clarendon Press).

Skocpol, T. (1979), *States and Social Revolutions: A Comparative Analysis of France, Russia and China* (Cambridge: Cambridge University Press).

Strang, D. (1991a), "Anomaly and Commonplace in European Political Expansion: Realist and Institutional Accounts", *International Organization*, Vol. 45. No. 2, pp. 143–162.

Strang, D. (1991b), "Global Patterns of Decolonization, 1500–1987", *International Studies Quarterly*, Vol. 35. No. 4, pp. 429–454.

Swatuk, L. (1996), "Power and Water: The Coming Order in Southern Africa", *Southern African Perspectives*, No. 58 (Cape Town, South Africa: Center for South African Studies).

Tandon, Y. (1998), "Globalization and Africa Options", *AAPS Newsletter*, Vol. 3. No. 1.

Thomson, J. and Krasner, S. (1989), "Global Transaction and the Consolidation of Sovereignty", in E. Czempiel and J. Rosenau (eds), *Global Changes and Theoretical Challenges: Approaches to World Politics for the 1990s* (Lexington, MA: Lexington Books).

Thomson, J.E. (1995), "State Sovereignty in International Relations: Bridging the Gap between Theory and Empirical Research", *International Studies Quarterly*, Vol. 39. No. 2, pp. 213–233.

Thompson, C.B. (2000), "Regional Challenges to Globalization: Perspectives from Southern Africa", *New Political Economy*, Vol.5. Issue 1, pp. 41–57.

Tilly, C. (ed.) (1975), *The Formation of National States in Western Europe* (Princeton, NJ: Princeton University Press).

Vayrynen, R. (2001), "Sovereignty, Globalization and Transnational Social Movements", *International Relations of the Asia-Pacific*,Vol. 1. No. 2, pp. 227–246.

Walker, R. (1988), *State Sovereignty, Global Civilization, and the Rearticulation of Political Space*, World Order Studies Program Occasional Paper. No. 18. (Princeton, NJ: Princeton University Center for International Studies).

Waltz, K. (1970), "The Myth of National Interdependence", in C. Kindleberger (ed.), *The International Corporation* (Cambridge, MA: MIT Press), pp. 205–223.

Waltz Weber and Biersteker, K. (1979), *Theory of International Politics* (Reading, MA: Addison-Wesley).

Weber, C. and Biersteker, T.J. (1996), "Reconstructing the Analysis of Sovereignty: Concluding Reflections and Directions for Future Research", in C. Weber and T. J.Biersteker (eds.) (1996), *State Sovereignty as Social Construct* (New York: Cambridge University Press).

Webber, M. (1964), *The Theory of Social and Economic Organization* (New York: Free Press.

Weiss, L. (1997), "Globalization and the Myth of the Powerless State", *New Left Review*, Vol. 1. No. 225, pp. 3–27.

Wendt, A. and Barnett, M. (1993), Dependent State Formation and Third World Militarization, *Review of International Studies*, Vol. 19. No. 4, pp. 321–347.

Young, C. (1994), *African Colonial State in Comparative Perspective* (New Haven: Yale University Press).

Zartman, I.W. (ed.) (1995), *Collapsed States*: The Disintegration and Restoration of Legitimate Authority, (Boulder: Lynne Rienner).

Chapter 7

The Environment and the New Globalization in Africa

John Mukum Mbaku

Introduction

As the first decade of the new millennium continues to unfold, Africa and Africans continue to face many serious problems. Among these are extremely high levels of poverty and deprivation, especially among rural communities; the absence of governance structures that adequately constrain the exercise of government agency and the ability of politicians and civil servants to engage in such opportunistic behaviors as corruption and rent seeking; the existence of resource allocation systems that stunt indigenous entrepreneurship and the creation of the wealth that Africans need to confront massive and pervasive poverty; and excessive exploitation of the continent's environmental resources and, agro-ecological degradation. Recent events in the Niger Delta region of Nigeria have forced the world to take a serious look at ecological degradation and its consequences on the African peoples.

However, it is important to emphasize that overexploitation of natural resources and environmental degradation – especially for the production of goods for export to the industrial market economies – is a continent-wide problem. As will be made evident in this chapter, the present patterns for the exploitation of Africa's natural resources and damage to its environment were set during the colonial period. First, we shall examine how patterns of resource exploitation that were established by European mercantile companies, with the help of the colonial state apparatus, have remained to this day. Second, we shall show that the overexploitation of the continent's environmental resources, primarily for the benefit of the metropolitan economies, has resulted in significant damage to Africa's environment. Increased globalization, which has been going on since the partition of the continent in the late 19th century, has produced trade patterns that have continued to impose severe damage on Africa's already fragile ecosystem. Third, we argue that poorly defined and unenforceable property rights in environmental resources – a consequence of the continent's inability to provide itself with locally-focused, relevant, and viable institutional arrangements – have been the main determinant of overexploitation and abuse, all of which have contributed not only to increased poverty in the continent, but have significantly endangered sustainability in the allocation of natural resources. Finally, we shall examine ways to help African countries improve the allocation of their natural resources, minimize damage to the ecosystem, and enhance their ability to participate in the new, post-Cold War global economy.

Colonialism and the Degradation of Africa's Environment

European partition of Africa and the subsequent establishment of colonies in the region had a significant impact on the development and exploitation of the continent's environmental resources. Colonialism was part of a global movement that brought Western institutions, particularly forms of resource allocation, to Africa and paved the way for the Europeans to exploit Africans and their resources for the benefit of the metropolitan economies. Despite the fact that most African countries have been independent for more than forty years, the patterns of resource exploitation established during colonialism remain in place and continue to govern national economies. Forces of the "new globalization" have reinforced these anachronistic economic governance structures, leading to the continued exploitation of the continent's environmental resources for the benefit of the developed economies. The result has been the further impoverishment of the African peoples and their relegation to the periphery of the global economy.

In the nineteenth century, Europeans forcefully annexed African lands and established colonies out of them. Usually, after some form of political administration was established in each colony, an effort was made to exploit the resources of the captured territories and provide raw materials for the industries of the metropolitan economies. However, at this time, most of the European countries that had colonies in Africa were either unwilling or unable to invest public funds in the exploitation of the resources of the colonies. Consequently, these governments turned to their private sectors for the human and physical capital necessary to bring the enormous colonial resources under control. The private sector was reluctant to commit to such risky ventures and as a consequence was not willing to provide the required capital. In order to make each colony an attractive investment opportunity for metropolitan entrepreneurs and enhance the ability of the latter to operate profitably in Africa, resident colonial officials were directed to offer prospective investors exclusive or *monopoly rights* to exploit, develop and market the resources of the new "possessions" (see, e.g., Rudin, 1938; Burns, 1963).

After the Berlin Conference of 1885 formally recognized British claims in the Niger Delta, it was determined that "the Government was not yet prepared to provide the costly administration that would be necessary if these immense areas were to be brought under control" (Burns, 1963, p. 158). The government subsequently adopted a strategy that called for the offer of *exclusive monopoly rights* to English entrepreneurs to "develop" the resources of the recently captured territories. The colonial government in what would later become the colony of Nigeria created monopolies out of the territories of the Niger Delta and assigned the rights to English mercantile firms. On July 10, 1886, the National African Company Limited (which later changed its name to the Royal Niger Company) was granted a Royal Charter to exploit and develop the resources of its concession for the benefit of the British economy. The colonies were expected to serve two important economic functions: (1) provide necessary raw materials for metropolitan industries; and (2) function as a receptacle for excess production from English factories.

Part of the conditions for offering the Royal Niger Company exclusive rights to such enormous territories was that the company would provide both the human and physical capital that was needed to effectively exploit and export to England, the resources of the concession. In creating each concession, the colonial government did not engage in voluntary and mutually beneficial exchanges with African land owners. Instead, the process involved the confiscation, usually through force, of African lands and the subsequent establishment of private property rights regimes that were then assigned to English mercantile companies. Through this process, land that was owned communally by African ethnic groups was captured and all the rights in it transferred to European entrepreneurs. Such a process introduced the exploitation of the continent's environmental resources for the benefit of the metropolitan economies that remains in effect today.

Throughout colonial Africa, Europeans used force to displace indigenous (i.e., African) peoples and occupy their lands. In the Cameroon River district, German planters forced out the Bakweri people from the lands enriched by the volcanic ashes from the Cameroon Mountain, and turned the captured properties into plantations that produced several types of crops for export to Germany. Many of the Bakweri, now unable to engage in their traditional pursuits – hunting and gathering – were forced to seek wage employment, becoming an important and critical source of cheap labor for German economic activities (see Rudin, 1938).

In each colony, the dominant method for the production of export crops (e.g., rubber, palm oil and kernel, cocoa, bananas, and coffee) determined the extent to which the property rights of indigenous groups in land were abrogated. In the African colonies with significantly large populations of European colonists or settlers (e.g., the four colonies that in 1910 became South Africa, the Rhodesias, Algeria, Angola, Mozambique, Kenya, and Namibia), most of the cash or export crops were produced on large plantations owned and managed by Europeans. In these colonies, most of the fertile and cultivable land was seized and reserved for Europeans. Since production on these plantations was labor intensive, the colonial government designed and implemented policies that enhanced the ability of plantation owners to obtain the labor they needed for their economic activities. Accordingly, land confiscation was undertaken partly to create landlessness in Africans, and discourage them from engaging in their traditional occupations in favor of wage labor on European plantations. In addition, the colonial authorities also imposed poll taxes (in some areas of the continent, so-called "hut" taxes were used) on Africans that could only be paid with European-sanctioned currency. Since the latter could only legally be obtained by engaging in occupations of a European nature (i.e., wage labor), many Africans were forced to hire themselves out to the settlers in order to obtain the currency needed to pay the taxes (see, e.g., Fredrickson, 1981; Rudin, 1938).

European attitudes towards African property rights in environmental resources at this time were appropriately expressed by then French Governor of Algeria General Bugeaud, when he declared in 1841 that "[w]henever the water supply is good and the land fertile, there we must place colonists without worrying about previous owners. We must distribute the lands [with] full title to the colonists" (Brace, 1964, p. 48). Of course, such an approach to the assignment of property rights was not unique to the French. All of the colonial governments in the continent used force to secure ownership of territories and their resources. The distinguished British colonial officer in Southern Africa, Earl Grey, expressed the feelings of most English settlers in the region towards the indigenous peoples and their resources, when he declared that whenever and wherever there arose a conflict between Africans and the colonists, especially in the allocation of environmental resources, the interests of the indigenous peoples should be ignored and that "facilities should be afforded the white colonist for obtaining the possession of land theretofore occupied by the Native tribes" (Magubane, 1979, p. 71). Throughout the continent, especially in areas that were considered to have significant potential for European entrepreneurial activities, settlers had similar sentiments. Usually, indigenous groups were uprooted from their ancestral lands, placed in special reservations created by the colonial government, and the unoccupied land reassigned to Europeans. Since most of the so-called "native reserves" were usually not economically viable, they became labor reservoirs for European economic activities. In fact, in Southern Africa, many of the reservations were located strategically close to either European farms or industrial centers. Colonial policies were designed to enhance the confiscation of African property rights in environmental resources and reassign them to Europeans, allowing the latter to exploit and "develop" these properties for the benefit of the metropolitan economies, as well as that of the Europeans resident in the colonies (see, e.g., Magubane, 1979; Fredrickson, 1981; Hutt, 1964; Mbaku, 1993, 1991).

During the colonial period, then, the allocation of Africa's environmental resources was controlled and monopolized by European entrepreneurs with the help of the resident colonial state. Two major types of property rights regimes could be recognized: (1) communal property (that is, tribal or ethnic lands); and (2) private property (Of course, the colonial state owned property. However, such ownership did not involve the massive exploitation of environmental resources). Most European property in the colonies was regulated by private property rights regimes, which were *well specified* and *properly enforced* either by the colonial government or by the mercantile company itself (see, Burns, 1963, for efforts by the Royal Niger Company to enforce its property rights against "encroachment" by African ethnic groups; and Rudin, 1938, for wars fought between German planters and the Bakweri people over land and land-use rights at the foot of the Cameroon Mountain). African ownership of environmental resources was mostly communal and the properties were exploited under a "tribal" or "customary" system that rarely created a "tragedy of the commons" (see Hardin, 1968; also Stevenson, 1991) until the arrival of colonialism. Many incoming Europeans viewed communally owned properties as unoccupied and hence, belonging to nobody. As a consequence, they believed they had the right to occupy or confiscate them.

At independence, most Africans believed that the new dispensation would change colonial trade patterns and enhance the ability of Africans to participate in global trade. However, most of the new leaders chose to retain the trade patterns inherited from the colonial state, allowing their countries to remain essentially suppliers of raw materials to the metropolitan economies and markets for the sale of excess output from the factories of their former colonizers. Although such economic dependency is a serious problem in Africa today, it is not a main concern of this chapter. In this chapter, we concern ourselves with the fact that as a result of *poorly specified and unenforced property rights* in environmental resources, the latter continue to be exploited excessively for the production of goods that benefit the European and other industrial market economies. In addition to the fact that such an approach to the allocation of the continent's environmental resources produces little or no benefits for African societies, it also imposes significant damage on the continent's ecosystem and endangers sustainability in the management of the environment. Part of this chapter, thus, would be devoted to an examination of the importance of well-defined property rights regimes to the efficient and effective allocation of resources and the management of the environment. We argue that the present effort by Africans to provide themselves with transparent, participatory and accountable governance structures, and resource allocation systems that enhance wealth creation, must include the establishment of more efficient property rights regimes in each country. Large-scale agro-ecological degradation, over-exploitation of environmental resources and other forms of environmental degradation that have become endemic in post-independence Africa have been caused primarily by the existence of "incomplete, inconsistent, or unenforced [or unenforceable] property rights regimes" (Hanna, Folke and Mäler, 1995, p. 15). Thus, to make certain that Africa's environmental resources are allocated efficiently and in socially optimal ways, and to ensure sustainability in the management of the continent's fragile ecosystem, Africans must engage in democratic institutional reforms to create complete property rights regimes which are consistent with (1) their relationship with the environment; (2) their values; (3) their customs and traditions; and (4) their concept of equity in resource allocation. The new property rights regimes, of course, must provide the African peoples with the opportunities to improve their living standards – that is, they must enhance their ability to participate in and benefit from the new global economy, so that they can secure the wealth they need to effectively confront massive poverty and deprivation. Unless Africans provide themselves with economic and political structures that are relevant to their realities, the "new globalization" is likely to (1) reinforce existing exploitative neo-colonial structures, (2) enhance the ability of the developed industrial countries to harvest Africa's natural resources for their own benefit, (3) impose significant ecological costs on African societies; and (4) further impoverish the African peoples and force them into a miserable existence on the periphery of the new global economy.

It is important to note that property rights are a part of each nation's institutional arrangements. Given the fact that most African countries do not currently have effective and viable institutional arrangements – those that properly constrain the exercise of government agency (i.e., minimize political opportunism, including corruption and rent seeking), enhance peaceful coexistence of groups, and promote entrepreneurship and the creation of wealth – this chapter will call for comprehensive institutional reforms, through democratic (i.e., people-driven, bottom-up, inclusive and participatory) constitution making, to create the appropriate laws and institutions, including well-specified property rights regimes, which reflect the people's customs, cultures, aspirations, worldview, and generally enhance their ability to live together peacefully and allocate their resources in an equitable and efficient manner.

Environmental Degradation in Africa: the Role of Property Rights

For many years, economists believed that overexploitation of environmental resources and environmental degradation were due primarily to communal ownership of natural resources. As a consequence, they called for privatization and the establishment of private property rights regimes as the appropriate way to minimize the "tragedy." Thus, countries in Africa, where the environment was continuously being abused, were advised to introduce private property rights regimes in their natural resources and ecosystems. The argument was that the private or sole owner would be more inclined to maximize *long-term* benefits from the exploitation of the resource, resulting in the necessary investment to improve the resource's productivity. Such an owner was also expected to engage in efficient and effective policing to minimize overuse. Proponents of this approach to the management of the environment believed that ownership of natural resources was limited to only two property rights regime types – *private* or *open access*. Management of the environment under the former was expected to minimize overexploitation; the latter, however, was considered the main source of the "tragedy of the commons" examined by Hardin (1968).

Research carried out since these arguments were first presented, however, has determined that there are other resource ownership types that can mitigate the problems of overexploitation of environmental resources and, ecological damage just as effectively as private ownership. In fact, effective access restrictions, appropriate incentive structures for market participants (e.g., guarantee of future claims to resource benefits), and proper enforcement of property rights can mitigate the problems of abuse under state, communal, or private ownership types. Research by Hanna, Folke and Mäler (1995, 19; also see Furubotn and Pejovich, 1974), has determined that:

- Property rights regimes do not exist as two opposing types but rather as combinations along a spectrum from open access to private ownership.
- Property rights regimes are not in themselves sufficient conditions for resource sustainability, but they are necessary conditions. Without specified rights to resource benefits, ownership is realized only upon capture. If the assurance to future claims to resource benefits is absent, no incentive exists to limit use.
- No single type of property rights regime can be prescribed as a remedy for problems of resource degradation and overuse. Both effective control and ineffective control can exist under any kind of regime. Effective property rights regimes are well specified, context-specific, and enforceable.

To deal effectively with resource overexploitation and environmental abuse, then, one should focus primarily on the design and adoption of effective property rights regimes – those that are well defined or specified, are context-specific, enforceable, and reflect the views of greater society about use and sustainability. For example, in dealing with the problem of environmental degradation in Africa, emphasis should be placed on reforms to provide each society with effective property rights regimes and incentive structures that minimize political opportunism and enhance the security of the owner's future claims to resource benefits – whether those owners are private individuals or a whole village or community. The property rights regimes produced could be private, communal, state or a combination of the above, as long as they are well specified, and the appropriate incentive structures are provided market participants in order to minimize overexploitation and maximize long-term benefits from the asset. The following examples may be instructive: Throughout most of Africa, the state, instead of the market, controls property rights assignments. After a regime change takes place through a coup d'état, the new government usually restructures property rights to benefit members of the new ruling coalition and punish the ousted regime and its supporters. A citizen who has just been granted ownership of say, a piece of property as reward for his support in the coup, is unlikely to seek to maximize long-term benefits from the asset or invest in its improvement. The new owner is aware that his rights could be abrogated or cancelled very easily if the government is itself displaced by another set of competitive elites. The present owner of record does not have the guarantee of future claims to the resource's benefits and therefore would take a myopic view to allocation and would want to maximize short-term benefits. Under such conditions, overexploitation would be the most likely outcome even if the resource were owned privately.

Where corruption is pervasive, as is the case in many African countries, many people may be able to secure important resources through paying bribes to the bureaucracy instead of engaging in mutually beneficial exchange with the owners of such assets. For example, an entrepreneur may be able to secure access to valuable public land by bribing civil servants, whose job it is to manage the properties for the benefit of society. Such ownership, however, is not secure and the new owner is likely to engage in overexploitation in order to extract as much benefits as possible before the illegal deal is uncovered or he loses favor with the incumbent regime. What these two simple examples have shown is that overexploitation can and does occur even when property is owned privately. Minimizing overexploitation of environmental resources requires reforms to provide each society with well specified property rights – including appropriate restrictions to access – and incentive structures that minimize opportunism by market participants.

Producing the effective property rights regime is similar to designing a society's laws and institutions. Like the institutional arrangements for a country, the outcome of the deliberations must reflect the goals and objectives of the greater society. In other words, whatever the property rights regime that a society chooses to have, it must be one that helps the people meet such goals as (1) equity in the distribution of wealth and income; (2) macroeconomic performance; and (3) efficiency and sustainability in the management of the environment. It is critical that society's desires/objectives for the long-term use of its resources (environment) be explicitly elaborated in the property rights regime in order to make certain that what is expected of those who use or exploit the resources – whether they are members of the society or foreigners – is not inconsistent with societal expectations (Hanna, Folke and Mäler, 1995).

A first step in creating a viable and effective property rights regime is to define the various stakeholders (i.e., the various individuals and groups that have an interest in the asset or its services) (Bromley, 1989). Through this discovery process, those designing the property rights regime can more accurately determine the rights and obligations of the several conflicting parties and provide rules that will efficiently govern use and maintenance of the resource, and allow for peaceful resolution of any conflict that may arise. The expected *property rules* must insure that the "rights and responsibilities are as congruent as possible" (Hanna, Folke and Mäler, 1995, p. 20). The resulting rules, of course, must minimize such behaviors as rent seeking, free riding, and other forms of opportunism (Runge, 1984).

The two most important determinants of overexploitation and environmental damage are (1) the nature of access to resources; and (2) the incentive structure that regulates the behavior of traders, and as a consequence, resource use. It is important to emphasize that the incentive structure must reflect long-term sustainability of both the resource in question and the overall environment. The latter goal is shared by many societies, including those in Africa (Jentoft, 1989; Pinkerton, 1989).

In producing a property rights regime for a society, it is important to insure that the distribution of decision-making authority regarding exploitation or use, and maintenance of the resource are consistent with ownership. For example, privately owned property should be managed by the owner or his agent; and resources that belong to a collectivity should be managed through the collective choice process. Recent research points to the fact that in the latter, a decentralized form of management is likely to be more efficient, since the process would make greater use of time-and-place information that is unique to each locality. Usually, people at the local level will be empowered and allowed to have greater input into policy decisions that directly affect their welfare (Ostrom, 1990). As already mentioned, as in all collective choice processes, rent seeking and other forms of opportunism are likely to be major problems. Appropriate institutional arrangements, however, can minimize these behaviors and improve efficiency in the allocation of resources (see, e.g., Mbaku, 1997; Brennan and Buchanan, 1985).

Colonialism as a Globalizing Force and Environmental Degradation in Africa

As examined earlier, following annexation of African territories, the colonial government proceeded to introduce private property rights in land and assign them to European mercantile companies. Then, it was believed that the establishment of private property rights regimes would significantly improve allocation of resources and economic conditions in the colonies. Converting communal lands into private property was expected to minimize overexploitation through effective control of access. However, it is important to note that access restriction is a necessary but not a sufficient condition for minimizing environmental abuse. To minimize overuse and abuse of resources, market participants must be provided with the appropriate incentive structures. Colonialism was not a mutually beneficial system, freely entered into by Africans. It was a brutal, opportunistic, exploitative and oppressive system imposed on the Africans by the Europeans. Property rights assignments were undertaken through force and not through the market. Thus, European entrepreneurs who were granted ownership (by the colonial government) of these confiscated African properties were in a constant struggle to prevent Africans from either gaining access to them or seizing them. In other words, the European entrepreneurial class, with the help of the resident colonial government, spent a lot of resources making certain that African groups did not develop enough violence potential to effectively challenge continued European monopolization of resource allocation in each colony (see, e.g., Burns, 1963; Rudin, 1938). Given such a hostile and politically unstable environment, most of the European entrepreneurs developed a *short-term* view of resource exploitation and as a consequence, engaged in levels of resource consumption that were higher than those that could have guaranteed sustainability and most importantly, preserved the environment.

The European entrepreneurial class in each colony was quite aware of the struggle by Africans for independence. The enterprise owners knew that control of governance and resource allocation systems by indigenous (i.e., African) elites would result in the nationalization of European properties and their eventual transfer to Africans. Thus, many of these Europeans did not see their future claims to resource benefits as secure and as a consequence engaged primarily in the maximization of short-term goals. The outcome was overexploitation and severe environmental degradation even though the properties were owned privately. It is important to note, then, that even if environmental resources are privately owned, they can still be overused if the market incentive structures are unable to guarantee resource owners future claims to benefits.

Several African colonies had large populations of European settlers, the majority of whom intended to remain in the continent permanently. In fact, in South Africa and Southern Rhodesia, many of these Europeans came to view themselves as Africans of European ancestry, with a distinct culture, and resented domination by the resident colonial power. In some of the southern African colonies that formed the Union of South Africa in 1910, Afrikaners (European colonists of Dutch-French-German ancestry) fought almost continuously with the resident English colonial government over language, culture, the treatment of Africans, and other policies. In each colony, the European settlers controlled, usually as private property, large parcels of land that had previously belonged to African ethnic groups. Many of these European settlers believed that they had "earned" the right to occupy these properties and looked forward to deriving *long-term* benefits from them and also hoped to eventually bequeath them to their offspring. Despite the fact that these colonists faced similar insecurities with respect to future claims on resource benefits – Africans continued the struggle to recapture their resources, the decision to make Africa their permanent home forced them to maximize long-term benefits from resource use. Of course, the settlers were aware that someday the colonies would be granted their independence. However, many of them hoped to manipulate the conditions of independence to insure that they retained their control of resource allocation and the properties that they had accumulated (Cf. the unilateral declaration of independence in the then British colony of Southern Rhodesia by settlers hoping to maintain control of governance structures and the allocation of resources). Thus, private ownership of environmental resources appears to have resulted in less overexploitation mostly in those colonies that had large populations of settlers. These Europeans viewed their future claims to resources as more secure (either because they hoped to be able to control property rights assignments even after independence or they believed in a so-called divine right to occupy these properties), and as a consequence, did not engage in the type of merciless exploitation of natural resources that was characteristic of other colonies. As has already been mentioned, the critical determinant of resource and environmental abuse is the incentive structure faced by market participants. If the incentives guarantee the resource owner's future claims to benefits, overexploitation is not likely to be the market outcome.

We must caution here that even though the allocation of environmental resources in settler-dominated African colonies may not have produced as much environmental degradation as was common in other colonies, resource use nevertheless was, for all intents and purposes, *not socially optimal.* Property rights regimes in these colonies did not reflect societal values, aspirations, concerns for equity and equality in the distribution of wealth and income, and the indigenous peoples' view of social justice. On the contrary, most of these property rights regimes exacerbated existing inequalities in the distribution of resources and contributed significantly to poverty and material deprivation among the African peoples. Although the pattern of allocation of environmental resources, including such things as water-use rights, land and mineral rights, may have created less of a free rider problem and subsequently less overuse, it concentrated income and wealth in the hands of a few groups, primarily Europeans, and caused significant marginalization and impoverishment of many indigenous groups and communities.

To summarize, during the colonial period, most European entrepreneurs maximized short-term economic objectives resulting in the overexploitation of the continent's natural resources. In those colonies that had large populations of European settlers, many of whom planned to remain in Africa permanently, many of them felt more secure about their future claims to resource benefits and as a consequence, took a long-term view of exploitation. Thus, overexploitation was less of a problem in these than in the other colonies. However, control of property rights assignments by settlers resulted in the concentration of wealth in European hands and the almost total exclusion of Africans from participating in economic processes. To reiterate, patterns of resource allocation in both forms of colonies concentrated income and wealth in European households and impoverished and marginalized African groups and communities.

The "integration" of the African economies into the global economy brought about by colonial forces beginning in the mid-1880s, produced several outcomes, virtually all of which were detrimental to the welfare of the African peoples. First, the alienation of African lands by colonial forces to European entrepreneurs created enormous hardships in many communities and significantly and negatively impacted the social, economic, and political development of the people. Second, patterns of exploitation of Africa's natural resources brought by the Europeans benefited exclusively resident European entrepreneurs and the metropolitan economies but imposed significant costs on the African peoples. Third, in most of the colonies, resource exploitation by the Europeans significantly damaged the environment and threatened the survival of many local communities. Finally, the resulting relationship between the colonial African economies and the global economy of the time was not a mutually beneficial one; instead, what emerged was an exploitative relationship which produced benefits mostly for the metropolitan economies, while imposing significant costs on Africa and its peoples.

Environmental Degradation in Africa: the Role of the "New Globalization"

For Africa, the "old" globalization began with the 1880s "scramble for Africa" by the European powers. The start of the "new" globalization can be traced to the demise of socialism in Eastern Europe, the collapse of the Soviet Union, and the "triumph" of capitalism. According to Held (1995, p. 20), globalization involves "dense networks of regional and global economic relations which stretch beyond the scope of any single state (even dominant states); extensive webs of transnational relations and instantaneous electronic communications over which particular states have limited influence; a vast array of international regimes and organizations which can limit the scope for action of the most powerful states ..." As argued by Idahosa (2004, p 95), these "networks and their institutional embodiments have resulted in the weakening of the prevailing expression of territorial sovereignty, and they have become subversive of economic, political, cultural, and social meaning of the nation-state." For the purposes of the discussion in this chapter, it is critical to recognize that the "new globalization" has (1) been accompanied by a significant and rapid expansion in the world economy, a process that has increased the demand for certain natural resources, including especially oil; (2) resulted in an expansion of world trade; (3) produced a highly integrated global financial system; (4) improved communications significantly; and (5) weakened many governments, especially those of the developing countries, making it much more difficult for local policymakers to have control over domestic policies. The new global economy is characterized by relatively easy flows of large volumes of trade, capital and knowledge across national borders. It must be recognized, however, that except for the export of certain categories of raw materials, notably those such as oil and several minerals that are critical inputs into productive economic activities in the developed economies, most developing countries, including especially those in Africa, still find it quite difficult to have access to the markets of the developed economies. It has been argued that the domination of national and international economic transactions by transnational companies does not augur well for the African state, especially in its efforts to develop and implement intervention programs aimed at improving the quality of life for various local constituencies.

How, then, has the "new globalization" affected environmental resource management in Africa? Transnational companies from the developed countries, many of which were invited by policymakers in the new countries to help "develop" national resources and provide the foundation for eventual industrialization and modernization, have actually become agents of environmental degradation. These companies, which operate in economies with poorly-specified property rights regimes, have teamed up with corrupt and opportunistic state custodians (especially in such areas as mining) to exploit national resources, not for the benefit of the citizens of these countries, but for that of the companies' shareholders (who are usually located in the home countries of these companies) and the parasitic bureaucrats and politicians in each African country. Through this process, the African peoples have been further impoverished, their ecosystems destroyed, their social structures corrupted or decimated, and their ability to create wealth for themselves severely stunted. The struggles of many nationality groups in the Niger Delta of Nigeria against transnational oil companies and the central government in Abuja and that of the Anglophones of Cameroon against various foreign business entities operating in the region and the central government in Yaoundé are cases in point.

As they did during colonialism, most African countries continue to specialize in the production and export of raw materials to the industrial market economies, primarily those in Western Europe. Present production patterns in these countries (especially those involving the extractive industries), as they did during the colonial period, generate a significant level of environmental pollution, lay waste large amounts of fertile agricultural lands, destroy ground water for many villages, saturate the air with significant amounts of dangerous pollutants, and in the process, deprive many of these peoples of the foundation for their economic growth and development. Management and exploitation of virtually all of the continent's natural resources remains firmly entrenched in the hands of Western-based transnational companies, a process that has allowed national economic governance to move from the nation-state to global corporations and international institutions, whose interests and objectives are often not congruent with those of the relevant stakeholder groups in the African countries. As a consequence, the activities of these global firms in the African countries fail to contribute positively to overall improvements in the quality of life for many poor and vulnerable communities since most of the benefits of their economic activities usually accrue to opportunistic and corrupt center elites (who are unwilling or unable to effect genuine pro-poor development policies in their countries) and the companies' share holders at home. Of course, this is to be expected, considering the fact that through out the continent, the people and communities where these resources are located are rarely, if ever, consulted by either the central government or the transnational companies that control the exploitation and allocation of the various resources. In the Niger Delta of Nigeria, for example, many ethnic groups have, during the last several years, been engaged in violent and bloody mobilization to force both the central government in Abuja and the transnational oil companies operating in the region to grant them more participation in the exploitation of their natural resources, as well as in the overall management of their environment. Unfortunately, as is common throughout the continent, the local people usually do not have the wherewithal to negotiate effectively with intrusive global capital. While there are many reasons for this state of affairs in the case of the Niger Delta, the most important include the fact that (1) the Nigerian polity, since independence in 1960, has failed to provide its citizens with the necessary structures to resolve conflict peacefully and in an equitable and efficient manner; (2) property rights in environmental resources are not well-specified, hence, ownership is in debate – in fact, while the various ethnic groups in the Niger Delta claim collective ownership of these resources, the central government in Abuja has assumed ownership and management of the resources, supposedly for the benefit of all Nigerians; and (3) a highly fractured, corrupt and weakened Nigerian state is not in a position to effectively control the activities of the various transnational companies that operate within its borders. As a consequence, globalization has only brought misery to many in the Niger Delta. While the exploitation of their natural resources has produced significant amounts of revenue for the central government in Abuja and made the oil companies quite rich, the process has permanently destroyed their traditional ways of making a living (particularly farming and fishing), seriously endangered their health through air, water, and land pollution, and left them with a very bleak future.

Many other areas of the continent, like the Niger Delta of Nigeria, are faced with similar problems – globalization, which was supposed to enhance local development and improve the quality of life for the people through the provision of more opportunities for trade and investment, has only brought misery and poverty. In most of these countries, environmental resources are unregulated common property, with virtually no restriction on access. Throughout the continent, national policymakers routinely grant permission to transnational companies to exploit these resources without bothering to consult the people on whose ancestral lands these resources are located. The claim, of course, is that these resources belong to the nation as a whole and that the central government is acting as the national custodian whose job it is to manage the revenues derived from exploitation for the benefit of the whole country. Unfortunately, as illustrated by the case of oil exploitation in the Niger Delta of Nigeria and the Anglophone region of Cameroon, virtually none of the oil royalties are actually used to develop the affected lands and their peoples. Instead, the various villages and communities are left to deal with the negative externalities (e.g., ecosystem degradation) of exploitation.

The continent's tropical forests, which are being used to harvest timber or cleared to grow coffee, cocoa, rubber, palm kernel and oil, and rubber, are considered common property – with unrestricted access. Additionally, most grazing pastures, water holes, including rivers and lakes, are considered common property to be shared with the continent's future generations. The bulk of these resources are used primarily to produce goods that are traded in the global economy. Recent research has determined that most of the tropical deforestation that occurs today, including that in Africa, derives from the use of tropical forests for agricultural purposes – particularly for the production of commodities for sale in the global economy (Chichilnisky, 1994).

Many examples exist, however, the Korup National Park (KNP), located between Cameroon and Nigeria and considered common property with no access restrictions, adequately illustrates the consequences of poorly defined and unenforced property rights regimes on environmental resources and globalization's menancing influence. The KNP is 60 million years old and is considered one of the oldest rain forests in the world. It is also one of the richest in biodiversity. For several years, it has been exploited as a common-property resource with open access, primarily to produce commodities such as palm oil, rubber, timber, and other tropical forest products for export to the industrial North. Poorly defined property rights and the absence of restrictions on use have resulted in excessive exploitation, primarily by transnational companies, of KNP's resources for export to Western Europe and other industrial countries and have severely damaged the forest's ecosystem (Ruitenbeck, 1990).

In Africa, tradition and custom have been used quite successfully to restrict access and minimize abuse and overexploitation of environmental resources. Tribal groups have been able to effectively constrain the activities of free riders and secure cooperative outcomes in the use of common-property resources, such as watering holes, land and forests. As argued by Mueller (1991, p. 326), "custom and tradition dictate the appropriate penalties to be meted out for deviant behavior." However, as African societies become dynamic and complex and the population is no longer stable, and as globalizing forces continue to change domestic social, economic and political structures, "new situations arise and the proper behavior and appropriate penalties should this behavior not be forthcoming are not always known" (Mueller, 1991, p. 326). To be able to effectively regulate socio-political interaction in such complex societies requires *explicit rules*. A well-defined property rights regime is such a set of explicit rules and can enhance the ability of society to allocate its resources efficiently and achieve sustainability. Thus, for today's more complex African societies, formal property rights regimes are needed to replace custom and tradition and to allow these countries to participate more gainfully in the global economy.

What are the consequences of incomplete, inconsistent, and unenforceable property rights regimes for African societies? One can identify the following: (1) exacerbation of the problem of the commons; (2) underpricing of the continent's environmental resources in the global marketplace; (3) overconsumption of these underpriced resources, primarily by the industrial North; (4) deforestation and other forms of ecological degradation; (5) significant inequities and inequalities in the distribution of the benefits of the environment; (6) exacerbation of general inequality in resource allocation; (7) social and political upheavals; and (8) a failure to deal in a more effective and beneficial way with the forces of globalization. Many economists have argued that the African countries can benefit from globalization (see, e.g., Fischer, 2001). However, for that to happen, these countries must engage in the reconstruction and reconstitution of the post-colonial state to provide institutional arrangements that adequately constrain the state, enhance peaceful coexistence of population groups, and promote entrepreneurship, especially among the citizens. A well-specified and enforced property rights regime is part of those institutional arrangements.

Today, in this era of the new globalization, many Africans no longer see their trade with the industrial North, especially in environmental resources, as contributing to economic growth and development. Instead, they see such trade as a continuation of the form of exploitation that began with colonialism and continues to this day. Such exploitation has destroyed the continent's development potential and resulted in significant levels of marginalization.

It has been argued that there is another consequence of Africa's poorly specified and unenforced property rights in environmental resources and its interaction with the forces of globalization (see, e.g., Chichilnisky, 1994) – trade patterns that cannot be easily explained. For example, small African countries with extremely scarce natural resources continue to export wood to European countries that have well maintained and better managed forests. In most African countries, forest resources are treated as unregulated common property with unrestricted access. The forest's depreciation as an asset is not considered by national governments. With the assistance of transnational companies, these forest resources are exploited intensively for products to export to the industrial North. As a consequence, important biodiversity reservoirs such as the KNP are gradually being destroyed in an effort to produce commodities for export to the industrial countries, many of which are more productive and have higher endowments of fertile agricultural lands than the African economies. In addition to the fact that this process destroys critical natural resources, it also leaves behind a significant level of environmental degradation, brings about what are irreversible changes in the cultural practices of many villages, and causes disruptions in the fabric of many societies.

How can Africa prevent its participation in the new global economy from damaging its environmental resources and endangering sustainability? The traditional approach to minimizing overexploitation of natural resources has been to increase the producer's costs through taxation. However, as research by Chichilnisky (1994) has determined, given present production patterns in most of Africa's rain forests, taxation will actually exacerbate the problem of overexploitation. Increased taxes would force the forest workers – most of whom are very poor and perform consignment work for the transnational companies – to engage in overproduction in order to compensate for the lower per unit prices that accrue to them as a result of the higher tax. When environmental resources are extracted by unskilled subsistence laborers, taxation only encourages them to extract more of the resource, not less. Consequently, taxation has not been an effective and reliable regulatory tool in the fight to manage consumption of Africa's environmental resources.

Work by Chichilnisky (1994) has confirmed the importance of well-specified property rights regimes to the allocation of environmental resources. Establishing a system of well-specified private property rights in land, accompanied by the appropriate incentive structures for market participants, can mitigate many of the problems of overexploitation and result in more efficient allocation. Of course, as has been emphasized in this chapter, efficiency in the allocation of environmental resources, including proper management of the environment, can be achieved with property rights regimes other than private ownership or those based on profit maximization. The critical issue is that each society provides itself with complete, consistent, and enforceable property rights regimes, and incentive structures to minimize opportunistic behaviors such as free riding and rent seeking. In other words, efficiency in allocation can be achieved under private, communal, and state property rights regimes, as long as these are well defined, access is adequately restricted, appropriate incentive structures are provided traders, and a fully functioning enforcement mechanism is provided.

Given the fact that the welfare and livelihoods of many African villages and/or ethnic groups are usually tied to the land that they occupy, the issue of effective and equitable management of the resources (e.g., oil, timber, minerals) found on those lands continues to challenge policymakers. Management by the central government (which usually sub-contracts actual exploitation of the resources to some transnational company) is currently the most popular approach to natural resource exploitation in the continent. Unfortunately, this approach has failed to allocate these resources in a socially equitable manner, deal effectively with the problem of environmental degradation, and significantly improve the quality of life for individuals in the affected regions and communities. A much more locally-focused approach, one that enhances the ability of the relevant stakeholders, that is, those in whose ancestral lands the resources are located and whose welfare is most likely to be affected by the actual exploitation of the resources, has been suggested (see, e.g., Mbaku, 2004). According to this approach, property rights should be *formally* restructured to produce *limited ownership* by the relevant stakeholders (e.g., the village where the resources are located) – henceforth, the village would be recognized by the national government as the legal owner of the land and the only one legally allowed to grant permission for its exploitation. Limited ownership implies that open access has been eliminated. Thus, even though the land (which may contain large deposits of oil or other valuable commodities) is communally owned (by the village or ethnic group), the individual villager no longer has unlimited access to it. Of course, exemptions can be made for certain activities such as hunting, gathering of firewood, non-commercial fishing, and food production, which are considered essential to village life. Which activities are to be exempt should be left to the villagers to decide through their collective decision making mechanism.

Since the present and future welfare of the village is tied to the land and its fruits, the village is most likely to design exploitation and/or utilization policies that will maximize long-term benefits from the asset, and thus avoid abuse, overexploitation and degradation. The collective decision making body of the village (e.g., the council of elders) can be called upon to develop and adopt rules (that are consistent with the village's goals for the environment and use of the land, and with equity in allocation) for the effective and socially equitable exploitation of the resource. The village can then hire, through the market, a manager to oversee the day-to-day management of the resource within the rules established earlier by the village. Such a manager can even be a multinational company, which will manage the property exclusively for the benefit of its owner – the village, and hence would be paid compensation based on the extent to which it meets certain goals (e.g., profit maximization, sustainability, preservation of hallowed grounds on which ancestral spirits rest, minimization of environmental degradation, etc.) set by the village's collective decision making body. Income earned through the management of the resources in question will accrue to the village and can then be taxed by the central government, allowing the latter to meet its redistributive functions. While the village council may seek assistance from the central government in its negotiations to hire a manager, it is important to note that the final decision on the person or organization to manage the resources and how exploitation should be undertaken, should be made by the relevant stakeholders only.

One could argue that while such a highly decentralized approach to ownership and management of environmental resources might work for the allocation of water-use rights, timber, grazing fields, and other "simpler" environmental goods and services, it might be problematic for engagement in more complex projects such as the exploitation of oil and the mining of various minerals. In addition, it could be argued that within such a decentralized framework, it might be quite difficult for groups of rural villages to successfully undertake the complex negotiations that are required to secure beneficial long-term contracts for the exploitation of such natural resources as oil. This, of course, need not be a problem given the fact that the villages' collective decision making bodies can hire teams of professional negotiators to represent them and work within parameters set by the villages. If the national government is democratic, the villages' representatives at the central government can assist in securing such a team of negotiators and make certain that the relevant stakeholders' values are maximized. Hence, it is important that the restructuring of property rights be made part of the process of state reconstruction to provide democratic governance structures within each African country. The important thing to note is that property rights should be restructured so as to allow local communities to own their resources and have a say in how they are allocated. It is only through such a process that Africans can deal more effectively with environmental resource overexploitation and ecosystem degradation and ensure the sustainability of their resources.

The restructuring of property rights in Africa will be expensive, time-consuming and difficult. We must recognize, however, that unless well-specified and enforced property rights structures are provided each society, overexploitation and ecological degradation will remain pervasive. Thus, the issue of producing more effective property rights regimes for the African countries should be considered as important as democratization and the provision of more transparent, accountable and participatory governance structures. Throughout the continent, Africans are currently engaged in institutional reforms to provide themselves with more effective governance and economic systems. To arrest the problems of underdevelopment and poverty in the continent, each emerging dispensation must be one that includes more effective property rights regimes. The latter, of course, must reflect the people's aspirations, traditions and customs, values, and their concern for issues of equity in the allocation of resources. In other words, the property rights regimes produced for each African society must reflect that society's values, minimize opportunism (and subsequently overuse), and at the same time, enhance equitable allocation of resources and environmental sustainability.

Regional Integration, the "New Globalization" and the Environment in Africa

It has been suggested that African states, weakened considerably by the forces of globalization, should strengthen themselves and enhance their ability and that of their economies to compete gainfully in the global economy by undertaking *economic integration.* Such integration, it is believed, would (1) enhance Africa's ability to negotiate at international forums, such as the WTO, which have a direct impact on the continent's welfare; (2) provide the continent with the wherewithal to effectively resist exploitation by transnational firms and international institutions (e.g., IMF and the World Bank); (3) allow Africa to mobilize its enormous resource endowments and use them to create the wealth that the continent needs to meet its various obligations; (4) improve its ability to effectively monitor the activities of transnational companies operating in the continent so as to force them to internalize all their costs and hence, minimize any ecosystem degradation associated with their various activities; and (5) significantly improve the continent's ability to withstand the negative forces of globalization. Thus, as Africans complete their first decade in the new century, the question is whether to maintain their position as an appendage to the European Union economy, favor the development of a multilateral trading system, or form a continent-wide economic (and perhaps political) union in order to reduce their dependence on the industrial market economies, have more control over the allocation of resources, and consequently over the management of their environment, and significantly improve their ability to benefit from the new globalization. These questions have been examined thoroughly elsewhere (Mbaku, 1995, 1997). In this section, we take the idea of integration a step further and show how African countries can combine integration with *changes in trade patterns* to significantly improve their participation levels in the new global economy, and reduce environmental degradation.

Regional economic integration has been suggested as a scheme that can be used by the African countries to improve their participation in the new global economy. It is argued that at the present moment, most African economies are small and not particularly viable. Through regional integration, however, these economies can increase their effective sizes and allow them to benefit significantly from a more enhanced exploitation of technological economies of scale, as well as effectively resist the negative influences of transnational companies and various international institutions. Larger markets made possible by integration are also expected to provide infant industries a more enabling environment to grow and eventually become competitive. In 1980, the OAU specifically advocated trade integration as part of its agenda for the development of the continent and today, the African Union (AU), the successor to the OAU, is promoting the same agenda. The Economic Commission for Africa (ECA) has accordingly sponsored three integration schemes: the Economic Community of West African States (ECOWAS), the Economic Community of Central African States (ECCAS), and the Preferential Trading Area for Eastern and Southern Africa (PTA-ESA) (Johnson, 1991; OAU, 1981). In addition, the SADC, a trade bloc comprising southern African countries, has become more viable since the demise of apartheid in 1994.

Economies of Scale and the Participation of Africa in Global Trade

Even if we assume that this time around African countries will succeed in establishing viable integration schemes, they may still not be able to participate effectively in global trade. Why? First, African economies must produce goods that are competitive globally in both price and quality. Second, as research has revealed (Chichilnisky, 1996, 1981), if specialization within each new and larger internal market (i.e., the integration scheme) is based on traditional comparative advantages, each member country will still be unable to benefit effectively from international trade, especially if the trading arrangement is made up primarily of poor, underdeveloped and primary-commodity exporting countries. Africa's comparative advantage is in the export of *resource intensive* goods that are produced with relatively *cheap, uneducated, and unskilled* labor. Such trade patterns, most of which were developed during colonialism, increase the continent's dependence on the industrial market economies and impose significant damage on Africa's fragile ecosystems. Research (see, e.g., Mbaku, 1997) now points to the de-emphasis of the export of cheap raw materials in favor of the production and export of *knowledge intensive* goods as a more effective trade strategy for the African countries in this era of globalization. Knowledge intensive goods are produced with highly skilled and well-educated labor; the process generally does not impose as much damage on the ecological system as does mining and quarrying, logging, and other traditional export industries in the African countries.

Chichilnisky (1996) argues that "while free trade in competitive markets leads to efficient solutions, when countries are large and have market power, this is no longer true. Free trade may not lead to Pareto efficient allocations when countries are large and have market power." Large countries with a significant level of market power usually behave like monopolistic firms and attempt to manipulate supply to maximize their revenues from exports. Thus, countries that have market power can impose restrictions on trade (e.g., tariffs) and generate additional benefits for themselves. Smaller countries can, of course, form trade blocs or large internal markets and gain the market power needed to manipulate supply to their advantage.

For an African trade bloc to be able to effectively manipulate supply, the new grouping must (1) produce goods that are competitive globally in both price and quality; and (2) possess enough output to dominate the global market for the product in question. At the moment, few African countries are able to produce goods (except raw materials) that can compete well in global markets, especially with respect to price and quality. The continent's comparative advantage continues to be in the export of primary commodities. It appears that even if the African countries succeed in forming viable integration schemes, these will still not be able to improve the continent's participation in the global economy if specialization is based on traditional comparative advantages.

Trade Diversion and Trade Creation: the Costs and Benefits of Integration

Trade integration can produce both costs and benefits. An important cost of trade integration is trade diversion, which usually leads to a reduction in the national welfare of member countries. Trade diversion can be illustrated using the hypothetical example of country A, which presently shops for widgets (a fictitious product) in a globally competitive economy. In other words, citizens of country A purchase widgets from the most competitive producer, be it local or foreign. Suppose that consumers in country A currently purchase their widgets from country B, the lowest-cost global producer of widgets. Now, let country A join a new integration scheme that includes country C, another producer of widgets; country B does not join this trade bloc. Although widget production in country C is cheaper than in country A, C's costs are higher than those in country B. Thus, when country A joins the union, it will be forced to stop buying widgets from the lowest cost producer (country B) and start purchasing them from a higher cost producer, country C. This is called trade diversion and represents a cost of integration. The formation of the trade bloc has resulted in decreased welfare for citizens of country A as a result of *trade diversion*.

However, the larger market size made possible by integration may lead to increased levels of competition and greater economic efficiency. Economies of scale made possible by the formation of a larger internal market can help member countries achieve production efficiencies leading to *trade creation* instead of diversion. For example, after the trade agreement is reached between countries A, C and others (but excluding country B), country C can expand its production of widgets due to increased trade with country A and become more efficient since it is now able to benefit from economies of scale. Country C expands production of widgets, and since it is now part of a common market with country A, it is no longer affected by tariffs on imports of widgets into country A, increases its trade with country A, and benefits from the lower average costs of production made possible by the expanding production. Production efficiency in country C now exceeds that in country B.

Chichilnisky (1996) has argued that economies of scale can mitigate trade diversion and constrain the tendency of regional integration schemes with market power to impose trade restrictions on non-members. In production, the envelope average cost curve (EnvAC) may be upward sloping, downward sloping, or horizontal. A declining EnvAC implies that the firm is encountering economies of scale or increasing returns. If these conditions obtain, then the minimum average total cost falls as plant size increases (see, e.g., McCloskey, 1985; Hochstein, 1993). These economies of scale are said to be internal to the firm and occur primarily when the production unit becomes more efficient as output levels rise. Many traditional industries such as commercial banking, power (electricity) generation, automobile manufacturing, and airlines, have exhibited economies of scale. These industries are prone to monopolization, which can produce significant social costs. Global trade in goods and services produced by these industries has come to be dominated and controlled by a few countries and firms.

In recent years, a new type of economies of scale, called *external* economies of scale, has emerged. These relate to the *size of an entire industry* within a given geographic area. Here, as the industry output increases, the average cost of the individual firm within the industry falls. We must note that even though the average cost curve of the individual firm is upward sloping, when the output of the industry expands, externalities are generated resulting in lower per unit costs of production for all the firms participating in the market. For example, in the production of consumer electronics, new knowledge about products and product technology spreads very rapidly throughout the industry leading to lower per unit costs of production for all firms. Even without *internal* (i.e., firm-specific) economies of scale in an industry, the latter can still be very competitive if it enjoys *external* economies of scale. Thus, significant external economies of scale can be present in a competitive industry. During the post-World War II period, many countries were able to achieve phenomenal rates of economic growth through export-led policies based on the production of *knowledge-intensive* goods in industries characterized by *external economies of scale*. Industries falling in this category include consumer electronics, computers and computer parts. Recently, an important new industry has emerged that is quite favorable to external economies of scale – the computer software industry. The latter, as has been shown by Chichilnisky (1996), is knowledge and (skilled) labor intensive. Such an industry should be quite appropriate for a region that has a lot of highly skilled and well-educated labor resources.

As mentioned earlier, most African countries presently specialize in the export of raw materials that are produced with cheap, uneducated and unskilled labor. In addition to the fact that such trade patterns place the African countries at the mercy of economic policies in the industrial market economies, they contribute significantly to environmental degradation. To improve African participation in the global economy, minimize continued environmental degradation, and place these economies in a position to more effectively deal with the vagaries of the new globalization, these economies must move away from specialization in the traditional areas in favor of the production of knowledge intensive goods using skilled and highly educated labor resources. Thus, national policies should be directed at providing the facilities for Africans to acquire the specialized knowledge and technological skills that they need to function effectively in industries such as software, consumer electronics, computer hardware, information technology and others that exhibit external economies of scale. Specialization in such knowledge intensive industries will not only significantly improve Africa's participation in the new global economy, but will reduce environmental damage since national economies will become less dependent on the exploitation of environmental resources.

Given the fact that public policy in most African countries during the post-independence period has been driven primarily by political opportunism on the part of civil servants, politicians and interest groups – these groups have manipulated public policies to enrich themselves at the expense of the rest of society–, it is important that the design of *new* education policy be made a national priority and handled as part of the effort to reconstruct the state. A highly decentralized policy would allow local communities to more efficiently determine their needs and design the programs to meet them. Under such a system, the federal or central government would serve primarily as a coordinator, helping integrate the country's communities into the fast-changing global technological environment.

The Policy Imperative in a Globalized World

The critical question to ask is: What should Africans and their leaders do in order to face globalization effectively and benefit from it? The experts, especially those at the IMF and the World Bank, have recommended that Africans make certain that they have sound macroeconomic policies, more effective governance systems (the good governance argument, which incidentally, has been endorsed by the African Union through its NEPAD initiative), reform their legal and financial systems, reduce government activities in the economy through privatization, liberalize prices and increase spending on infrastructure. Some experts believe that African countries should place emphasis on trade liberalization so as to open their economies to foreign investors, as well as invest heavily in human capital formation. The latter can be achieved by increasing expenditures on education, especially at the primary and secondary school levels and providing improved access to basic health care, clean water, affordable housing, balanced nutrition, and opportunities for entrepreneurial activities. Such improved access is especially critical for hitherto marginalized and excluded groups and communities such as women, youth, rural inhabitants, urban poor, and minority ethnic groups.

The future of environmental-friendly production is in knowledge-based and skill-intensive goods. In order for Africa to enter these industries competitively, it must arm itself with well-trained and skilled labor resources. In addition, given the nature of the modern marketplace, which is gradually being taken over by technology-based marketing systems (e.g., the Internet), it is important that Africans develop competencies in the various new technologies in order to function efficiently and effectively in the new global economy. Of course, one cannot talk of human capital formation in Africa without mentioning the constraining role played by HIV/AIDS, which during the last several decades, has wiped out a lot of the continent's highly educated and trained labor resources. Hence, it is important that African countries initiate and implement public health policies that will significantly reduce the incidence of HIV/AIDS and minimize its deleterious effects on human development.

Other experts (e.g., Mbaku and Ihonvbere, 2003), while agreeing that economic and political integration can provide Africa with the wherewithal to confront, in an effective manner, the forces of globalization, have argued that efforts to integrate African economies must be preceded by comprehensive institutional reforms through democratic constitution making to provide institutional arrangements that reflect the relevant stakeholders' interests, values, aspirations, cultures, customs, and worldviews. Reconstruction and reconstitution of the neocolonial state are imperative given the fact that these structures were established by the European colonialists to enhance their ability to exploit Africa, its peoples, and its resources for the benefit of the metropolitan economies. These despotic and exploitative institutions were never intended to enhance the ability of Africans to govern themselves effectively or allocate their resources in an equitable and efficient manner.

While domestic reforms are expected to significantly improve the ability of Africans to participate effectively and gainfully in the global economy, it is important to note that Africa will remain vulnerable to the caprices of various global rules and institutions, which presently are being designed without the effective and full participation of Africans. Like those at the domestic level, global rules and institutions must be designed to enhance the ability of relevant stakeholders to advance their individual and collective values. As has been indicated for constitutional reform in Africa (see, e.g., Mbaku and Ihonvbere, 2003), the only way to obtain laws and institutions that reflect the values and collective interests of the relevant stakeholders is make certain that the process through which the rules are selected is democratic. Hence, the selection of global rules and institutions must be undertaken through a participatory, inclusive, bottom-up, and people-driven process. The process must not be dominated and controlled, as it has been in the past, by the G-7 or any other such economic grouping. Instead, all relevant stakeholders, including especially those who historically have been marginalized and excluded, should be provided the facilities to participate fully and effectively in the design and implementation of global rules. Thus, global institutions must be democratized so that all relevant stakeholders, regardless of their position in the international division of labor, are granted a full and effective voice. Through such a truly participatory process, economically weaker nations and societies can have an impact on the choice of the rules and institutions that govern the international economy, making certain that the resulting global governance system is one that reflects their interests, desires, relationship with their environment, customs, cultures, and worldview.

The participatory process for institutional reforms mentioned above is supposed to restructure the global governance system and make it less oppressive to and exploitative of developing countries, including those in Africa. Given the fact that the developed countries were primarily responsible for developing this anachronistic global system, and for many years, reaped significant benefits from it, it is incumbent upon them to shoulder most of the responsibility for and take an active role in providing an enabling environment within which it can be properly reconstructed and reconstituted (Fischer, 2001). As part of that process, the economic North is called upon to: (1) provide free and unobstructed access to their markets to African exports, especially the continent's agricultural output – this calls for the elimination of all tariffs and other impediments to trade for the African countries; (2) stop all arms sales, especially to war-torn regions in the continent and help local communities in peace building efforts; (3) contribute generously to the continent's war against HIV/AIDS; and (4) assist in the development of human capital, especially by contributing to the improvement of access to primary education to all African children.

Conclusion

The colonization of Africa produced trade patterns that had and continue to have significant impact on the exploitation of the continent's environmental resources. In addition, these trade patterns, most of which were retained after independence, have contributed significantly to environmental degradation in the African countries. Colonialism was an oppressive, exploitative and coercive system imposed on the Africans by Europeans. Given such an economic and political environment, most of the European entrepreneurs who operated in the colonies developed a short-term perspective on resource allocation and as a consequence engaged in overexploitation. In those colonies in which there were large populations of European settlers, the latter, who planned to make Africa their permanent home, had a different relationship with the lands that had been captured from the Africans. These Europeans tended to have a long-term view of resource exploitation. Unfortunately, the patterns of resource allocation in settler-dominated colonies did not reflect the goals and objectives of the Africans. Wealth and income distribution, like that in the other colonies, reflected primarily the interests and objectives of the Europeans.

Today, most of the continent's environmental resources, especially its rainforests, are being decimated in order to produce commodities that are traded in the global economy. Taxation has been recommended as a tool to prevent North-South trade from damaging Africa's fragile environment. Unfortunately, taxation has actually exacerbated the problem and increased ecosystem damage in the continent. Research has shown that the most effective way to minimize the problems of overexploitation and environmental damage is to provide each African society with well-specified, consistent, complete and enforceable property rights regimes (see, e.g., Chichilnisky, 1994). One needs to note, however, that the choice should not be restricted to private and state ownership. Design of the property rights regime is more important than what it is. Regardless of the type of property rights regime adopted, in order to minimize opportunism, prevent environmental degradation, and insure the socially-optimal allocation of resources, the appropriate regime must (1) reflect the goals and objectives of greater society; and (2) be congruent with society's objectives for equity, macroeconomic performance, and sustainability of the environment. Of course, the appropriate incentive structures must be provided market participants to make it much more difficult for them to engage in opportunistic behaviors. With the appropriate access constraints and incentive structures, a communal property rights regime should function just as efficiently as one based on private ownership. As has been argued by Brennan and Buchanan (1985), the behavior of market participants or traders, and as a consequence, market outcomes, is determined by the incentive structures that they face. The most effective way to deal with the "tragedy of the commons," then, is to design and adopt property rights regimes that adequately constrain the behavior of market participants and produce the outcomes that society desires.

Since research points to improvements in institutional arrangements – including property rights regimes – as the most effective way to minimize overexploitation of the continent's resources and provide for more efficient management of the environment, it is critical that the present transition begin with state reconstruction to provide these necessary structures – transparent, accountable, and participatory governance structures; and complete, consistent, and well-defined property rights regimes. A state that is well constrained will minimize corruption and the manipulation of property rights assignments by bureaucrats and politicians who are seeking ways to enrich themselves and their supporters. In addition, appropriate institutional arrangements will reduce the type of political and economic instability that forces market participants to take a short-term view of resource allocation and thus, engage in overexploitation.

In recent years, regional integration has been suggested as a scheme to improve economic growth and Africa's participation in the global economy. It is also argued that regional integration will improve the ability of Africans to more effectively confront the new globalization and benefit from it. The basic argument is that individual African economies are small and not particularly viable and that formation of large internal markets through integration would significantly increase the effective size of the African economies and allow them to benefit from technological economies of scale. The larger markets made possible by integration are also expected to provide a more enabling environment for infant industries to mature and become more competitive globally. We have argued in this chapter that even if African countries succeed this time in forming viable integration schemes, the latter would not be very beneficial to Africans if specialization is based on the export of primary commodities produced with cheap, unskilled and poorly educated labor. In order for integration schemes to serve as effective frameworks for development in the continent, Africans must move away from the export of raw materials and specialize in the production of knowledge-intensive goods, using skilled and highly educated labor. Research should be directed at helping the African countries develop appropriate structures to provide their labor resources with the education and skills needed for the production of knowledge-intensive goods. Specialization in the production of knowledge intensive goods should significantly reduce environmental damage (since African countries will no longer have to depend so much on the exploitation of environmental resources) and allow these countries to function more competitively in the new global economy.

References

Brace, R.M. (1964), *Morocco, Algeria, Tunisia* (Englewood-Cliffs, NJ: Prentice-Hall).

Brennan, G. and Buchanan, J.M. (1985), *The Reason of Rules: Constitutional Political Economy* (Cambridge: Cambridge University Press).

Bromley, D.W. (1989), *Economic Interests and Institutions: The Conceptual Foundations of Public Policy* (Oxford: Basil Blackwell).

Burns, Sir A.C. (1963), *History of Nigeria* (London: George Allen).

Chichilnisky, G. (1981), "Terms of Trade and Domestic Distribution: Export Led Growth with Abundant Labor", *Journal of Development Economics*, Vol. 8, pp. 163–192.

Chichilnisky, G. (1994), "North-South Trade and the Global Environment", *American Economic Review*, Vol. 84, No. 4, pp. 851–874.

Chichilnisky, G. (1996), "Trade Regimes and GATT: Resource Intensive vs. Knowledge Intensive Growth", *Economic Systems* merged with *Journal of International and Comparative Economics*, Vol. 20, pp. 147–181.

Fischer, S. (2001), "The Challenge of Globalization", Speech delivered at the France-Africa Summit, Yaoundé, Cameroon,19 January, 2001.

Fredrickson, G.M. (1981), *White Supremacy: A Comparative Study in American and South African History* (Oxford: Oxford University Press).

Furubotn, E.G. and Pejovich, S. (eds) (1974), *The Economics of Property Rights* (Cambridge, MA: Ballinger Publishing Company).

Hanna, S., Folke, C. and Mäler, K.-G. (1995), "Property Rights and Environmental Resources", in S. Hanna, and M. Munasinghe (eds), *Property Rights and the Environment* (Washington DC: The World Bank), pp. 15–29.

Hanna, S. and Munasinghe, M. (1995), "Property Rights and Environmental Resources", in S. Hanna and M. Munasinghe (eds), *Property Rights and the Environment* (Washington, DC: The World Bank), pp. 3–11.

Hardin, G. (1968), "The Tragedy of the Commons", *Science*, Vol. 162, pp. 143–148.

Held, D. (1995), *Democracy and Global Order: From Modern State to Cosmopolitan Governance* (Stanford, CA: Stanford University Press).

Hochstein, A. (1993), *Microeconomics: An Advanced Introduction* (Lewiston, NJ: Thompson Educational Publishing, Inc).

Hutt, H.W. (1964), *The Economics of the Color Bar* (London: Institute for Economic Affairs).

Idahosa, P.L.E. (2004), "A Tale of Three Images: Globalization, Marginalization, and the Sovereignty of the African-Nation State", in J.M. Mbaku and S.C. Saxena (eds), *Africa at the Crossroads: Between Regionalism and Globalization* (Westport, CT: Praeger), pp. 93–119.

Jentoft, S. (1989), "Fisheries Co-management: Delegating Responsibility to Fishermen's Organizations", *Marine Policy*, Vol. 13, No. 2, pp. 137–154.

Johnson, O.E.G. (1991), 'Economic Integration in Africa: Enhancing Prospects for Success', *The Journal of Modern African Studies*, Vol. 29, No. 1, pp. 1–26.

Magubane, B.M. (1979), *The Political Economy of Race and Class in South Africa* (New York: Monthly Review).

Mbaku, J.M. (1991), "Property Rights, European Colonialism, and Rent Seeking in Africa", *The European Studies Journal* (U.S.), Vol. 8, No. 1, pp. 25–45.

Mbaku, J.M. (1993), "Markets and Economic Origins of Apartheid in South Africa", *The Indian Journal of Social Science*, Vol. 6, No. 2, pp. 139–158.

Mbaku, J.M. (1995), "Changing Global Trade Patterns and the Further Marginalization of Africa", *Business & the Contemporary World*, Vol. 7, No. 3, pp. 77–90.

Mbaku, J.M. (1997), *Institutions and Reform in Africa: The Public Choice Perspective* (Westport, CT: Praeger).

Mbaku, J.M. (2004), *Institutions and Development in Africa* (Trenton, NJ: Africa World Press).

Mbaku, J.M. and Ihonvbere, J.O. (eds) (2003), *Transition to Democratic Governance in Africa: The Continuing Struggle*, (Westport, CT: Praeger).

McClosky, D. (1985), *The Applied Theory of Price* (New York: MacMillan).

Mueller, D.C. (1991), "Choosing a Constitution in East Europe: Lessons from Public Choice", *Journal of Comparative Economics*, Vol. 15, No. 2, pp. 325–348.

OAU (Organization of African Unity) (1981), *The Lagos Plan of Action for the Economic Development of Africa 1980–2000* (Geneva: International Institute of Labor Studies).

Ostrom, E. (1990), *Governing the Commons: The Evolution of Institutions for Collective Action*, (Cambridge: Cambridge University Press).

Pinkerton, E. (ed.) (1989), *Cooperative Management of Local Fisheries: New Directions for Improved Management and Community Development*, (Vancouver: University of British Columbia Press).

Rudin, H.R. (1938), *Germans in the Cameroons, 1884–1914*, (New Haven, CT: Yale University Press).

Ruitenbeck, H.J. (1990), *The Rainforest Supply Price: A Step Towards Estimating a Cost Curve for Rainforest Conservation*, Development Research Program Working Paper No. 29, London School of Economics.

Stevenson, G.G. (1991), *Common Property Economics: A General Theory and Land Use Applications* (Cambridge: Cambridge University Press).

Chapter 8

The New Globalization and HIV/AIDS in Africa

Amy S. Patterson

Introduction

Although it may be tempting to term HIV/AIDS the first disease of globalization, in reality the spread of epidemics has always been facilitated by the tools of globalization such as travel, trade, and migration. As early as the 1340s, Europeans associated the spread of plague with ships and refugees (Hunter, 2003, p. 126). The high incidence of sexually transmitted infections (STIs) in the United States and Western Europe immediately after World War I reflected the return of soldiers after the war (Hunter 2003, p. 165). While sharing similarities with these epidemics, HIV/AIDS is further shaped by the globalization that has occurred since the Cold War. HIV/AIDS interfaces with the system of international capitalism, widespread technological advances, migration, the expansion of institutions of global governance, and the development of transnational advocacy networks.

The forces of globalization are never neutral. For example, economic integration has been asymmetrical, with Western Europe, North America, and parts of Asia benefiting much more than sub-Saharan Africa and parts of Latin America (Barnett and Whiteside, 2002, p. 353; Blake, 2005, pp. 417–419; van de Walle, 2001, p. 6). Because of these uneven benefits, the chapter argues that some aspects of globalization have facilitated the spread of HIV/AIDS in Africa and complicated the continent's ability to address the pandemic.[1] Yet, because globalization has also encouraged the formation of transnational advocacy networks, facilitated greater knowledge on AIDS in Africa, and led to the formation of international institutions to combat the disease, this chapter also asserts that globalization may provide new opportunities in the AIDS battle. The chapter begins with background on HIV/AIDS in Africa. Next, it examines how globalization has contributed to the spread of the disease. Finally, it demonstrates how some aspects of globalization provide a way forward for addressing the pandemic.

1 I use both *pandemic* and *epidemic*. An epidemic occurs when the incidence of a disease exceeds the expected rate in a particular area. A pandemic is an epidemic affecting multiple countries. I use the word pandemic when discussing AIDS across Africa, but epidemic when describing the disease in a particular country.

HIV/AIDS in Africa

In 2006, the Joint United Nations Program on HIV/AIDS (UNAIDS) estimated that there were 39.5 million people living with HIV/AIDS worldwide; the pandemic has already claimed more than 25 million lives. Since the discovery of the first AIDS cases in 1981 in the United States, HIV/AIDS has become the leading cause of death worldwide among people aged 15 to 59. Although the first people with AIDS tended to be middle class, young, white American men, today 95 percent of those with HIV/AIDS live in low- and middle-income countries. In 2005, women were almost half (48 percent) of people worldwide with HIV/AIDS; in sub-Saharan Africa, women were 59 percent of individuals living with the disease. UNAIDS estimates there are three HIV-positive African women for every one HIV-positive African man. Although the continent only has 11 percent of the world's population, in 2005, it had 63 percent of the world's people living with HIV/AIDS and 91 percent of the world's children with HIV/AIDS (Kaiser Family Foundation, 2006, p. 1).

Almost all African countries have HIV prevalence rates near or above 1 percent. The prevalence rate is the percentage of a population with HIV at any given time. Prevalence rates are usually given as a percentage of a particular population group. Because UNAIDS uses adults fifteen to forty-nine years old as its population group, this chapter does the same when it provides prevalence rates. Public health officials and AIDS experts rely on prevalence data instead of AIDS case data because in many African countries, medical personnel are not legally required to report AIDS cases and not all citizens use medical services. Because it is impossible to test a country's entire population, prevalence data often rely on samples of population subgroups, such as women attending antenatal clinics. These percentages are then extrapolated to the larger population (Patterson, 2006, p. 4). There is great variation across the continent in terms of prevalence levels. For example, Ghana's HIV rate has remained under 3 percent since the mid-1990s, but Swaziland's has hovered above 33 percent. South Africa, the country with one of the world's largest HIV-positive populations, had approximately 5.5 million HIV-positive citizens in 2005, and infection levels among pregnant women continue to rise (UNAIDS, 2006, pp. 10–21).

While some countries such as Uganda, Rwanda, Botswana, Kenya, and Zimbabwe have experienced declines in HIV prevalence in recent years, these small declines have done little to overcome the negative effects of AIDS on African citizens, societies, and economies (UNAIDS, 2006, pp. 14–21). Because the time period between HIV infection and the onset of AIDS-identifying opportunistic infections such as pneumonia, esophageal candidiasis, and tuberculosis (TB) can be eight to ten years, the continent is now experiencing the loss of individuals infected roughly a decade ago. This fact also means that the impact of new HIV infections today will be felt years from now. The pandemic is eroding the gains made since the 1970s in life expectancy, the under-five mortality rate (per 1,000 life births), and the human development index (HDI).[2] In 2006, the United Nations Development Program (UNDP) reported that the under-five mortality rate had increased since 1970 in Zambia and remained roughly equal to its 1970 level in Rwanda and Zimbabwe (UNDP, 2006a, pp. 317–318). Seven countries with HIV prevalence levels over 20 percent – South Africa, Namibia, Botswana, Swaziland, Lesotho, Zimbabwe, and Zambia – experienced a decline in HDI between 2000 and 2004 (UNDP, 2006a, pp. 290–291). In 2006, life expectancy for Zimbabwean women was thirty-four years, one of the lowest levels in the world (It is thirty-seven years for men). Food shortages, forced migration, high inflation rates, and pervasive unemployment have exacerbated the negative impact of AIDS in this country, which has a 20 percent HIV prevalence rate (UNAIDS, 2006, p. 11). Even Botswana and South Africa – two countries without Zimbabwe's dire economic problems – face declining life expectancy rates.

Because HIV prevalence levels have yet to stabilize in many countries, the exact impact of these changes on life expectancy and HDI is difficult to discern. As of 2006, the loss of thousands of adults in their most productive years of life has created roughly 12 million African orphans. The education and healthcare sectors have been negatively affected, with school attendance and enrollment among children infected with or affected by HIV/AIDS lower than those without exposure to the disease. In some countries, AIDS causes up to half of deaths of healthcare workers, a fact which hinders the AIDS fight. Many businesses in Africa report that HIV/AIDS will negative impact their "bottom line" in the next decade, because of the loss of trained workers, the increase in health insurance costs, and the work days lost when employees must care for the ill or attend funerals (Patterson, 2006, p. 7). Because the disease erodes people's hope for the future, personal investments in property or education may be set aside, to the detriment of overall economic development. The untimely death of parents with knowledge about farming and food production may contribute to a decline in overall food production and an increase in hunger (de Waal, 2003; de Waal, 2006, p. 91).

AIDS has an uneven impact on African society, most drastically affecting the poor, marginalized, and women. Even women who are HIV-negative may spend many hours each day caring for ill family members. The financial crisis that occurs when the household's breadwinner is sick or has died may cause women to engage in survival sex to support their children. Parents may remove girl children from school so the girls can provide more labor in the household or work in the market for their parents; families in AIDS-affected households may forgo education for all children because of the lack of money to pay school fees (Siplon, 2005, pp. 23–27). Patriarchal norms that limit women's ability to demand monogamy or condom use from their sexual partners have contributed to the high HIV prevalence rate among married women in several high-prevalence countries. In 2006, for example, the Ugandan AIDS Commission reported that the highest percentage of people contracting HIV/

2 The Human Development Index (HDI) measures a country's achievements in three areas: health (life expectancy at birth), education (adult literacy rate and school enrollment ratio), and standard of living (GDP per capita). The measure is given on a scale of 0 to 1, with a higher score indicating a higher level of development (Patterson, 2005, p. 228).

AIDS were married (Bagala, 2006). It is clear that the magnitude of the pandemic will affect the continent for decades.

The Interaction of the "New Globalization" and HIV/AIDS in Africa

Broadly understood, globalization has contributed to the spread of HIV/AIDS throughout Africa. To be clear, though, it is not that globalization has *caused* the AIDS pandemic. AIDS is caused by the human immunodeficiency virus (HIV), a retrovirus which is spread through sexual contact or the exchange of blood through contaminated needles, blood transfusions, or blood products. I assert that there are four overall ways that globalization has made individuals more vulnerable to HIV transmission: (1) labor migration to export-oriented industries; (2) African states' adoption of neo-liberal economic policies; (3) the increased power of the World Trade Organization (WTO) and its Trade-Related Intellectual Property Rights (TRIPS) Agreement; and (4) donors' increasingly volatile interest in Africa after the cold war. These factors also have made it more difficult for African states to address the pandemic.

Labor Migration to Export-Oriented Industries

Migration to mines and industries that produce for export has facilitated the spread of HIV/AIDS has most affected the southern African countries of Botswana, South Africa, Swaziland, Namibia, Zimbabwe, and Lesotho. These countries also have higher levels of economic development (as measured by GDP per capita) than countries in East, Central, or West Africa. Southern Africa has been more integrated into the global economy than other parts of the continent, particularly through the region's exports of mining commodities such as gold, diamonds, and copper and more recently, labor-intensive manufactured goods such as apparel. Transportation infrastructure between southern African countries is more developed than in other African regions, with roads and railroads moving migrants across borders, primarily into South Africa.

In search of cheap labor, the gold and diamond mining industries in South Africa heavily recruited male migrants from neighboring countries, with an average 300,000 coming into the country in the early 1970s. This number declined to 200,000 in the 1980s, though many experts speculate it has increased since the end of apartheid in 1994 and Zimbabwe's sharp economic decline. As of 2004, the South African government estimated that there were between three and five million undocumented migrants in the country (United Nations, 2004, p. 57).

Men compose almost all of the migrants in the mining industry, and often married men are not been allowed to bring their families into South Africa. Migrant communities lack social cohesion; migrants live far from their spouses, families, and friends in single-sex hostels (Barnett and Whiteside, 2002, p.117). Poor living situations and the stresses associated with mining work increase the men's vulnerability to HIV. Catherine Campbell (2003, pp. 28–30) describes the migrant experience:

> Living and working conditions in the mines are dangerous and highly stressful... Compound life is dirty and overcrowded, with no space for privacy or quiet... Opportunities for leisure are few. Some workers spend time in the African townships near the mines; others avoid them as dangerous places. Drinking and sex are two of the few diversionary activities easily available on a day-to-day basis... Even more stressful than life outside of work, however, is the time spent in the mines themselves... Many [workers] had witnessed accidents in which friends and co-workers had been either killed or injured... Men referred to the accidents in a fatalistic way, and this sense of powerlessness is an important feature of the contextual backdrop against which miners' sexual identities are negotiated.

Because of their closely confined living and working conditions, miners were quite vulnerable to TB infection, and most had the disease at some point. TB is the most common opportunistic infection associated with AIDS in sub-Saharan Africa and the leading cause of death of HIV-positive people. HIV and TB reinforce each other: HIV can activate latent TB, while TB infection accelerates the progression of HIV to AIDS (Stillwaggon, 2006, p. 59).

It was not only the poor health of miners that exacerbated their vulnerability to HIV infection. Migrants engage in sex with local sex workers out of boredom, loneliness, and the ever-present concern about safety. These communities attracted poor women who moved in search of employment, and often ended up working in the sex trade. Migrant community members may have concurrent sexual relations: the migrant may have a wife in his village and a girlfriend (or two) in the migrant community. He also may engage in occasional relations with sex workers. The large number of individuals in the sexual network increases the likelihood that if any member of the network is HIV-positive the virus will rapidly spread to others. Poor nutrition further heightens vulnerability to HIV: research shows that malnutrition promotes HIV replication and contributes to greater risk of HIV transmission (Stillwaggon, 2006, p. 47). The labor migration which resulted from South Africa's export-oriented mining economy contributed to the spread of HIV.

A similar process has occurred with labor migration to more recently developed export-oriented industries. The WTO and the US African Growth and Opportunity Act (passed in 2000) have sought to encourage foreign direct investment (FDI) in Africa. As part of the US legislation, producers in Africa can export their goods into the United States with few, if any, trade restrictions. As production abroad has become more efficient because of instant communication and rapid transportation, investors from the West and Asia have built export-oriented factories in several African countries. Between 1990 and 2003, FDI to Africa increased from $2.2 billion to $13.8 billion. While this is a sizeable increase, Africa received only 2 to 3 percent of global FDI flows in 2005, a decline from its peak of 6 percent in the mid-1970s. Of non-oil producing countries, Swaziland, Mauritius, Uganda, and South Africa have experienced the greatest increases in FDI, most of it going to enclaves of export-oriented industries. These industries rely heavily on imported technology and they have limited linkages to the rest of the economy. Therefore, the ability of these industries to foster long-term economic development in these countries is debatable (UNCTAD, 2005, pp. 4, 11). Exports of footwear, toys, sportswear, nuts, apparel, and cut flowers have increased to the United States, with Botswana,

Uganda, Tanzania, and Mozambique benefiting from this expanded trade (US Trade Representative, 2006).

Research on these industries is somewhat limited, but reports indicate that these firms tend to hire female workers. A similar trend is evident in the *maquiladoras* of Mexico and Central America (ver Beek, 2001). Female workers are often willing to take lower paying jobs than men and they are less likely than men to unionize or to demand better working conditions. For factory managers trying to keep costs low, hiring women is wise financial decision. However, the migration of women to urban areas for these jobs may contribute to HIV transmission. As with male migrants, women far from home may be more likely to engage in casual sex. Furthermore, because the wages they receive may be insufficient to support themselves and their children, these women may trade casual sexual favors with male supporters for food or rent money (Wines, 2004; Whiteside, 2005, p. 113). While FDI throughout Africa creates jobs, it also can disrupt social structures and limit the options that workers have in very impoverished countries where trade unions often are weak and workers lack economic and political options.

The Adoption of Neoliberal Economic Policies

A second outcome of globalization has been the implementation of neo-liberal structural adjustment policies, the introduction of which coincided with the rapid spread of HIV throughout the continent. Throughout the 1980s, economic growth across Africa remained stagnant, at roughly 1.7 percent annually. High oil prices and the decline in demand for Africa's export commodities during the 1970s caused many African states to turn to the IMF and World Bank for loans to meet their balance of payments shortfalls. Africa's debt increased from roughly $11 billion in 1970 to $120 billion in the early 1980s (UNCTAD, 2004). By the early 1980s, however, a general consensus emerged among the IMF, World Bank, bilateral donors, and commercial banks that loans to poor countries were increasingly risky without major structural changes to those countries' economies. Beginning in 1979 with Senegal, most sub-Saharan African countries agreed to neo-liberal policy conditions in order to obtain additional loans. These structural adjustment policies, sometimes called the "Washington consensus," typically included concessions to encourage FDI; trade liberalization; currency devaluation; income and consumption tax increases; liberalization of commodity markets; privatization; and cuts in government spending.

Although most African countries did not fully put in place all of these policies, cuts in state spending to reduce fiscal deficits and currency devaluations were the most widely and comprehensively implemented. Fiscal deficits across the region declined from an average of 10 percent of GDP in the 1980s to roughly 4 percent in 1997 (van de Walle, 2004, p. 31). However, despite some progress on macroeconomic policy, African debt continued to increase, to a high of $317 billion by the late 1990s. It was only in 1997 that annual GDP growth rate rose above 3 percent. However, the overall GDP growth rate for the continent was a meager 0.1 percent for the 1990 to 2003 period (UNDP, 2005, p. 269). Despite structural adjustment, most African countries remain poor and continue to have relatively stagnant economies.

Decreases in African states' spending on healthcare have shaped the AIDS pandemic. Because of budgetary constraints, many primary healthcare services were eliminated in the 1980s, particularly in poor and remote regions. Between 1980 and 1985, spending on health, education, and welfare declined 26 percent throughout the continent; health spending itself declined from 5.5 percent of national budgets in 1972 to 2.8 percent in 1988. Many African countries implemented user fees for healthcare, including fees for some of the most basic services like childhood immunizations and prenatal care. In Kenya, for example, charges for patients to clinics providing care for STIs led to a 35 to 60 percent decline in patient attendance (Lurie et al., 2004, p. 209).[3] This decrease was one factor contributing to the rise in HIV infections in the country. Studies show that STIs increase a person's vulnerability to HIV infection, since STIs compromise the epithelial defense against disease in genital tissues (Stillwaggon, 2006, p. 63).

Declines in spending on health throughout the 1980s and early 1990s also contributed to the emigration of healthcare professionals. Medical personnel, particularly nurses, are in high demand in the United States, United Kingdom, and Canada, where aging populations and nursing shortages have led Western hospitals to "recruit" nurses from primarily English-speaking African countries. The number of foreign nurses admitted to the United States increased from 4,700 in 1982 to over 16,000 in 1990. In 2004, Malawi, a country with a 14 percent HIV prevalence rate, had 64 percent of its nursing positions, 91 percent of its OB/GYN positions, and 92 percent of its pediatrician slots vacant (Dugger, 2004). The World Health Organization (WHO) reported that the world needs four million additional healthcare workers to adequately fight AIDS; only 3 percent of the world's healthcare workers live in Africa, though almost two-thirds of all people with HIV/AIDS live on the continent (Smith, 2006). African doctors and nurses who chose not to emigrate are often overworked and underpaid.

The lack of healthcare personnel contributes to the overall decline in Africa's healthcare capacity. But this lack of capacity is reflected in other ways too. For example, rural clinics often lack basic supplies, such as clean needles, refrigerators (and electric generators or batteries) to keep medicines cold, and clean water. Funding shortages make it harder to provide HIV testing and to support AIDS treatment with antiretroviral drugs (ARVs). Preventing medical transmission of HIV through blood transfusions and injections also is more difficult with limited funds. In 2003, the WHO estimated that 30 percent of the 16 billion injections given annually worldwide are unsafe because of the reuse of equipment (Stillwaggon, 2006, p. 43). The lack of African states' resources means that donors provide roughly 50 percent of all healthcare services in Africa (van de Walle, 2001, p. 100).

Structural adjustment also has had more indirect effects on AIDS, by contributing to situations which put individuals at higher risk for HIV infection. Increases in urban unemployment have contributed to a rise in poverty throughout the continent (van de Walle, 2001, p. 87). Poverty makes people more vulnerable to disease, because it limits their access to primary healthcare and it hampers their ability to attain good nutrition. Individuals are more susceptible to any type of viral infection if they suffer

3 The percentage depended on the clinic and region of the country.

protein deficiencies and lack specific micronutrients such as iron, zinc, and vitamins (Stillwaggon, 2006, p. 32). As African states devalued their currencies throughout the mid-1990s, food prices increased with overall inflation, making it more difficult for poor urban citizens to afford adequate calorie intake. In 2003, roughly 30 percent of all people in sub-Saharan Africa were undernourished (UNDP, 2006a, p. 308). In rural areas, subsistence farmers experienced economic shocks with the decline in state-subsidized fertilizers, seeds, and credit. Coupled with the increased promotion of export-oriented agriculture and land privatization, the end of these subsidies harmed the poorest farmers, many of whom turned to urban migration to supplement their farming incomes. Rural-urban migration increased the avenues for sexual transmission of HIV. One outcome of such migration is that HIV rates tend to be higher along major transportation routes, in trading villages, in border towns, and in fishing camps (Lurie et al., 2004, p. 209).

Over the past two decades, poverty has increased throughout Africa. In 2004, twelve sub-Saharan African countries had over 50 percent of their populations living in poverty (This amounted to half of the countries for which UNDP provided data) (UNDP, 2005, pp. 224–225). Coupled with cuts in healthcare spending, poverty has contributed to diseases that make Africans more vulnerable to HIV infection. For example, STIs are more common in poor populations because of the lack of sanitation for personal hygiene, the lack of access to STI clinics, and the lack of information about their treatment. Poor citizens living in crowded urban neighborhoods often lack access to clean water and sanitation. Water borne parasites, malaria, and TB thrive in such conditions. UNDP (2006a, p. 308) reports that in 2005, 44 percent of Africans lacked access to clean water and 63 percent did not have adequate sanitation. Although these numbers have improved since1990, when 52 percent had no access to water and 68 percent lacked adequate sanitation, positive changes in these areas have been minimal. Individuals who are infected with parasites such as hookworm, filarial worm, and schistosomiasis have greater vulnerability to HIV infection than those without such parasitic infections. Malaria also increases HIV vulnerability: "HIV viral loads are significantly higher in malarial patients than in HIV-infected persons without malaria" (Stillwaggon, 2006, p. 48) Greater funding for sanitation, clean water, and de-worming programs is essential to fight some of the disease co-factors that increase Africans' risk of HIV infection. Yet, UNDP (2006b) reports that at the current rate of providing water and sanitation services, clean water will be available to just half the Africans who need it in 2040; sanitation will not reach this number of Africans until 2076.

The WTO and the TRIPS Agreement

When 123 countries formed the WTO in 1995, multinational corporations pushed for the new institution to protect intellectual property rights (IPRs). The United States and the European Union (EU) supported this inclusion because these Western countries have a comparative advantage in the trade of computers, pharmaceuticals, and entertainment products which rely on IPR protection. Placing IPRs under WTO jurisdiction allows Western countries to use trade sanctions to force adherence to IPRs. Many African states joined the WTO in 1995, in the hope that free trade would boost African exports. Since African states are IPR consumers, not producers, the risk of the TRIPS Agreement for public health in Africa may not have been apparent (Halbert and May, 2005, pp. 196–200). At the time of WTO formation, few state leaders realized, or cared to admit, the possible magnitude of the AIDS crisis. Moreover, there were few drugs that could treat HIV/AIDS. However, one year after the WTO's formation, new AIDS treatments became available in the West. The "highly active antiretroviral therapy" (HAART) utilized protease inhibitors, nucleoside reverse transcriptase inhibitors, and nonnucleoside reverse transcriptase inhibitors in combination to suppress HIV replication in the body. HAART decreased the incidence of transmission of HIV from mother to child and led to plummeting death rates in the West. Between 1995 and 1997, AIDS deaths in the United States decrease by over two-thirds (Smith and Siplon, 2006, p. 42). Private insurance and/or government programs, such as the US Ryan White CARE Act, made these expensive drugs available to patients. In poor countries, however, the cost of ARVs ranged from $10,000 to $15,000 per year per patient, making HAART inaccessible to all but a handful of wealthy individuals. The TRIPS Agreement protected the patents of pharmaceutical companies which produced ARVs, gave these companies a monopoly on production, and enabled them to set high prices.

However, Article 30 of the TRIPS Agreement allows countries to break patents under conditions of a "national health emergency." A country may then engage in parallel importing or compulsory licensing. In the former, the country imports lower priced drugs from another country instead of from the producer. Compulsory licensing allows the country to pay the patent holder a "reasonable royalty," after which it can produce generic versions of the drug. In the late 1990s, India, Brazil, and Thailand began to produce generics through compulsory licensing, but many African countries lacked the production facilities to do the same. Further, when some countries such as Ghana made plans for compulsory licensing, they were quickly discouraged by US and EU trade negotiators, who threatened to enact trade sanctions against them (Thomas, 2002). When South Africa passed the Medicines Act of 1997 to engage in compulsory licensing to produce AIDS and TB drugs, forty domestic and international pharmaceutical companies sued the government. Although the case was dropped in 2001, prices for ARVs remained extremely high throughout Africa until 2003. The lack of access to ARVs in poor countries meant that by 2003, only 400,000 people needing ARVs in poor countries (and only about 7 percent of Africans) were receiving the drugs. By 2006, this number had increased to 1.3 million, with 17 percent of HIV-positive Africans who needed treatment getting it (UN General Assembly, 2006). As I illustrate below, other aspects of globalization – transnational advocacy networks, global media attention, and the formation of global institutions to fight AIDS – facilitated this gradual change to providing ARV access. However, the delay in providing ARVs in Africa because the TRIPS Agreement allowed companies to set high prices meant thousands of Africans died of AIDS.

Inconsistent Interest in Africa

Globalization after the cold war helped to divert donors' attention away from African development to other issues and global regions. Although the continent has always been subject to shifts in first-world interest, the cold war provided a lengthy period during which the United States and the Soviet Union paid attention to the continent. When the cold war ended, the global media, the United States, and the EU focused on the rise of democratization and free markets in Eastern Europe and the former Soviet Union. This shift had several implications. First, the demise of communism legitimated free markets and trade, and US policymakers began to focus on "trade not aid" in their interaction with poor countries. Second, since US concern about the spread of communism in Africa ended with the cold war, US policymakers no longer saw the continent in terms of its strategic value. While official development assistance (ODA) to Africa increased significantly in the 1980s when cold war tensions reignited and when structural adjustment policies were implemented, by 1994, ODA to Africa had declined significantly. In 1994, 14.6 percent of ODA from the United States went to Africa, less than 1 percent more than went to Eastern Europe during the same year. In 1997, the amount of ODA was equal in real terms to the level of aid in 1983. Furthermore, ODA averaged 5 percent of an African country income in 1997, down from 10 percent in the 1980s (Lancaster, 2000, pp. 211–213; Tarnoff and Nowels, 2004, p. 10). Declines in ODA and its shift in focus to market development and democratization meant that donor governments paid limited attention to the rapidly escalating AIDS pandemic. In 1996, for example, donors and national governments spent only $292 million to fight AIDS in low- and middle-income countries (UN General Assembly, 2006, p. 6). Multilateral and bilateral donors remained relatively silent about AIDS, lacking institutions and funding mechanisms to address the impending crisis.

The terrorist attacks of September 11 helped increase interest in Africa and HIV/AIDS among Western policymakers, who feared that failed states would become the safe havens of terrorists. Because several African states face political, economic, and social pressures, policymakers have become more concerned about the continent's stability. One factor which may potentially exacerbate poverty, conflict, and political competition in some places on the continent is AIDS. As a result of this shift in paradigm, ODA from the United States grew between fiscal year 2002 ($17 billion) and fiscal year 2003 ($21 billion). (These numbers exclude amounts going to Iraq in 2003.) By fiscal year 2004, 18.3 percent of US ODA went to Africa, an increase of 4 percent since 1994. Between 2002 and 2004, the biggest increases were for global health, though these increases were not consistent across all health programs. For example, there was very little increase in the budgets for family planning, child survival, maternal health, and other infectious disease programs. AIDS spending, on the other hand, tripled (Tarnoff and Nowels, 2004, p. 10). In 2006, multilateral and bilateral donors and national governments spent approximately $8.3 billion on AIDS programs in low- and middle-income countries. While the increase in funding is crucial for fighting AIDS, it is important to notice that attention to AIDS in Africa reflects changes in how the West views its strategic interest in the continent. The danger of framing Africa (and its AIDS pandemic) in this light is that when Western interests change, funding for AIDS programs may decline. Building a sustainable fight against the pandemic will require long-term commitment from the West and African states.

In summary, globalization has contributed to the AIDS pandemic in several ways. It has encouraged labor migration to mining towns and export-producing enclaves. Neoliberal economic policies have led to increased unemployment and poverty. The WTO's promotion of drug company patents meant that ARV treatment remained too costly for most HIV-positive Africans. Structural adjustment policies constrained the ability of African states to fight AIDS, particularly during the 1980s and early 1990s, when states cut healthcare budgets. Even though twenty-seven of forty-eight African countries increased healthcare spending between 1995 and 2003, state capacity remains a huge challenge (Patterson, 2006, pp. 83–84). Over the past twenty-five years, Africa has experienced a progressive loss of state capacity, "with civil services characterized by pervasive absenteeism, endemic corruption, politicization, declining legitimacy, and low morale" (van de Walle, 2004, p. 50). The AIDS battle requires not only healthcare workers, but state infrastructure and educated and well-paid civil servants at all levels of government. Yet, this requirement is not met when millions of Africans live abroad, including 47 percent of all college-educated Ghanaians and 38 percent of all college-educated Kenyans (Dugger, 2005). Bilateral and multilateral donors have not paid sufficient attention to African state building as part of structural adjustment policies. Furthermore, through their inconsistent attention to the continent during the 1990s, Western donors made it more difficult to develop a proactive plan to fight the disease.

While donors now provide more resources for the pandemic, Africa still is burdened by over $200 billion in debt. Africa's debt burden and high level of poverty mean that donors are essential to the AIDS fight. In some states, donors provide over 80 percent of the AIDS funds (UNCTAD, 2004; Patterson, 2006, p. 89). The "Geneva consensus" (i.e., AIDS policies that come from UNAIDS, which is headquartered in Geneva) accompanies such funds. To prevent HIV transmission, the consensus has stressed individual behavior change through activities such as abstinence until marriage, monogamy in relationships, and condom use, but it has downplayed larger contextual factors such as poverty and Africans' poor health that shape the pandemic. Africa's overall economic marginalization in the era of post-cold war globalization shapes the pandemic and international, state, and local responses to it.

Using the Tools of Globalization to Fight AIDS in Africa

While globalization has exacerbated the factors which make people vulnerable to HIV infection, the phenomenon also provides avenues through which to fight the disease. To conquer AIDS and its long-term effects on societies, economies, and families, it will be essential to utilize the tools of globalization such as the global media, transnational advocacy networks, and international organizations. This section will focus on how the AIDS fight has begun to move along this path.

Global Media and the Mobilization of Western Interest

The media have been crucial for making citizens in industrialized countries aware of the AIDS pandemic in Africa. Satellite technology, CNN, and 24-hour news outlets have made it easier for Westerners to see pictures of AIDS clinics, Africans living with AIDS, and children affected by the disease. While such imagery can reinforce the stereotypes of Africa as a poor, conflict-ridden, and "primitive" continent (Keim 1999, p. 14), media coverage has been crucial for making political leaders and citizens in the West aware of the magnitude of AIDS. In 2004, 51 percent of people surveyed in the United States reported seeing a considerable amount of television coverage on the global AIDS pandemic, and 59 percent said that AIDS had "gotten worse" in Africa (Kaiser Family Foundation, 2004; Patterson, 2006, p. 137). While these statistics say nothing about how strongly people in the United States held these opinions, these numbers demonstrate growing citizen concern about AIDS. More specifically, this public awareness enabled US policymakers and advocacy groups who wanted more funds to fight AIDS to build support for the US President's Emergency Plan for AIDS Relief (PEPFAR), which the US Congress passed in 2003. PEPFAR provides $15 billion over five years to fifteen focus countries that are hard hit by HIV/AIDS. Twelve of these countries – South Africa, Zambia, Tanzania, Namibia, Nigeria, Kenya, Mozambique, Rwanda, Côte d'Ivoire, Botswana, Ethiopia, and Uganda – are in Africa; the other three are Haiti, Guyana, and Vietnam.

PEPFAR's emergence reflected the political mobilization of evangelical Christians who had overwhelmingly voted for George W. Bush in the 2000 election (den Dulk 2006). Evangelical Christians reported learning about AIDS from media reports, but also through missionaries who lived and worked in Africa, short-term mission trips they (or their family and friends) had made to the continent, and denominational newsletters and websites. By 2001, the relative ease of gaining information about Africa and traveling to the continent heightened awareness about AIDS. Christian development organizations such as World Vision began to highlight AIDS to their financial supporters and they organized short-term trips to the continent to educate pastors of large American churches about the pandemic.[4] When the White House began to design its AIDS plan in late 2002, there was strong support in the US Congress for what eventually became PEPFAR. The tools of globalization – airline travel, rapid communication, and the internet – facilitated this US interest in AIDS.

The global entertainment industry also heightened awareness about AIDS and Africa's poverty. Bono, the lead singer for U2, helped to cofound the organization Debt, AIDS, Trade, Africa (DATA). The advocacy group capitalized on Bono's popularity to educate people in the West about Africa and to advocate for pro-Africa policies in Washington and London. Bono's trips to Africa received widespread media attention in the United States, and they encouraged other celebrities such as Brad Pitt and Angela Jolie to travel to Africa and to publicize relief and development work there. The Live 8 concert before the Group of Eight industrialized countries

4 Serge Duss, Director of Public Policy and Advocacy, World Vision, interview with author, Washington, DC, March 18, 2005.

met in July 2005 to discuss African debt relief also called attention to the continent's economic plight (Takiff, 2005).

It would be naïve to assume that such activities have much direct impact on the AIDS fight. In reality, celebrity and media attention to Africa often focus on the worst of the continent's problems and such attention can be fleeting. Despite these limitations, this attention is crucial because it keeps the pandemic on the political agenda in the West, particularly in the United States, which provides the largest amount of money to fight AIDS globally. As demonstrated above, US foreign assistance programs can increase or decrease relatively easily as perceptions about national interests change. Western citizens and policymakers must continue to perceive that combating AIDS is in their nations' interests. This perspective is crucial because AIDS in Africa is not a short-term problem which will be solved in a few years; the disease will affect several generations. To lessen the pandemic's effects, additional resources are essential: UNAIDS estimates that $22.1 billion will be needed in 2008, more than twice what was spent in 2005 (UN General Assembly, 2006, p.17). Western policymakers will only allocate those types of funds if their constituents continue to care about AIDS. Thus, mobilizing Western citizens through media coverage and celebrity advocacy is an important tool in the AIDS fight, since the beneficiaries of ODA – poor, marginalized individuals in countries far from Washington, London, or Brussels – have no voice in Western politics.

International Organizations

While the World Bank, IMF, and WTO constrained the ability of states to address AIDS in the 1980s and 1990s through the implementation of structural adjustment policies and the protection of IPRs, such international organizations such as UNAIDS and the Global Fund to Fight AIDS, Tuberculosis and Malaria have been crucial for coordinating AIDS efforts. Formed in 1996, UNAIDS brings together ten UN agencies.[5] With its secretariat working in more than seventy-five countries, UNAIDS advocates for more political attention to AIDS, collects HIV prevalence data, and coordinates the efforts of multilateral and bilateral donors. UNAIDS has provided technical advice to countries facing mounting HIV prevalence levels and it has mobilized NGOs to educate citizens about AIDS, to advocate for additional funding, and to care and support people with the disease.

In recent years, UNAIDS has helped to frame the disease in ways most pertinent to the West. After the terrorist attacks on the United States in 2001, Peter Piot, UNAIDS coordinator, realized that policymakers in the West would pay greater attention to AIDS if the disease were tied to national security concerns. In particular, he asserted that countries with health crises could become havens for terrorists, warlords, and insurgents, since health crises such as AIDS erode the economic and social fabric

---

5 The ten agencies are the UN High Commission for Refugees, the UN Children's Fund, the World Food Program, the UN Development Program, the UN Fund for Population Activities, the UN Office of Drug Control, the International Labor Organization, the UN Educational, Scientific, and Cultural Organization, the World Health Organization, and the World Bank

of a nation. At approximately the same time, some scholars published research which linked disease, resource scarcity, and global security (See Price-Smith, 2002; International Crisis Group, 2001; Ostergard, 2002). In late 2002, the US Central Intelligence Agency reported that rising HIV rates in China, Ethiopia, India, Nigeria, and Russia pose a security threat to those countries' regions and the United States (Altman, 2002). To be clear, while Al-Qaeda had found refuge in the failed state of Afghanistan, empirical studies have yet to determine that AIDS increases global insecurity (Barnett, 2006). However, the perception that disease and global security are intertwined helped mobilize support for increased funding for AIDS.

UNAIDS also provided the institutional structure through which public health experts and AIDS activists could push for a new global funding mechanism to combat AIDS, TB, and malaria. By 2001, UNAIDS officials had helped to build political support for a UN General Assembly Special Session on HIV/AIDS. At the session, all UN member states agreed to the "Declaration of Commitment on HIV/AIDS," which emphasized a multisectoral approach to AIDS, the need to provide HIV prevention and ARV treatment, and the importance of developing a funding mechanism for AIDS programs. Officials at UNAIDS, WHO, and the UN Secretary General's office built support for the Global Fund to Fight AIDS, Tuberculosis and Malaria among Western donors and received a US pledge of $200 million before the 2001 special session (Patterson, 2005, pp. 179–184). Since its first grants in 2003, the Global Fund has approved over $6.6 billion for programs in 136 countries (Of this amount, it has dispersed roughly $2.9 billion to 129 countries). Approximately 58 percent of Global Fund money awarded during the first five rounds of grants has been for AIDS programs; Sub-Saharan Africa has gained 56 percent of all grants during the five rounds. Of its funds allocated, 48 percent has gone for medicines and commodities and 22 percent has been used for human resources (Global Fund, 2006).

Unlike many UN agencies or bilateral donors, the Global Fund does not administer programs. Instead, it requires applicant countries to form a country coordinating mechanism (CCM) composed of state officials, civil society representatives, academics, and bilateral and multilateral donor officials. The CCM writes the country's grant proposal, a process which is intended to increase civil society representation in AIDS policymaking and to make government more accountable for health spending. A Technical Review Panel composed of physicians and public health experts meets in Geneva to judge proposals and award grants. Thus, grants from the Global Fund are not subject to the same political or strategic calculations that bilateral aid programs often are.

To pay for its grants, the Global Fund relies on donations from bilateral donors, individuals, and corporations. While this dependence makes the Global Fund more independent in its decisions, it also makes the institution vulnerable to the whims of domestic politics within its donor countries, particularly since it lacks a built-in constituency in the West. Organizations such as DATA have tried to advocate for the Global Fund, and former US Senate Majority Leader Bill Frist, retired US Representative Jim Kolbe, and current US Representative Barbara Lee have been strong supporters of the organization in the US Congress. Yet despite these advocates, the relationship between the Global Fund and the US bilateral program PEPFAR has been unclear at times. While the United States provides the most money to the Global Fund of any industrialized country, this amount is often less than many Global Fund supporters would like (Patterson, 2006, pp. 148–149). Additionally, PEPFAR's 2003 authorizing legislation limits the size of the US contribution to the Global Fund to one-third of all money the fund receives annually. While intended to encourage other industrialized countries to give more to the Fund, this earmark limited the US contribution to the institution in 2004 (Copson, 2005).

The Global Fund demonstrates how one aspect of globalization – integration through multilateral institutions – can be positive for the AIDS fight. The Global Fund seeks to support local initiatives and encourage creativity in public health solutions through its application process. It aims to promote consensus building, compromise, and transparency within countries, and as such, recognizes that health issues cannot be merely solved through the application of technical solutions. Health problems also must be addressed through the policy process, which involves setting priorities, allocating resources, and deciding what a society values. Both the Global Fund and UNAIDS institutionalize the AIDS fight, providing staff with expertise about AIDS and actors with political interests in the AIDS fight. Furthermore, by working in multiple countries, these global institutions enable Western states to shape AIDS programs in countries even where they have no bilateral programs. While this may be negative, if Western states do not listen to local voices or only support the "Geneva consensus," these global institutions also help to increase the likelihood that powerful states will continue to be concerned about AIDS in poor countries. This is particularly true if donor countries see that the Global Fund's grants are essential for the success of their own bilateral AIDS programs. For example, because PEPFAR concentrates on AIDS, it must rely on Global Fund-supported TB treatment and testing programs in PEPFAR-focus countries. Since roughly one-third of HIV-positive people globally are co-infected with TB, and since TB is the leading killer of AIDS patients in Southern Africa, any success in fighting AIDS in the most hard-hit countries must include large TB components (Patterson, 2006, p.140). A positive outcome of globalization, the integration of bilateral programs and Global Fund-funded projects, is essential for both programs to achieve success.

The Global Fund also has tapped into the globalization of consumer products through its so-called (Product) RED. Unveiled in late 2005 and started by Bobby Shriver and Bono, the product line seeks to capitalize on the buying power and consumerism of citizens in wealthy countries to benefit AIDS programs globally. Producers of items purchased predominantly in wealthy countries (e.g., Converse shoes, Gap clothes, Armani bags, and American Express credit cards) have agreed to give a certain percentage of their RED profits to the Global Fund. For example, the Fund receives 50 percent of profits from Gap's RED product line. Bono, Penelope Cruz, and Dakota Fanning have publicized (Product) RED in the United Kingdom and the United States, through editorials in newspapers, news interviews, and appearances on television talk shows (Gordon, 2006).

The Transnational Advocacy Network and Treatment for People with HIV/AIDS

Transnational advocacy networks are composed of actors working on an issue who are bound together by shared values, a common discourse, and dense exchanges of information and services (Keck and Sikkink, 2004, pp. 222–226). These networks frame issues, bring new ideas, norms, and discourses into policy debates, and monitor compliance with international agreements. Transnational networks often link international and domestic NGOs, and use their expertise in issue areas to persuade and socialize global actors to accept their policy ideas. While their impact varies, a network's activities can lead to changes in policy, not only in the states they target, but also in other states and international organizations. A transnational advocacy network composed of AIDS activists, public health experts, human rights advocates, people with HIV/AIDS, and representatives of development organizations has become a crucial actor in global AIDS policymaking. The network is evident in the aforementioned mobilization of citizens to support PEPFAR or the development and marketing of (Product) RED. However, the network has been the most effective in its advocacy of ARV treatment in poor countries. By 2003, the so-called AIDS treatment movement had strongly influenced the treatment policies of donor states and international organizations.

By 1998, the gap between people with AIDS in industrialized countries who had access to life-saving ARVs and individuals with AIDS in the developing world without drug access had become wide (Smith and Siplon, 2006, p. 45). At the 1998 International AIDS Conference, Western AIDS activists began to call for greater access to ARVs in poor countries. At roughly the same time, political activists formed the Treatment Action Campaign (TAC) in South Africa. TAC's initial activity was to challenge the pharmaceutical industry's case against the South African Medicines Act, which allowed compulsory licensing of AIDS drugs. Through the use of mass protests and savvy media interviews, TAC humanized the cost of the lack of ARV treatment for thousands of South Africans with AIDS. The organization reframed the treatment issue as a moral crisis, and argued that human lives were being lost because the TRIPS Agreement protected the drug companies' ability to make high profits (Cameron, 2005, p. 177). Because of the efforts of TAC, the pharmaceutical industry dropped the lawsuit against the South African government in 2001. In 1999, AIDS activists globally formed the Health Global Access Project Coalition (or "Health GAP"), an organization which collaborated closely with TAC, Partners in Health, Médicins sans Frontières (Doctors without Borders), AIDS Coalition to Unleash Power (ACT UP), Health Action International, and Consumer Product Technology (Smith and Siplon, 2006, p. 60).

The coalition highlighted the lack of treatment in poor countries and the high prices of ARVs at global media events. For example, when South Africa hosted the 2000 International AIDS Conference, TAC-organized protestors gained international media attention with their conference speeches and their protests outside the meeting. The media paid close attention to the event because it was the first time the biennial AIDS meeting was held in Africa, and because President Thabo Mbeki had questioned the link between HIV and AIDS earlier that year. One of the highlighted speakers at the conference was the HIV-positive Nkosi Johnson, a black South

African teenager who had battled HIV/AIDS his entire life and whose plight had been publicized nationally and globally. Nkosi ended his speech with the powerful words: "We are all the same… We love and we laugh, we hurt and we cry, we live and we die. … Care for us and accept us" (Wooten, 2004, p. 205).

Nkosi's speech, TAC protests, Mbeki's denial of the seriousness of AIDS, and the drug companies' callousness to the need for cheap ARVs galvanized the treatment movement. These events also helped mobilize other organizations which had previously paid limited attention to AIDS: human rights groups began to focus on treatment as a basic human right; development organizations argued that without treatment years of progress in Africa's socioeconomic development would be lost; faith-based organizations asserted that there were religious and humanitarian reasons that AIDS treatment should made available. Activists portrayed drug manufacturers as profit-mongers, and Western governments which supported the companies, as inhumane. Protesters in the United States linked the Clinton Administration to the pharmaceutical industry, since the United States had supported the lawsuit against South Africa and had threatened trade sanctions against poor countries if they engaged in parallel importing or compulsory licensing. To call attention to these US actions, Health GAP staged protests at campaign rallies for then presidential candidate Al Gore in 2000 (Behrman, 2004, pp. 140–154).

The movement also relied on knowledge and expertise to shape the debate about treatment in poor countries. While price was a huge obstacle to ARV access, some Western policymakers argued that the complicated regimens that HAART required of patients would be impossible to follow in resource-poor countries among uneducated patients. Through their pilot treatment programs in poor communities in Haiti and South Africa, Partners in Health and Doctors without Borders provided empirical evidence that poor patients can adhere to complicated drug regimens. Their successful programs debunked the "treatment is not feasible" assertion (Farmer, 2005, p. 18; Irwin et al., 2003, p. 77). AIDS experts such as Dr. Alan Berkman of the Columbia School of Public Health argued that treatment and prevention programs must be implemented together. Treatment gave citizens an incentive to get tested for HIV; without testing, people could easily spread the virus to others. He also maintained that it was essential to keep HIV-positive individuals alive, since they are the most effective advocates for HIV prevention and since they are productive workers and caregivers for children (Berkman, 2001).

By the UN General Assembly Special Session in 2001, these arguments had swayed many states that treatment in poor countries could no longer be ignored. The success of compulsory licensing and generic ARV production in Brazil demonstrated that poor countries could produce their own ARVs and administer large scale treatment programs (Smith and Siplon, 2006, p. 49). The 2001 Declaration of Commitment to HIV/AIDS reaffirmed the need for treatment in poor countries as crucial for the AIDS fight. The Global Fund and PEPFAR have put this policy into practice; the Global Fund through the large percentage of money it spends on ARVs and PEPFAR, through the requirement that 55 percent of its funding be used for ARV treatment (Office of Global AIDS Coordinator, 2004). The treatment movement was a significant factor leading to these outcomes, primarily because it moved the debate about treatment from the technical issue of IPRs to the moral issue of patients' lives. This new understanding enabled poor states and activists to push for further implementation of Article 30 of the TRIPS Agreement that allows parallel importing and compulsory licensing. Moreover, as PEPFAR tries to treat two million people with AIDS by 2008, it has increasingly had to rely on cheaper generic ARVs (PEPFAR requires such generics to meet FDA approval first, a process which critics claim slows their use). The entry of generics into the market has created competition, driving down the price of the first-line triple combination therapy to less than $200 per patient per year (Patterson, 2007).

Although the number of Africans with access to ARVs has increased greatly since 2000, the vast majority of HIV-positive people on the continent who need treatment still cannot get it. The transnational advocacy network must continue to hold donors and African states responsible so that treatment becomes more readily available. Several tasks remain: The network must lobby donors and drug companies to make pediatric ARVs, which are more difficult to administer and often more expensive, available to the thousands of African children who need them. Additionally, the network must play a watchdog role, making sure that the US Congress when it reauthorizes PEPFAR in 2008, provides adequate funding for ARVs, including second-line treatment regimens which are more expensive. To achieve these goals, the network will need to capitalize on the tools of globalization, such as the internet, global AIDS conferences, media coverage of AIDS, the global dissemination of knowledge about the disease, and interconnections among states, nonstate actors, and international organizations such as UNAIDS and the Global Fund.

Conclusion

As a complex collection of phenomena, globalization has interacted with HIV/AIDS to shape African society for years to come. Through the spread of trade networks and FDI, Africa has been pulled into the global economy, though not to the same extent as other regions. Africans have migrated to export-producing enclaves in search of jobs, but this migration has fueled the conditions of urban overcrowding, poor housing, and social dislocation under which individuals become more vulnerable to disease. Africa's integration into the capitalist system facilitated debt and, by the 1980s, subjected the continent to the neoliberal consensus of international financial institutions. Structural adjustment policies, particularly cuts in government spending on social services, made it more difficult for African states to provide adequate health care for their citizens. With increased poverty and decreased primary healthcare, Africans became more vulnerable to health problems, including STIs, parasitic infections, TB, and malaria. Co-infection with these diseases and poor nutrition increased vulnerability to HIV, and contributed to the rapid spread of the disease in some African countries. The WTO and TRIPS Agreement made treating AIDS and other disease more expensive, since it protected the IPRs of Western companies at the expense of poor, politically powerless Africans. And the West's sporadic attention to the continent after the cold war meant it did little to curtail the impending AIDS pandemic until the twenty-first century.

While globalization has had negative ramifications for AIDS in Africa, it also presents opportunities. New international institutions have formed to address AIDS: UNAIDS politicizes the disease and provides needed data for an effective AIDS fight and the Global Fund raises and allocates money to combat the pandemic. The global media and international celebrities have called attention to AIDS, a crucial factor for mobilizing Western citizens to pressure their elected officials. Transnational advocacy networks have used the media, international communication, global travel, and international institutions to push for more just AIDS policies. As these networks become sophisticated and widespread, they have the potential to challenge the negative effects of globalization. The fact that only three years after activists demanded treatment at the 2000 AIDS conference the US Congress passed PEPFAR testifies to the power of such networks against the negative forces of globalization. Maintaining the interest, energy, and power of such networks as AIDS enters its third decade will be essential for the future health of Africa's citizens.

References

Altman, L. (2002), "AIDS in 5 Nations Called Security Threat", *New York Times*, 1 October, p. A6.

Bagala, A. (2006), "Married Couples Top HIV Infection Rates", *The Monitor* (Kampala). 4 December, available at <http://allafrica.com/stories/printable/200612041050.html>.

Barnett, T. (2006), "A Long Wave Event: HIV/AIDS, Politics, Governance and Security: Sundering the Intergenerational Bond?" *International Affairs*, Vol. 82, No. 2, pp. 931–952.

Barnett, T., and Whiteside, A. (2002), *AIDS in the Twenty-First Century: Disease and Globalization* (New York: Palgrave Macmillan).

Behrman, G. (2004), *The Invisible People: How the U.S. Has Slept Through the Global AIDS Pandemic, the Greatest Humanitarian Catastrophe of Our Time* (New York: Free Press).

Berkman, A. (2001), "Confronting Global AIDS: Prevention and Treatment", *American Journal of Public Health*, Vol. 91. No. 9, pp. 1348–1349.

Blake, C. (2005), *Politics in Latin America* (New York: Houghton Mifflin).

Cameron, E. (2005), *Witness to AIDS* (New York: I. B. Taurus).

Campbell, C. (2003), *"Letting Them Die": Why HIV/AIDS Prevention Programs Fail* (Bloomington IN: Indiana University Press).

Copson, R. (2005), *The Global Fund and PEPFAR in U.S. International AIDS Policy: Implications for Africa*, Paper presented at the African Studies Association Conference, Washington, DC, 17 Nov.

de Waal, A. (2006), *AIDS and Power: Why There Is No Political Crisis-Yet* (New York: Zed Books).

—— (2003), "How Will HIV/AIDS Transform African Governance?", *African Affairs*, Vol. 102, No. 206, pp. 1–23.

den Dulk, K. (2006), "Evangelical Elites and Faith-based Foreign Affairs", *Faith and International Affairs*, Vol. 4, No. 1, pp. 21–29.

Dugger, C. (2004), "An Exodus of African Nurses Puts Infants and the Ill in Peril", *New York Times*, 12 July, p. A1.

—— (2005), "Study Finds Small Developing Lands Hit Hardest by 'Brain Drain'", *New York Times*, 25 Oct., p. A10.

Farmer, P. (2005), *Pathologies of Power: Health, Human Rights, and the New War on the Poor* (Berkeley: University of California Press).

Global Fund to Fight AIDS, Tuberculosis and Malaria (2006), "Monthly Progress Update – 15 November 2006," Available at <http://www.theglobalfund.org>.

"The Globalization Index" (2006), *Foreign Policy*, November/December, pp. 74–81.

Gordon, D. (2006), "Buying Our Way to a Better World", *Toronto Star*, 28 Oct. at <http://web.lexis-nexis.com/universe/document?_m=926bd16be1fd14889d71-d4cfa0bf8>

Halbert, D., and May, C. (2005), "AIDS, Pharmaceutical Patents and the African State: Reorienting the Global Governance of Intellectual Property," in A. Patterson (ed.) *The African State and the AIDS Crisis* (Aldershot, UK: Ashgate Publishing)

Hunter, S. (2003), *Black Death: AIDS in Africa* (New York: Palgrave Macmillan).

International Crisis Group (2001), "AIDS as a Security Threat", at <http://www.crisisgroup.org/library/documents/report/archives/A400321_19062001.pdf>.

Irwin, A., Millen, J., and Fallows, D. (2003), *Global AIDS Myths and Facts*, (Cambridge, MA.: South End Press).

Kaiser Family Foundation (2006), "HIV/AIDS Policy Fact Sheet", at <http://www.kff.org>.

—— (2004), "Survey of Americans on HIV/AIDS. Part One – Global HIV/AIDS. Summary and Chart Pack", at <http://www.kff.org/hivaids/7093.cfm>.

Keck, M. and Sikkink, K. (2004), "Transnational Advocacy Networks in International Politics: Introduction", in K. Mingst and J. Snyder (eds) *Essential Readings in World Politics*, 2nd edn (New York: Norton Press).

Keim, C. (1999), *Mistaking Africa: Curiosities and Inventions of the American Mind*, (Boulder, CO: Westview Press).

Lancaster, C. (2000), "Africa in World Affairs", in J. Harbeson and D. Rothchild (eds) *Africa in World Politics: The African State System in Flux*, 3rd edn (Boulder, CO: Westview Press).

Lurie, P., Hintzen, P., and Lowe, R. (2004), "Socioeconomic Obstacles to HIV Prevention and Treatment in Developing Countries: The Role of the International Monetary Fund and the World Bank", in E. Kalipeni, S. Craddock, J. Oppong and J. Ghosh (eds) *HIV & AIDS in Africa: Beyond Epidemiology* (Malden, MA: Blackwell Publishing).

Office of Global AIDS Coordinator (2004), *The President's Emergency Plan for AIDS Relief: U.S. Five Year Global HIV/AIDS Strategy*, at <http://www.state.gov/s/gac/rl/or/44535.htm>.

Ostergard, R. (2002), "Politics in the Hot Zone: AIDS and National Security in Africa", *Third World Quarterly*, Vol. 23, No. 2, pp. 333–350.

Patterson, A. (ed.) (2005), *The African State and the AIDS Crisis*, (Aldershot, UK: Ashgate Publishing).

Patterson, A. (2006), *The Politics of AIDS in Africa* (Boulder, CO: Lynne Rienner Publishers).

——. (2007), "The UN and the Fight Against HIV/AIDS", in P. Harris and P. Siplon (eds) *The Global Politics of AIDS* (Boulder, CO: Lynne Rienner Publishers).

Price-Smith, A. (2002), *The Health of Nations: Infectious Disease, Environmental Change, and Their Effects on National Security and Development* (Cambridge, MA: MIT Press).

Siplon, P. (2005), "AIDS and Patriarchy: Ideological Obstacles to Effective Policy Making", in A. Patterson (ed.) *The African State and the AIDS Crisis*, (Aldershot, UK: Ashgate Publishers).

Smith, R. and Siplon, P. (2006), *Drugs into Bodies: Global AIDS Treatment Activism* (Westport, CT: Praeger).

Smith, S. (2006), "Wanted in AIDS Fight: 4 Million More Workers", *Boston Globe*, 21 Aug., available at <http://www.boston.com/news/global/health_science/articles/2006/08/21/wanted_in_aids_fight>.

Stillwaggon, E. (2006), *AIDS and the Ecology of Poverty* (New York: Oxford Press).

Takiff, J. (2005), "Plugged In", *Philadelphia Daily News*, 28 June, available at: <http://web.lexis-nexis.com/universe/document?_m=ed655a1c67a584322a1268cea8ae9ee6&_docnum=3&wchp=dGLbVlz-zSkVb&_md5=e5663e1b0887315c47b1b039006e92e6>.

Tarnoff, C. and Nowels, L. (2004), "Foreign Aid: An Introductory Overview of U.S. Programs and Policy", *CRS Report for Congress* (Washington, DC: Government Printing Office).

Thomas, C. (2002), "Trade Policy and the Politics of Access to Drugs", *Third World Quarterly*, Vol. 23, No. 2, pp. 251–264.

UNAIDS (2006), *UNAIDS/WHO AIDS Epidemic Update, December 2006*, available at <http://www.unaids.org/en/HIV_data/epi2006/default.asp>

UNCTAD (2004), "New UNCTAD Study Makes Case for African Debt Write-Off", press release, at <http://www.unctad.org>.

—— (2005), *Economic Development in Africa: Rethinking the Role of Foreign Direct Investment*, UN Conference on Trade and Development, Geneva.

UNDP (2005), *Human Development Report 2005. International Cooperation at a Crossroads: Aid, Trade and Security in an Unequal World*, United Nations, New York.

—— (2006a), *Human Development Report. Beyond Scarcity: Power, Poverty and the Global Water Crisis*, available at: <http://hdr.undp.org/hdr2006/statistics/indicators/10.html>.

—— (2006b), "Power Point Presentation for Media", available at: <http://hdr.undp.org/hcr2006/press/HDR2006_Full_ENGLISH_OCt26.ppt>.

UN General Assembly (2006), "Declaration of Commitment on HIV/AIDS: Five Years Later", *Report of the Secretary General*, March 24, 2006, Available at: <http://data.unaids.org/pub/Report/2006/20060324_SGReport_GA_A60736_en.pdf>.

United Nations (2004), *World Economic and Social Survey 2004: International Migration* (New York: United Nations Printing Office).

US Trade Representative (2006), "Trade Facts: US-Africa Trade", at <http://www.agoa.gov>.

van de Walle, N. (2001), *African Economies and the Politics of Permanent Crisis, 1979–1999* (New York: Cambridge University Press).

—— (2004), "Economic Reform: Patterns and Constraints", in E. Gyimah-Boadi (ed.) *Democratic Reform in Africa: The Quality of Progress* (Boulder, CO: Lynne Rienner Publishers).

ver Beek, K. (2001), "Maquiladoras: Exploitation or Emancipation? An Overview of the Situation of Maquiladora Workers in Honduras", *World Development*, Vol. 29, No.9, pp. 1553–1567.

Whiteside, A. (2005), "The Economic, Social, and Political Drivers of the AIDS Epidemic in Swaziland: A Case Study", in A. Patterson (ed.), *The African State and the AIDS Crisis* (Aldershot, UK: Ashgate Publishers).

Wines, M. (2004), "Women in Lesotho Become Easy Prey for H.I.V." *New York Times*, 20 July, p. A1.

Wooten, J. (2004), *We Are All the Same: A Story of a Boy's Courage and a Mother's Love* (New York: Penguin Press).

Chapter 9

Weaving Together the Threads of the New Globalization: The Lessons

George Klay Kieh, Jr.

Introduction

The various chapters in this volume have attempted to examine the impact of the "new globalization" on Africa. Addressing various frontier issues – debt, human rights, development, state sovereignty, the environment and the HIV/AIDS pandemic – each chapter deciphers the nature and dynamics of the problematique and then situates them within the bowels of the phenomenon. Specifically, there were two major overarching questions: What are the travails of each of the frontier issues? What is the impact of the "new globalization" on the issue?

Against this background, the purpose of this chapter is three-fold. First, it will summarize the major findings of the various chapters. Second, it will draw the lessons that are common to the various chapters. Third, it will suggest some ways in which Africa could address and mediate the deleterious effects of the phenomenon.

The Summation

Debt

The chapter offers major findings about the impact of the "new globalization" on Africa in the area of debt. Clearly it appears that the advanced capitalist states and their international financial institutions – International Monetary Fund(IMF) and the World Bank – have grudgingly come to the realization that the once vaunted "Structural Adjustment Programs" (SAPs) and their associated "therapeutic toolboxes" of economic openness to foreign private investment and trade, the "dismantling of the social safety net," currency devaluation, increase in interest rates, downsizing the public sector, freezing employment in the public sector and freezing wages in the public sector have not been able to heal the endemic sclerosis of the economies of African states; hence, the "movers and shakers" of the global economy have devised multilateral and bilateral "debt forgiveness plans": At the multilateral level, the Heavily Indebted Poor Countries Initiative (HIPCI) is ostensibly designed to waive the debts owed to the "Bretton Woods institutions" – International Monetary Fund(IMF) and the World Bank. Similarly, the United States and other advanced capitalist states have designed their own "debt forgiveness plans" for Africa. The logic of the two clusters is that those African states whose debts are forgiven can use the money for debt servicing to help fund their respective national development programs – education, health care, etc. In other words, the professed goal of "debt forgiveness" is to redirect the financial resources of African states from debt servicing to national socio-economic development.

However, the various multilateral and bilateral plans have some major shortcoming. A critical issue is the fact that the plans are not opened to all African countries that are being strangulated by the asphyxiating effects of servicing odious debts. Instead, in order for an African state to qualify for "debt forgiveness," it must fulfill criteria designed by the advanced capitalist states and their multilateral financial institutions. Another problem is that the plans do not include Western commercial banks, which have made huge profits from indebted African states through debt servicing. Also, the schemes are being implemented in the context of the neo-colonial African state. The problem is that it is this construct that has provided the enabling environment for the contracting of these odious debts by African states. Hence, in order for "debt servicing" to have any meaningful impact on the affected African states, it must take place within the bowels of a democratically reconstituted state in Africa. If this is not done, the custodians of the various neo-colonial African states will not direct the "dividends of debt forgiveness" to funding social and economic programs. In the same vein, there would be no mechanisms in place to restrain the capacity of the members of the bureaucratic wing of the ruling classes of African states from contracting new debts.

The Travails of Human Needs

During the "old globalization," Africa was plagued by, among other things, mass abject poverty, low standard of living, the lack of access to health care, safe drinking water and acceptable sanitation, vulnerability to diseases and low life expectancy. Overall, life in Africa, to paraphrase Hobbes (2002), was "short, nasty and brutish." The state which should have been the bulwark of protection for its citizens against the venalities of the "old globalization" served as the phenomenon's reliable collaborator. The neo-colonial African state as a handmaid of the "old globalization" was an albatross that made it difficult for people-centered development to take place on the continent.

Against the backdrop of Africa's travails during the "old globalization," one of the major arguments of the proponents of the "new globalization" is that the phenomenon would, inter alia, provide economic opportunities, improve the standards of living and create wealth throughout the world (Solimano, 1999). In effect, the proponents of the "new globalization" have unequivocally asserted that the phenomenon would be based on the framework of a "positive sum game" in which Africa would reap handsomely from the "dividends. As the annual human development reports recurrently show, human development in Africa is the lowest in the world irrespective of the indicators that are employed. Even the imposition of the neo-liberal model of socio-economic development has worsened the state of basic human needs on the continent. So, life on the continent for the preponderant majority of Africans remains what Ramsay (1993, p. 3) calls "a struggle for survival."

Human Rights

The promotion and the protection of comprehensive human rights have always been the mainstay of the existence of the African peoples. For example, the national liberation struggles were hoisted on the common goal of ushering in a post-colonial order in which the political, civil, economic, social and cultural rights of the peoples of Africa would be respected. However, during the epoch of the "old globalization" the continent's various authoritarian regimes suppressed, repressed and violated the political and civil rights of their citizens with impunity. Similarly, in the economic and social arenas, the African peoples were the targets and victims of structural violence. This was evidenced by high rates of unemployment, excruciating poverty, gross inequities in wealth and income, limited access to health care, safe drinking water and sanitation and overall low standard of living. Culturally, in some cases, the state was transformed into an ethnic construct beholden to the particularistic agenda of a dominant ethnic group. In cases such as Rwanda, the resultant polarizing relationship between and among ethnic groups led to the commission of acts of genocide.

With the advent of the "new globalization," the issue of human rights has been placed on the agenda. For example, some sectors of the international community have made the respect for human rights an element of their relationships with African states. In the case of the European Union, it has made the respect for human rights a cornerstone of its relations with African states. The organization's aid program to African states has the respect for human rights as one of its major eligibility requirements Also, the United Nations and various regional and sub-regional organizations have intervened in civil conflicts in various African states – Somalia, Liberia, Sierra Leone, Guinea Bissau, Lesotho, Cote d' Ivoire, Guinea Bissau, the Democratic Republic of the Congo and Sudan, among others – as expressions, among other things, of their concerns for the protection of human rights. Another indication of the emergent global interest is the establishment of the International Criminal Court as the judicial form for bringing to justice those would violate human rights.

However, there are major challenges that need to be addressed if the promotion of human rights would become an enduring feature of the African landscape. First, the promotion of human rights needs to transcend the emphasis on political and civil liberties or "first generation human rights" and incorporate economic, social and cultural rights. This is because it is important to treat human rights as multidimensional and the composite of various freedoms.

Second, international actors like the United States need to be consistent in the application of human rights standards in their relations with African states. For example, in the case of the United States, it has not consistently linked its rhetorical commitment to the promotion of human rights on the continent to praxis, especially in matters involving its African client regimes in countries such as Nigeria, Rwanda and Uganda. That is, when the client regimes in these states violate human rights, the

United States usually remains silent. However, when violations are committed by non-client regimes, the United States is then quite vocal in its condemnation.

Third, there is an urgent need for the acceleration of the pace of human rights education in various African states. There is the imperative to broaden the scope of the various human rights education programs that are currently being pursued by non-governmental organizations in various African states. The foci should be on the need to reach the totality of the population and the expansion of the curriculum to include the multiple dimensions of human rights. Undertaking human rights education is indispensable to the creation and maintenance of new democratic orders in African states.

National Development

The "new globalization" has transformed the national development arenas of African states in several major ways. First, the state is no longer the sole actor in the governance of national development. There is now the emergence of local and global non-governmental organizations as competing actors. In essence, the governance of national development has become decentralized. Clearly, given the enormity of the national development project, there is no doubt that the state alone cannot shoulder the responsibility. However, the rise of non-governmental actors was propelled by factors that promote conflict rather than cooperation between the state, on the one hand, and local and non-governmental organizations, on the other. Specifically, non-governmental actors emerged against the backdrop of the widely held belief in the international system that the African state was incapable of managing the national development project because of its multiple pathologies – corruption, inefficiency, etc. Accordingly, non-governmental organizations were portrayed as the "saviors" that would ultimately rescue Africans from the abyss of the crises of underdevelopment and the grip of a corrupt and ineffective state. In short, non-governmental organizations emerged as alternative managers of the national development arena. Also, the development-based non-governmental organizations are "foot soldiers" in the promotion of neo-liberal orthodoxy and its attendant anti-people agenda. Clearly, this is paradoxical in light of the claims by non-governmental organizations that they are committed to improving the lives of the majority of Africans.

Second, the rise of non-governmental organizations as alternative centers of power in the development sector of African states has widened the continent's web of dependencies. For example, in various African countries, non-governmental organizations, especially the global ones, have carved up various territories for themselves in the development arena. Effectively, this represents efforts to wrestle away control from the state in these sectors. However, the resultant effect is that the citizens of the various states increasingly come to depend on NGOs rather than the state for the provision of services in these sectors. Undoubtedly, the poor record of performance of the majority of African states and the weaknesses engendered by the debilitating effects of neo-liberalism have hamstrung the capacities of African states to resist the erosion of their sovereign control over various aspects of their development sectors.

Third, NGOs have become the loci for development aid from the "global North." This is because the "global North" is determined to circumvent the African state and deal with local and global NGOs as the "new overlords" in the development sector of African states. However, the evidence shows that NGOs are not the institutional panaceas to the development crises that have, and continue to bedevil the continent. This is because some of the NGOs have performed poorly. Also, some have not demonstrated the requisite experience in dealing with the daunting challenges of development. In this vein, these NGOs have made several critical mistakes in terms of project implementation. Yet, others have not been transparent and accountable in the disbursement of funds and the overall implementation of projects.

State Sovereignty

The sovereignty of the African state has been one of the major casualties of the "new globalization" as reflected by several cases. In the area of economic and social policy-making, African states have lost their capacity to make independent decisions. This is because, among other things, the Bretton Woods Institutions – the International Monetary Fund and the World Bank – decide the direction of these policies. For example, under the "Structural Adjustment Programs" (SAPs) and their attendant conditionalities, the affected African states followed the policy prescriptions mandated by the IMF and the World Bank. One of the major prescriptions was the dismantling of the "social safety net." This had profound implications for critical social areas such as education and health care. Importantly, the loss of autonomous policy-making power has increased the irrelevance of the African state and made it even more distant from the preponderant majority of Africans.

Another example is the increasing prevalence of intervention in internal conflicts in African states. During the "old globalization", African states that were afflicted by civil conflicts, especially civil wars, had the uninhibited ability to address these problems in the manner of their choosing. However, since the advent of the "new globalization," "humanitarian interventions" in civil conflicts have become commonplace. For examples, the United Nations intervened in Somalia, the Economic Community of West African States, the African Union and the United Nations intervened in Liberia, and the United Nations intervened in Sierra Leone and the Democratic Republic of the Congo. The rationale for "humanitarian interventions" is that they are ostensibly designed to either arrest or mitigate the tides of violence and its associated cataclysmic consequences, especially for the civilian populations. So, in effect, African states that are plagued by violent civil conflicts no longer have the blanket freedom of operation they enjoyed during the "old globalization."

The Environment

The environmental degradation conundrum that has beset Africa since the colonial era is being worsened by the "new globalization." During the colonial era, the imperialist powers had no regards for the ecological damage their economic policies and practices were visiting on the continent. With their absolute control over the various colonies, the imperialist powers had *carte blanche* power to plunder and pillage Africa's vast economic resources for the benefits of their respective "mother countries," without any regards for sustainability. Accordingly, the air, land and waterways were polluted by the profit – maximization machine of the colonial state and its citizens, who owned businesses in the colony.

Interestingly, throughout the post-colonial era, the African ruling classes have failed to design and implement effective policies, including property rights and environmental regulations that would help to address the ecological consequences of the exploitation of the continent's natural resources by metropolitan-based multinational corporations. In fact, consistent with their compradorial role, the African ruling classes have given multinational corporations a virtual "blank check" to exploit natural resources without any regards for the environmental consequences. For example, in the oil-rich Niger Delta Region of Nigeria, Shell is inflicting serious damage on the environment. For example, rivers in the region have been polluted, thereby affecting the health of the residents of the area. Each time Nigerians living in the region have protested, the neo-colonial Nigerian state has marshaled and unleashed the full fury of its repressive apparatus against them. Importantly, given the burgeoning increase in the rate of poverty throughout the continent, the poor and the dispossessed have engaged in "survival-based activities" such as the burning of coal. These activities are contributing to environmental degradation because they involve the cutting of trees and the pollution of the air and land. Also, with Africa's increasing importance as a supplier of oil to the metropolis, various multinational corporations from the metropolis are engaged in a "mad rush" of oil exploration. Clearly, this would accelerate the pace of environmental degradation on the continent. This is because there is no evidence that the African states in which these new deposits of oil are being discovered are showing any inclination to developing robust regulatory systems to contain the acquisitive impulse of these oil-based multinational corporations. Instead, the ruling classes in these countries are more concerned with what they see as an immense opportunity to further enrich themselves by stealing from the public's coffers.

The HIV/AIDS Pandemic

The HIV/AIDS pandemic reflects an example of the rare duality of the "new globalization" – what I termed the "misery-opportunity tension." On the one hand, the phenomenon has contributed to the spread of the pandemic through migration and the other movement of peoples across increasingly shrinking borders. For examples, migrant workers, peacekeepers and prostitutes have been among the major conveyors of the virus.

On the other hand, the "new globalization" provides some opportunities for combating the pandemic. For example, various transnational advocacy groups consisting of members from various countries, sub-regions and regions of the world have been established. These groups are playing pivotal roles in the promotion of public awareness and education about the virus. Also, these groups are at the forefront of the efforts to mobilize international efforts to fund research and engage in various activities that are intended to address the disease. Also, the vast improvements in technology have led to the expansiveness of communications. Through the efforts of various media outlets – television, radio and the movies – , the pandemic has been a major issue on the global agenda. Another benefit is the significant progress that has been made in the development of a knowledge base about the disease. Coupled with this is the marked advancement in the conduct of research pertaining to the disease. One of the outcomes has been the development of various drugs to help contain the disease. However, this achievement is being undermined by the fact that poor people, who are afflicted by the disease, do not have the money to buy the very expensive drugs. Although efforts are being made to develop generic drugs and to subsidize the cost, large metropolitan-based pharmaceutical corporations are making huge "financial windfalls" from the sale of various HIV/AIDS drugs.

The Lessons

What are the major lessons that have been learned thus far from the impact of the "new globalization" on Africa? First, the phenomenon is ubiquitous both in terms of its territorial and sectoral expanse. That is, the phenomenon has succeeded in incorporating all of the various actors – state and non-state – into the global capitalist system either willingly or unwillingly. Clearly, there are variations in the levels of incorporation: Some actors are more integrated into the international capitalist architecture than others. For example, the "Newly Industrializing States" (NICs) such as South Korea, Singapore and Taiwan are more integrated into the system than are the preponderant majority of African states. Also, the phenomenon covers virtually every sector – from cultural to military-security. In essence, the phenomenon is akin to a suzerain with an extensive international reach.

Second, Africa does not have the requisite structures and policies in place to mediate and address the deleterious effects and consequences of the phenomenon. Broadly, the neo-colonial state in Africa is not designed to protect the continent and its peoples from exploitation and marginalization. Instead, the failed "Berlinist state" (Kieh, 2007) is designed to sustain and enhance the plundering and pillaging of the continent. Against this background, African states are not positioned to impact the agenda of the "new globalization." Hence, African states are basically spectators and recipients of the after effects of the phenomenon's tidal waves.

Third and related, because Africa is not advantageously positioned in the global political economy and its "division of labor," the "dividends" of the "new globalization" are being disproportionately reaped by the metropolis. As Chinery-Hesse (2001:149) notes, "[African] countries, as their increasingly poor populations prove, appear the most vulnerable players, or the greatest casualties of the globalized world economy."

The Way Forward

Since African states are being impacted by the cascading effects of the "new globalization" and they cannot escape the extensive reach of the phenomenon, what are some of the steps they need to take in order to position the region to effectively mediate and address the effects of the phenomenon? I would suggest four interlinked approaches. First, the neo-colonial state in Africa needs to be deconstructed, rethought and democratically reconstituted, so that it can play an effective role as an advocate, defender and provider for the majority of the peoples of the continent. Generally, this would require a process of transformation that would ultimately change the nature, mission, character, structures, processes, values, rules and policies of the neo-colonial state. Central to the transformative process must be a resounding rejection of the neo-liberal ideology and its anti-people, anti-development and anti-democracy agenda. This type of pro-people state construct would make the protection of the interests of the peoples of Africa its primary *raison d'etre*. In turn, the peoples of Africa would develop a stake in the state and will come to view it as their own. Hence, they would legitimize it and give it the requisite support it needs to defend their interests against the venalities of the "new globalization." In short, only a democratically reconstituted state with a pro-people, pro-development and pro-democracy agenda can mediate and address the effects of the "new globalization" in the supreme interests of the African peoples. Importantly, the possibility and success of the democratic reconstitution project would require a new cadre of committed, dedicated, nationalistic and pan-African oriented leaders who would be prepared to place the interests of the peoples of Africa before the narrow agenda of using state power to foster the private accumulation of capital.

Second, African states need to formulate and implement effective modalities that would promote substantive integration at the regional and sub-regional levels. This would entail, among other things, a serious engagement in the process of deepening integration in the various sectors. Importantly, there must be the will to address the political ramifications of the integration process, including surrendering state sovereignty to regional and sub-regional entities over policy-making in various sectors. It is foolhardy for African states to keep using the "sovereignty card" to hamstring the process of deeper integration, when their respective sovereignties have already been eroded by the "new globalization." So, it is much more advantageous for African states to develop "collective sovereignty" within the broader context of regionalism.

Third, the Pan-African agenda needs to be revived and tailored to the exigencies of the "new globalization" and its "world order." Within the context of Pan-Africanism, Africans on the continent and those in the diaspora around the world should develop closer ties and bounds, and bring their collective resources to bear in helping to strengthen the continent.

Fourth, there is an urgent need to rethink "Third World solidarity" for the purpose of organizing a united front in the interests of the peoples on the margins of the "new globalization." This would require, among other things, the restructuring of the "Non-Aligned Movement" and the "Group of '77." The ostensible goal should be to create a single multi-purpose organization that can serve as vehicle for protecting, defending and promoting the interests of the peoples of the third world, especially against the vagaries of the "new globalization." Such an arrangement would enable third world states to collectively exercise their sovereignty in a meaningful way. Importantly, with their vast natural resources as the fulcrums, third world states through such collective arrangement would be able to impact, mediate and shape the direction of the "new globalization" in ways that benefit their peoples.

References

Chinery-Hesse, Mary (1993), "Divergence and Convergence in the New World Order", in Adebayo Adedeji (ed.), *Africa Within the World: Beyond Dispossession and Dependence* (London: Zed Books).

Hobbes, Thomas (2002), *Leviathan* (New York: Broadview Press).

Kieh, George Klay (2007), "Introduction: The Terminally Ill Berlinist State", in G. Klay Kieh, Jr. (ed.), *Beyond State Failure and Collapse: Making the State Relevant in Africa* (Lanham, MD: Lexington Books).

Ramsay, Jeffress (1993), "Introduction", *Africa* (Guilford, CT: Dushkin Publishing Group).

Solimano, Andres (1999), *Globalization and National Development at the End of the 20th Century: Tensions and Challenges*, World Bank Policy Research Working Paper No. 2137 (Washington D.C.: World Bank).

Index

For Product Safety Concerns and Information please contact our EU
representative GPSR@taylorandfrancis.com
Taylor & Francis Verlag GmbH, Kaufingerstraße 24, 80331 München, Germany

www.ingramcontent.com/pod-product-compliance
Ingram Content Group UK Ltd.
Pitfield, Milton Keynes, MK11 3LW, UK
UKHW021720240926
475702UK00029BA/1681
* 9 7 8 1 1 3 8 3 8 2 8 0 0 *